READING 4QMMT

NEW PERSPECTIVES ON QUMRAN LAW AND HISTORY

SOCIETY OF BIBLICAL LITERATURE

SBL

SYMPOSIUM SERIES

Gail R. O'Day, Editor

Number 2

READING 4QMMT

NEW PERSPECITVES ON QUMRAN LAW AND HISTORY

edited by
John Kampen and Moshe J. Bernstein

John Kampen
Moshe J. Bernstein
editors

Reading 4QMMT
New Perspectives on Qumran Law and History

Scholars Press
Atlanta, Georgia

Reading 4QMMT
New Perspectives on Qumran Law and History

edited by
John Kampen
Moshe J. Bernstein

Library of Congress Cataloging in Publication Data
Reading 4QMMT : new perspectives on Qumran law and history / John Kampen, Moshe J. Bernstein, editors.
p. cm.— (SBL symposium series ; no. 2)
Papers presented at the 1994 Annual Meeting of the Society of Biblical Literature and at the 1994 Annual Meeting of the Association for Jewish Studies.
Includes bibliographical references and indexes.
ISBN 0-7885-0222-0 (cloth : alk. paper). — ISBN 0-7885-0223-9 (pbk. : alk. paper)
1. Dead Sea scrolls. 4Q—Congresses. 2. Qumran community. I. Kampen, John. II. Bernstein, Moshe J. III. Society of Biblical Literature. Meeting (1994) IV. Association for Jewish Studies. Meeting (1994 : Boston, Mass.) V. Series: Symposium series (Society of Biblical Literature) ; no. 2.
BM488.5.R43 1996
296.1'55—dc20 95-51505
CIP

Printed in the United States of America
on acid-free paper

Contents

List of Abbreviations

The citations of biblical and rabbinic texts employ SBL abbreviations. A separate list of abbreviations for Qumran texts follows below.

AB	Anchor Bible
ABD	*The Anchor Bible Dictionary* (6 vols.; ed. D. N. Freedman; New York: Doubleday, 1992)
Ag. Ap.	Josephus, *Against Apion*
AJSRev	*Association of Jewish Studies Review*
ANRW	*Aufstieg und Niedergang der römischen Welt*
Ant.	Josephus, *Jewish Antiquities*
AUSS	*Andrews University Seminary Studies*
BA	*Biblical Archaeologist*
BARev	*Biblical Archaeology Review*
BDF	F. Blass and A. Debrunner, *A Greek Grammar of the New Testament and Other Early Christian Literature* (trans. and ed., R. W. Funk; Chicago: University of Chicago Press, 1961)
BJS	Brown Judaic Studies
CRINT	Compendium Rerum Iudaicarum ad Novum Testamentum
DSD	*Dead Sea Discoveries*
EncJud	*Encyclopaedia Judaica (1971)*
HTR	*Harvard Theological Review*
HUCA	*Hebrew Union College Annual*
ICC	International Critical Commentary
JBL	*Journal of Biblical Literature*
JES	*Journal of Ecumenical Studies*
JJS	*Journal of Jewish Studies*
JQR	*Jewish Quarterly Review*
JR	*Journal of Religion*
JSOTSup	Journal for the Study of the Old Testament–Supplemental Series

JSPSup	Journal for the Study of the Pseudepigrapha–Supplemental Series
JSJ	*Journal for the Study of Judaism*
J.W.	Josephus, *Jewish War*
NovT	*Novum Testamentum*
NovTSup	Novum Testamentum, Supplements
NTS	*New Testament Studies*
OTP	*The Old Testament Pseudepigrapha* (2 vols.; ed. J. H. Charlesworth; Garden City: Doubleday, 1983)
PAAJR	*Proceedings of the American Academy of Jewish Research*
RevQ	*Revue de Qumran*
RB	*Revue Biblique*
SBLRBS	Society of Biblical Literature Resources for Biblical Study
SBLSP	*Society of Biblical Literature Seminar Papers*
SR	*Studies in Religion*
STDJ	Studies on the Texts of the Desert of Judah
SNTSMS	Society for New Testament Studies Monograph Series
TDNT	*Theological Dictionary of the New Testament*
WUNT	Wissenschaftliche Untersuchungen zum Neuen Testament
ZTK	*Zeitschrift für Theologie und Kirche*

QUMRAN TEXTS

CD	Damascus Document (also known as Zadokite Fragments)
DJD III	M. Baillet, J. T. Milik, and R. de Vaux, *Les 'Petites Grottes' de Qumrân: Exploration de la falaise, les grottes 2Q, 3Q, 5Q, 6Q, 7Q à 10Q, le rouleau de cuivre* (Discoveries in the Judaean Desert of Jordan III; Oxford: Clarendon, 1962)
DJD V	J. M. Allegro (with the collaboration of A. A. Anderson), *Qumrân Cave 4, I (4Q158-186)* (Discoveries in the Judaean Desert of Jordan V; Oxford: Clarendon, 1968)
DJD VII	M. Baillet, *Qumrân Grotte 4, III (4Q482-4Q520)* (Discoveries in the Judaean Desert VII; Oxford: Clarendon, 1982)

DJD X	E. Qimron and J. Strugnell (in consultation with Y. Sussmann and with contributions by Y. Sussmann and A. Yardeni), *Qumran Cave 4, V: Miqṣat Maᶜaśe Ha-Torah* (Discoveries in the Judaean Desert X; Oxford: Clarendon, 1994)
DJD XIII	H. Attridge *et al.*, *Qumran Cave 4, VIII: Parabiblical Texts, Part I* (Discoveries in the Judaean Desert XIII; Oxford: Clarendon, 1994)
1QH	The Hymns
1QpHab	Pesher Habakkuk
1QS	Community Rule
1QSa	Rule of the Congregation or the Messianic Rule
4QMMT	מקצת מעשי התורה (line and section numbers are cited according to the DJD X edition)
4QpNah	Pesher Nahum (DJD V)
4QpPs^{a}	Pesher on Psalms (DJD V)
4QS	Manuscripts of the Community Rule found in Cave 4
11QT	Temple Scroll

Preface

The impetus for this collection of essays was the long-awaited appearance of the official edition of 4QMMT by Elisha Qimron and John Strugnell. Over the decade since MMT was presented in 1984 at the International Conference on Biblical Archaeology in Jerusalem, its tantalizing contents circulated unofficially among interested scholars, but few were willing to publish the results of their initial inquiries and fewer were given permission to include data from MMT officially in their publications.

Having reasonable assurances that the DJD edition of 4QMMT would appear in the summer of 1994, the co-chairs of the Qumran Section for the Annual Meeting of the Society of Biblical Literature, Eileen Schuller and John Kampen, began to plan a special session to present a variety of perspectives and issues concerning this new text for the benefit of the members of the SBL and AAR in attendance. The Program Committee of the Society recognized the significance of this document, and the resulting session was introduced and chaired by Eileen Schuller. A similar interest on the part of the Association for Jewish Studies was evident, and Lawrence Schiffman and Moshe Bernstein proposed a panel discussion on 4QMMT to focus on different areas from the SBL session. The resulting session at the Association's annual meeting in Boston in December 1994 was chaired by Baruch Levine. The only person to present a paper in both programs was Lawrence Schiffman, one of which is included in this volume. While a number of the contributors to this volume are members of both SBL and AJS, combining the presentations for the two associations helped to broaden the focus of the present volume and to assure its interdisciplinary character. The papers by Kampen, García Martínez, Qimron and Schwartz were presented at SBL, and those by Bernstein, Elman, Eshel and Schiffman at AJS.

The editors would like to thank all those who contributed essays to this volume, and especially Professor Elisha Qimron, one of the "parents" of MMT according to one of our writers, for his participation in the SBL session on 4QMMT. We are grateful to Professors Eileen

Schuller and Baruch Levine for chairing the sessions at which the papers were read and to Professor Florentino García Martínez for his contribution to the bibliography. Dr. Richard T. White provided valuable aid in converting a variety of word-processing files into a common format, and Mr. Avi Shmidman provided support on a variety of computer-related issues. Ms. Judith C. Bernstein furnished editorial assistance beyond that which is customarily expected from the wife of an editor. Our sincere thanks to all of them.

We are deeply grateful to Professor Gail R. O'Day, editor of the new SBL series "Symposium," for accepting this collection as one of the first volumes in the series, and to the staff of Scholars Press for their able and helpful assistance in the production of this volume.

Introduction

JOHN KAMPEN AND MOSHE J. BERNSTEIN

To judge from the scholarly hullabaloo which accompanied both its non-publication and its subsequent release to the public, 4QMMT is one of the most significant documents to be reconstructed from the thousands of fragments found in Cave 4 at Qumran. The controversies surrounding the process of its publication have received extensive publicity. The text itself has become the subject of additional controversy as its contents have become more readily available. MMT's final publication occurred when many of the assumptions which had been broadly shared among a majority of the scholars involved in Qumran studies were becoming the subject of an extensive reevaluation. At the same time, Hershel Shanks, one of the key non-academic players in the controversy concerning access to the unpublished material from Qumran in general and MMT in particular, belittled the significance of the document in his popular journal, *Biblical Archaeology Review,* with an article entitled "MMT as the Maltese Falcon," and accompanied a transcription of the DJD text and translation with the heading "For This You Waited 35 Years."[1]

Six manuscripts of this composition (4Q394–399) have been identified by the editors, John Strugnell and Elisha Qimron, in the official DJD publication.[2] They provide a reconstruction of approximately 130 extant lines when integrated into a composite text. Both the transcriptions of each of the individual manuscripts and the reconstructed composite text are included in the DJD edition. On the

---

1 "Falcon," *BARev* 20 (November/December 1994) 48–51, 80, 82; "35 Years," *ibid.*, 56–61.

2 E. Qimron and J. Strugnell (in consultation with Y. Sussmann and with contributions by Y. Sussmann and A. Yardeni), *Qumran Cave 4, V: Miqṣat Maʿaśe Ha-Torah* (Discoveries in the Judaean Desert X; Oxford: Clarendon, 1994), abbreviated in this volume as DJD X.

basis of paleographic analysis, these fragments can be dated from 75 BCE to 50 CE. There is no reason to believe that any of these copies are autographs.

The reconstructed composite text is divided into three sections: (A) the calendar at the beginning; (B) the list of laws; and (C) the homiletic-paraenetic conclusion.[3] The meaning and significance of each of these sections is the occasion of considerable debate, and a number of the essays in this volume are evidence of that fact. The editors of 4QMMT also hypothesize an opening formula for the original composition which is now entirely lost.[4]

The fragments of 4QMMT were among those from Cave 4 found or purchased by the Palestine Archaeological Museum between 1953 and 1959. The six manuscripts "had been identified, transcribed, materially reconstructed and partly combined into a common text by 1959."[5] The first references to this unique text can be found in the writings of J. T. Milik.[6] He considered it to be "written in a neo-classical Hebrew with features, however, proper to the Mishnaic dialect . . . ."[7] Labelling it 4QMishn(ique) he reproduced words and phrases from it in his commentary on the Copper Scroll.[8] Since his citations included the reference to the *muṣaqot* (analogous to rabbinic *niṣṣoq*, "poured liquids"? [see Elman's essay in this volume]) in 4QMMT B 55–57, that text was cited both by Yadin and Baumgarten in discussions of Qumran halakhah.[9] After those initial revelations, however, there was virtual silence surrounding MMT for two decades.

Elisha Qimron first described the text in detail during the 1984 International Conference on Biblical Archaeology in Jerusalem.[10] In

---

3 DJD X, 109–11.

4 DJD X, 1.

5 DJD X, ix.

6 J. T. Milik, "Le travail d'édition des manuscrits du Désert de Juda," *Volume du Congrès; Strasbourg 1956* (VTSup 4; Leiden: Brill, 1957), 24. Note also the collective articles by M. Baillet et al., "Le travail d'édition des fragments manuscrits de Qumrân," *RB* 63 (1956) 65, and P. Benoit et al., "Editing the Manuscript Fragments from Qumran," *BA* 19 (1956) 94.

7 J. T. Milik, *Ten Years of Discovery in the Wilderness of Judaea* (tr. J. Strugnell; London: SCM, 1959), 130.

8 DJD III, 225.

9 Y. Yadin, *The Temple Scroll* [Hebrew] (Jerusalem: Israel Exploration Society, 1977), 2.150; J. M. Baumgarten, "The Pharisaic-Sadducean Controversies about Purity and the Qumran Texts," *JJS* 31 (1980) 164.

10 E. Qimron and J. Strugnell, "An Unpublished Halakhic Letter from Qumran,"

their published reports, Qimron and Strugnell described the language and content of the new text while working on the final version of its reconstruction and publication. It took yet another ten years before the official publication appeared. In the meantime a photocopy of the editors' handwritten reconstruction of the text began to circulate, so that it became known to many Qumran scholars prior to its official publication. Some "unofficial" publication efforts resulted from these circulated copies.[11]

Lawrence Schiffman of New York University, one of the scholars given official access to these texts, began to write articles discussing the text and its implications for an understanding of the history of Judaism.[12] An invitation to Yaʿakov Sussmann to aid the editors in the analysis of the halakhic elements in the text resulted in an extensive article in Hebrew.[13] Many of the scholars who were in possession of unofficial copies of the text were reluctant to publish material concerning it, however. Their reluctance was due, on the one hand, to the uncertainty regarding legal issues of access and, on the other, to the expectation that the official published version was imminent. With the appearance of the text as DJD X, these questions of access no longer hinder the study of the remnants of this important document. What must be made clear at this initial presentation of MMT is the wealth of material it contains. Now that MMT is available to the full

Biblical Archaeology Today (ed. Janet Amitai; Jerusalem: Israel Exploration Society/Israel Academy of Sciences and Humanities in cooperation with ASOR, 1985) 400–407; E. Qimron and J. Strugnell, "An Unpublished Halakhic Letter from Qumran," *The Israel Museum Journal* 4 (1985) 9–12.

[11] The best known efforts are those of Z. J. Kapera in "Appendix A," *Qumran Chronicle* 2 (December, 1990) 2–9 and R. H. Eisenman and J. M. Robinson, *A Facsimile Edition of the Dead Sea Scrolls* (Washington: Biblical Archaeology Society, 1991) xv-xvi and xxxi, Figure 8. The circulation of both of these editions was stopped. The text then appeared in R. H. Eisenman and M. Wise, *The Dead Sea Scrolls Uncovered: The First Complete Translation and Interpretation of 50 Key Documents Withheld for Over 35 Years* (Shaftesbury/Rockport/Brisbane: Element, 1992) 182–205. A point of dispute was the extent to which these editions relied on the photocopied texts. The publication of B. Z. Wacholder and M. G. Abegg, *A Preliminary Edition of the Unpublished Dead Sea Scrolls: The Hebrew and Aramaic Text from Cave Four* (Washington: Biblical Archaeology Society, 1995), fasc. 3, which includes the six MSS of 4QMMT was also delayed due to a lawsuit.

[12] E.g., L. H. Schiffman, "The New Halakhic Letter (4QMMT) and the Origins of the Dead Sea Sect," *BA* 53 (1990) 64–73.

[13] Yaʿakov Sussmann, "The History of Halakha and the Dead Sea Scrolls — Preliminary Observations on *Miqṣat Maʿase Ha-Torah* (4QMMT)," [Hebrew] *Tarbiz* 59 (1989–90) 11–76.

scrutiny of the world of Qumran scholarship, it will doubtless be the subject of many future articles on a broad variety of themes.

Any evaluation of this document must now begin with Qimron and Strugnell's *editio princeps,* which is accompanied by an extensive commentary and supplemental studies, including an English translation of the article by Yaᶜakov Sussmann on halakhah already mentioned above. In his essay in this volume, Elisha Qimron provides a glimpse of a few of the difficult issues the editors faced in the editing and reconstruction of this text. An elaboration of Strugnell's viewpoints found in Appendix 3 of DJD X can now be found in the published form of his paper from the 1993 Notre Dame Conference.[14] Subsequent research must take into account the viewpoints articulated in that article as well as the essays of Qimron discussed in the *editio princeps.*

The connection between Section A, the calendrical portion of the work, and the rest of the composition remains a matter of debate. That it is found only in the fragments of MS A (4Q394) raises questions about its original relationship to the remainder of the composition. In his essay in this volume, Lawrence Schiffman argues that this copy of the Qumran calendar was placed at the beginning of the treatise by a scribe in the process of making a copy of the remainder of the composition. This calendar then existed independently and in its essential features resembles other versions of the Qumran calendar available to us. Hanan Eshel, on the other hand, suggests a different road leading to the inclusion of the calendrical text in this document.

Both in the *editio princeps* and in the emerging body of secondary literature concerning this important composition, the central legal portion has received the most discussion. It is also the longest section in the preserved manuscripts. The scholar and layperson who have not had the oppportunity to develop some understanding of halakhah and its significance for the history of Second Temple Judaism might easily overlook the importance of this material. The contents of MMT B are legal; they assert a variety of principles in the observance of halakhah, generally with the implication that the opponents of the author hold views at variance with those asserted in the document. In such disputes, minute details are most often the crux of the issue. Every

---

[14] J. Strugnell, "MMT: Second Thoughts on a Forthcoming Edition," in *The Community of the Renewed Covenant: The Notre Dame Symposium on the Dead Sea Scrolls* (ed. E. Ulrich and J. VanderKam; Notre Dame: University of Notre Dame Press, 1994) 57–73.

serious student who wishes to understand MMT's contents, as well as its significance within the history of Second Temple Judaism, must be prepared to enter into a painstaking study of such seemingly insignificant technicalities.

One of the notable features of some of the halakhot in MMT is their similarity to stipulations attributed to the Sadducees in the rabbinic tradition. This has been argued by Lawrence Schiffman in other contexts.[15] Yaakov Elman's contribution to this volume is an important case study demonstrating the caution which must be exercised in the comparative study of sectarian and rabbinic halakhah, as well as the importance of evaluating halakhic data against the background of archaeological realia. In this volume Schiffman compares the halakhic requirements of 4QMMT with those specified in other works from Qumran, while Moshe Bernstein considers the question of the legal biblical exegesis of MMT.

One of the difficulties faced by the interpreter of MMT is the identification of its genre. Although termed a "halakhic letter" in Qimron and Strugnell's first publications, that characterization may legitimately be questioned. Although MMT contains a variety of rulings held by its authors on legal issues, it is clearly not a prescriptive legal text resembling some other Qumran compositions such as CD/4QD or 1QS/4QS. Those prescriptive legal texts at Qumran do not mention opposing halakhic opinions. The introduction of the views of the opponents into section B, the bulk of MMT, creates a polemical tone, accentuated by the constant juxtaposition of "we" and "you" and/or "they," discussed in several of the essays in this volume. If Section C, the "hortatory epilogue," did not exist, one might label MMT as a text which describes legal disputes. The presence of that last non-legal segment of the document, however, makes it clear that this document defies any simplistic classifications.

While MMT is frequently referred to as a letter, Strugnell himself has noted that the fragmentary remains of the opening lines of Section B are not of an epistolary character. While a definitive reconstruction of the incipit is difficult, he proposes that it is based on Deut 1:1, even though it is more likely the introduction to this collection of laws

---

[15] Schiffman, "The New Halakhic Letter," 68–71; id., *Reclaiming the Dead Sea Scrolls* (Philadelphia and Jerusalem: The Jewish Publication Society, 1994) 73–76, 252–55.

within a larger composition which is no longer preserved.[16] Rather than a treatise or epistle, Strugnell proposes that Section B comprises a free-standing collection of laws, perhaps modeled on the book of Deuteronomy. This proposal, however, disregards the combative aspect of Section B, the fact that it is not merely a collection of laws but part of an argument. Even in terms of nomenclature and genre, then, we have much yet to learn about MMT.

Many of the issues concerning the identity of the proponents and opponents of the viewpoints advanced in 4QMMT find their focus in a discussion of Section C, dubbed "the hortatory epilogue." In this volume, for example, Daniel Schwartz's critique of the way 4QMMT is used to construct a history of the Pharisees is rooted in this section. Hanan Eshel also utilizes the material in this section for his reconstruction of the early stages of the history of the Hasmonean period. Further analysis of the historiography and sociology of MMT is required in order to integrate this work into perceptions of that larger complex we know as Qumran.

Section C receives the least amount of attention in the *editio princeps*. As pointed out by Strugnell, a sustained discussion of the theology of the work is a desideratum. The fact that Qimron and Strugnell even propose a different ordering of the fragments in Section C forms the basis of the article by F. García Martínez in this volume. Many of the issues concerning this section must await a more sustained literary and theological analysis of the text. Preliminary work such as Bernstein's observations concerning the use of Scripture in Section C provides the foundation for such subsequent study.

The essays in this volume attempt to evaluate the significance of 4QMMT for understanding the history and literature of Qumran as well as for assessing its significance for subsequent Jewish and Christian history. Since the origins of Christianity are rooted in Jewish sectarianism of the first century CE, it is not surprising that this text provides new material which is also significant for the development of the early Christian movement. Kampen's essay in this volume evaluates three examples where this may be the case.

We can observe even within this collection of initial studies on MMT how many major interpretive issues are subject to disagreement. There is still no consensus on the historical implications of MMT; on the meaning and significance of its halakhah against the background

---

[16] Note also the comments of Kampen in his essay in this volume.

of other late Second Temple and early rabbinic legal material; on its utilization of the Hebrew Scriptures; on the relationship of its halakhot to that scripture; even on its title and genre. Many other issues will no doubt surface as patient study of MMT bears its expected fruit. It is the hope of the editors that this collection of essays will encourage further study and examination of this fascinating text which has only recently come to the attention of the academic community as a whole.

The Nature of the Reconstructed Composite Text of 4QMMT

ELISHA QIMRON
Ben Gurion University of the Negev
Beer Sheva, Israel

The six manuscripts of 4QMMT found in Cave 4 at Qumran were divided among approximately one hundred fragments. It was Professor Strugnell who initially identified these fragments, successfully locating most of the larger pieces and joining to them many of the smaller fragments. From the very beginning of my work with Strugnell, I took upon myself the task of placing all of the fragments in their appropriate location, thereby almost fully reconstructing the available text. The complicated work of reconstruction continued throughout the duration of my research and even into the proof-reading stage. The reconstruction of approximately 130 extant lines of MMT probably constitutes 40% of the composite text.

The publication of the composite text of MMT is the first attempt to fully reconstruct any composition from Qumran utilizing all of the available manuscripts. Editing these minute fragments was a difficult and complicated task requiring a number of years to complete. From the outset it was clear to us that a conscientious editing of these manuscripts would necessitate a thorough study of both content and language, as well as require extensive comparison with all the relevant parallels in the literature of early Judaism. Thus both laborious technical work and extensive scholarly research were required for the reproduction of the published text. Some passages remain a matter of conjecture since no reconstruction based on fragmentary evidence can ever be considered for certain to be an exact reproduction of the original text. Reconstruction is no more than an educated guess on the basis of the scholar's knowledge and intuition. The composite text of our edition therefore should not be used independently, but rather must always be consulted together with the individual manuscripts and commentary presented in its publication.

Examples of the Reconstruction

Let me discuss three passages which demonstrate the nature of this text and the way in which it was reconstructed.

1. *4QMMT B 9–11.* Only a portion of these lines have survived. In fact, only two groups of words are extant: אותה מיום ליום ("it from one day to the following one") and החלבים והבשר ביום זוב[חם] ("the suet and the flesh on the day when they are sacri[ficed]"). The fact that there is no preserved heading designating the subject of this particular law makes any reconstruction difficult. Yet, one can infer from the wording that this law concerns the designated time in which the sacrificial food can be eaten.[1] Such a controversial law does indeed occur in 11QT 20:12–13: ביום ההוא תא[כל ולו]א ת[בו]א ע[ליה] השמש ("on that day it shall be ea[ten before] the sun [goes down]"). This law in the Temple Scroll legislates the time in which it is permitted to eat the cereal offering, i.e., that day. This law was the basis of my idea for restoring שהמנ[חה נאכלת] ("that the cereal offer[ing is to be eaten]") at the beginning of line 11. Strugnell rather read at this point שהם ("that they").

The biblical source of this controversy is the passage in Lev 7:15: ובשר זבח תודת שלמיו ביום קרבנו יאכל לא יניח ממנו עד בקר ("And the flesh of his thanksgiving sacrifice of well-being shall be eaten on the day that it is offered; none of it shall be left until morning"). The controversy focused on the limits of the day; does it end in the evening or in the morning? The Rabbis ruled that in sacrificial matters the day ends in the morning, while the Dead Sea sectarians maintained that it always ends at sunset.[2] This led me to assume that the word יניח ("leave") or the like should be restored in line 10. Fortunately, I succeeded in finding the word שמניחים ("that they leave") on a tiny fragment containing parts of several letters belonging to lines 9 and 11. These letters establish the placement of this fragment as certain.

Note that I was originally misled by the biblical source to restore the heading of the law as [ואף על תודת] זבח השל[מים] ("[and also

---

1 See my discussion in DJD X, 150–52.

2 *M. Zebaḥ.* 6:1.

concerning the thanksgiving] sacrifice of well-[being]"). This error was perpetuated in all the unauthorized copy-editions of the composite text. Only later did I realize that the definite article preserved in the word שהמנ[ח]ה ("that the cereal offer[ing]") in line 11 must imply that the word מנחת ("cereal offering") already had been found in the heading, rather than תודת ("thanksgiving"). If my earlier proposal were correct one would expect to read in line 11 שמנחת התודה ("that the cereal offering of the thanksgiving"),[3] rather than שהמנחה ("that the cereal offering") with the definite article, as it is found in the relevant fragment. The definite article has a demonstrative function and often indicates that the noun governed by it has been mentioned before. Hence it here designates the earlier appearance of the word מנחה ("cereal offering"), thereby justifying its use in the reconstruction of line 9.

2. *4QMMT B 21–23.* These lines comprise the most extensive reconstruction of this text which we attempted. In fact, most of this portion of the text is reconstructed. The preserved text is extant on several tiny fragments, none of which contains more than two whole words. No direct physical joins between these fragments are possible. In order to indicate the uncertainty in combining such fragments I utilized a special kind of bracket, ⟦ ⟧. The reconstruction was achieved through the following processes: First, I read the word עורות ("hides") in line 18. Only the entire top part of the letters has survived; Strugnell suggested the reading אורות ("lights"). Next I discovered that parts of the words עורות and עור ("hide" in the singular) are also found on several tiny fragments. I assumed that this word must be the basis of some controversial law. The placement, then, of these tiny fragments in the composite text and the restoration of the missing portions was based on the controversial laws found in the Temple Scroll concerning the hides of ritually pure animals.[4] The rabbinic halakhah ruled that only the flesh transmits defilement, not the hides and bones (even the hides of impure animals), while the Dead Sea sectarians (and the Samaritans) maintained that the hides of impure animals as well as those of pure animals which have not died by ritual slaughter do

---

[3] Editor's note: While the letter ה, the definite article in Hebrew, does not appear in the first word of the construct chain, its presence on the second word implies the definiteness of the first.

[4] 11QT 51:4–5. See my discussion in DJD X, 154–56.

spread contamination (as does the flesh).[5] The fact that the fragments which contain the word עורות were derived from two separate manuscripts of 4QMMT provides further confirmation for this suggested arrangement. Since this reconstruction is based on the Temple Scroll, it contributes very little which is new to our understanding of this actual law from Qumran. It however does seem that 4QMMT also refers to the hides of ritually impure animals, a detail not explicitly mentioned in the Temple Scroll, but which does occur in the Samaritan legal literature.

3. *4QMMT C 18–24.* This section is preserved in only one of the larger fragments of the papyrus, 4QMMT^{e}. There is no parallel text extant in any of the other manuscripts and its placement is therefore physically unknown. Strugnell assumes that 4QMMT^{e} originally contained fewer than ten lines in each column. Since the fragment being discussed has seven preserved lines, it could not be added to either of the two columns of this manuscript which already each contain eight preserved lines. Strugnell therefore located this fragment at the beginning of Section C (preceding the aforementioned two columns).[6]

It was Menachem Kister who first suggested the present placement of this fragment. His conclusion was based solely on considerations of content. He noticed that the blessings and curses mentioned in C 18–22 refer to the blessing and curses in C 14–15. Furthermore, in C 25–26 we read: זכור [את] דויד שהיא איש חסדים [ו]אף היא [נ]צל מצרות רבות ונסלוח לו ("Think of David who was a man of righteous deeds [and] who was [therefore] delivered from many troubles and was forgiven"). This assertion is a more detailed version of the general statement in the preceding lines in the fragment under discussion: זכור את מלכי ישרא[ל] והתבנן במעשיהמה שמי מהם שהיא ירא[את התו]רה היה מצול מצרות והם מב[ק]שי תורה [נשו]אי עונות ("Think of the kings of Israe[l] and contemplate their deeds: whoever among them feared [the To]rah was delivered from

---

5 For the rabbinic tradition see *m. Ḥul.* 9:1–2. For Qumran see 11QT 51:4–5 (note the discussion by Y. Yadin, *The Temple Scroll* [Jerusalem: Israel Exploration Society, 1983] 1.338–41). For the Samaritan view, see *Abraham Geiger's Gesammelte Abhandlungen in hebräischer Sprache* (ed. S. Poznanski; Warsaw, 1910) 70–82.

6 J. Strugnell, "MMT: Second Thoughts on a Forthcoming Edition," *The Community of the Renewed Covenant: The Notre Dame Symposium on the Dead Sea Scrolls* (eds. Eugene Ulrich and James VanderKam; Notre Dame: University of Notre Dame Press, 1994) 67–70. See my comments in Appendix 2, DJD X, 201–202.

troubles; and these were the seekers of the Torah whose transgressions were [for]given." Note the direct continuation between the two fragments from a contextual point of view. Note also that ונסלוח לו ("and was forgiven") in line 26 refers to נשואי עונות ("whose transgressions were forgiven") in line 25. While Strugnell and Stegemann disagree with Kister on the basis of physical considerations, Bezalel Porten believes that papyrology in fact supports Kister's placement of this fragment.

I hope that these examples have provided you some idea of the special problems confronted in reconstructing such a text as 4QMMT. We all know that any reconstruction, however learned and brilliant, is merely an educated guess. Scholars of the Dead Sea Scrolls must now decide if the proposed reconstruction of this text is viable. I anxiously await the critical judgement of my esteemed colleagues concerning my attempted reconstruction of the text of 4QMMT.

4QMMT in a Qumran Context[1]

FLORENTINO GARCÍA MARTÍNEZ
Qumran Institute, Rijksuniversiteit Groningen
Groningen, Netherlands

The reading of various forewords and appendices to the long awaited volume of the *editio princeps* of 4QMMT[2] by Elisha Qimron and John Strugnell has left me with the impression of being witness to the quarrels of a couple who, after the love has become sour, are fighting for the custody of the only child. The judge has assigned the custody of this child to Qimron (he is the only owner of the copyright of the book!) but Strugnell has cared longer for the child and at the end he knows better.

One of the most telling disagreements of the two editors is the different order assigned to one of the two main fragments of 4QMMT^e (4Q398), the papyrus copy to which we owe most of the hortatory section of the document. The paragraph formed by fragments 11 to 13 is placed by Strugnell at the beginning of the hortatory section in his initial transcription of the individual manuscripts in the DJD edition,[3] before the passage formed by fragments 14 to 17.[4] Qimron, on the other hand, in the composite text locates it below the right part of frgs. 14–17, thereby forming the bottom portion of col. i of this fragment.[5] As the editors explain in Appendices 2 and 3 respectively, this placement in the composite text was suggested by Menahem Kister on the basis of its content and supported by Bezalel Porten on material

[1] Paper read at the SBL meeting, Chicago, November 1994. I have kept the form of the oral presentation, adding only some bibliographical references. I want to thank John Kampen for the revision of the English text.

[2] DJD X.

[3] Designated as fragment 1 in the description of the manuscript, DJD X, 28. See the text at DJD X, 36.

[4] Designated as fragment 2 in the description of the manuscript.

[5] In the composite text frgs. 14–17 are listed as C 9–16 and 25–32 while frgs. 11–13 comprise C 18–24.

grounds.[6] Supported by Hartmut Stegemann, Strugnell, while recognizing that the context seems to favour this position, argues that the material shape of the manuscript demands that frgs. 11–13 should be located before frgs. 14–17, a place which would be "just as plausible on grounds of context."[7] The arguments of both sides are very strong indeed. In favour of Qimron's position is, as Strugnell recognizes, the smooth flow of thought from the quotation of Deuteronomy on the blessings and curses to the blessings and curses concerning the days of Solomon and subsequent Israelite history, thereby linking frgs. 11–13 with the preceding text. Stylistic motifs such as the repetition of "remember" in C 23 and 25 and of "delivered from troubles" in C 24 and 26, which link the fragment to the following text, can also be cited. The shape of the two main fragments appears to support Strugnell's position.

In Appendix 3 of the *editio princeps* Strugnell furthermore states:

> This volume does not contain a chapter on the theology and tradition-history of Section C, a counterpart perhaps to Qimron's lengthy treatment of the legal background of the laws. A running commentary on some details in Section C is included, but not a thorough attempt to understand the relations between the language and theological traditions of this section and those of works which we expect to be near it chronologically and in thought, i.e., Daniel, *1 Enoch*, the *Divre Hammeʾorot*, the *Damascus Document*, and the *Temple Scroll*. Such an important study remains to be done.[8]

He then concludes:

> In any case, I suspect that this problem will not be solved until the missing chapter on the theological background of Section C is written, perhaps to give us an answer to this major difficulty.[9]

Let me state clearly at the beginning: I am not attempting to provide such an important study in this essay. Nor do I intend to resolve the problem of the ordering of the fragments. This is ultimately a material problem and, as Qimron says, only a microscopic inspection of the

---

6 DJD X, 201–206.

7 DJD X, 205. See now also John Strugnell, "MMT: Second Thoughts on a Forthcoming Edition," *The Community of the Renewed Covenant: The Notre Dame Symposium on the Dead Sea Scrolls* (eds. Eugene Ulrich and James VanderKam; Notre Dame: University of Notre Dame Press, 1994) 67–70.

8 DJD X, 205.

9 DJD X, 206.

fibers can conclusively prove which one of the two possibilities is correct.[10] My purpose is more simple. I want to examine some of the concepts of the hortatory section of MMT from the perspective of the Qumran writings, to see whether they point to a *Qumranic* or to a *pre-Qumranic* setting for the document. This question is based on Strugnell's inference that his ordering of the fragments is important precisely because it reveals the pre-Qumranic character of MMT.

It is clear from the list of related works which Strugnell quotes (no one of them is of undisputed Qumranic origin) that he is inclined to place the hortatory section (if not the legal section) of MMT in a pre-Qumranic setting. This inclination is apparent already in his chapter on the literary character and historical setting of MMT, in which repeatedly it is said that MMT is a document emanating from a group "either identical with, or ancestor of, the Qumran group,"[11] or "MMT is a group composition, originating in the Qumran group, or in one of its antecedents."[12] Strugnell states it even more forcefully in his review (with Daniel Harrington) of the book *The Dead Sea Scrolls Uncovered* by Robert Eisenman and Michael Wise:

> The whole exhortation is important in that it is contemporary with and reflects the thought of the slightly pre-Hasmonean and pre-Qumranic material found also in other texts (see "Words of the Luminaries," Daniel 9, Ezra 9).[13]

On the other hand, even a cursory reading of the chapters written by Qimron on the language and the halakhah shows that he places MMT not in a pre-Qumran group but right inside Qumran. As he rather bluntly says: "The 'we' group is clearly the Dead Sea Sect."[14]

This is the issue I wish to address in this paper, although the limitations of the available time preclude its exhaustive treatment in a systematic way. I will therefore limit myself to the analysis in a Qumranic context of two terms which appear in the disputed fragment and which provide additional evidence for determining which of the

---

[10] DJD X, 202.

[11] DJD X, 117.

[12] DJD X, 121.

[13] D. J. Harrington and J. Strugnell, "Qumran Cave 4 Texts: A New Publication," *JBL* 112 (1993) 495. See now also John Strugnell, "MMT: Second Thoughts on a Forthcoming Edition," 70–73.

[14] DJD X, 175.

two positions is more likely. These two topics are represented by the expressions אחרית הימים and מעשי התורה.

I

Before we begin with this exercise we must examine the text of the fragment (4QMMT C 18–24),[15] since there are a few places where I do not agree with either the translation or the reconstruction found in the *editio princeps*. Some of these differences are very minor and do not modify the meaning, such as the rendering "from the days" in C 19, following apparently the uncertain variant of MS D (מיומ[י]), rather than translating the phrase בימי ("in the days of"), found in the composite text based on MS E. Other differences are of greater consequence.

a) On C 21 Qimron recognizes that אחרית הימים is not preceded (as is usual in the OT and often in Qumran) by the preposition *bet*. He himself notes: "The phrase וזה הוא אחרית הימים (rather than ובאחרית הימים or the like) is, however, awkward."[16] But he nevertheless translates, "And this is *at* the end of days" (emphasis added), implying the presence of the letter *bet*, of which there is no trace in the manuscript. We will see later that the phrase as it is found in the text is an important clue to the Qumranic or pre-Qumranic context of the composition.

b) Also on C 21 we find the verb שוב, with two prepositions *bet* and *lamed*. While Qimron provides the translation "when they will return to Isra[el] [forever . . .]," the manuscript reads שישובו בישראל לת[. . ., where the last word is broken. It is true that in the Hebrew of Qumran some of the prepositions seem to be interchanged,[17] but in this case the interchange of *bet* with *lamed*, or of על and אל implied in Qimron's translation "return to Israel," seems to be unjustified due to the use of the *lamed* again in the same sentence. Hence the locative meaning of שוב in the *editio princeps* is retained by the *lamed* (cf. C 15, "return to Him"). The expression is paralleled in 1QS 5:22, לשוב ביחד לבריתו ("to return within the Community to his covenant"), and should be translated in the same way. In view of the uses of

---

[15] Also identified as 4QMMT^{e} (4Q398), frgs. 11–13 above.

[16] DJD X, 61.

[17] See, e.g., L. H. Schiffman, "The Interchange of the Prepositions *bet* and *mem* in the Texts from Qumran," *Textus* 10 (1982) 37–43.

שוב לתורה ("convert to the law") in 4Q171 (4QpPs^{a}) 1–2 ii 2–3 or שוב אל תורת מושה ("revert to the law of Moses") in 1QS and CD,[18] the reconstruction of לת]ורה at the beginning of C 22 does not seem to be too far-fetched.[19] The whole sentence should thus be translated: "when they return *in* Israel to the law." This meaning fits the context perfectly, making it unnecessary to employ the special meaning of "and not be cancelled" for ולוא ישובו אחור in C 22 (if *vera lectio*). The well-attested meaning of this phrase in the Bible and in Qumran, "to withdraw, to depart from,"[20] offers a perfect antithesis to "return to the law."

c) I also view the reconstruction of the beginning of C 24 as problematic, "feared [the To]rah," not because of the lack of exact parallels to the expression, but simply because it seems to me materially impossible to fill the lacuna of almost 3 centimetres with only five letters, even in the irregular hand of this manuscript. Biblical use and Qumran parallels would rather commend a reconstruction, "feared [God and observed the l]aw", or the like.

d) The presence of a *vacat* after 4QMMT C 24 cannot be resolved, of course, because it depends on the material ordering of the fragments. For Qimron it is the base line of the bottom of the column; for Strugnell it would be a *vacat* line. Greater coherence of thought appears evident if we assume (with Strugnell) a full stop in C 24 after "and these were seekers of the Torah," than if we (with Qimron) continue the sentence with "whose transgressions were forgiven." After all, the kings of Israel in C 23 are not portrayed as an impious lot whose transgressions need to be forgiven, but rather are presented as pious models who feared God, observed the Law (see previous paragraph on this reconstruction) and were delivered from troubles. Therefore they are honoured with the title, "seekers of the Law," a clear allusion to the priestly title of Mal 2:7.

---

18 1QS 5:8; CD 15:9,12; 16:1,4.

19 A reconstruction already proposed in R. Eisenman and M. Wise, *The Dead Sea Scrolls Uncovered: The First Complete Translation and Interpretation of 50 Key Documents Withheld for Over 35 Years* (Shaftesbury: Element, 1992) 199–200, whose translation seems to be closer to the original: "when (those) in Isra[e]l are to return to the La[w of God]."

20 See, e.g., 1QH 13:18,19.

II

With the text and translation of the fragment established we can explore the first of the two selected topics: אחרית הימים. This expression deserves investigation because there is a growing consensus that most of the biblical uses of the expression אחרית הימים are devoid of eschatological connotations, but that in the Qumran writings the expression has a clear eschatological meaning. In the latter texts it is still disputed as to whether the period of time so designated covers only the last days before the final bliss or refers also to the time after the judgment. The presence of the eschatological character of the expression, or its absence, can help us establish whether the composition is Qumranic or pre-Qumranic. A recent article by A. Steudel surveys all of the uses of the expression in the Qumran corpus, thereby facilitating our task of comparing its usage in MMT and other Qumran literature.[21]

In the hortatory section we find the phrase אחרית הימים in C 14, the word באחרית in C 16 and the already mentioned expression וזה הוא אחרית הימים in C 21. The fragmentary nature of C 16 precludes its value to us for this analysis.[22] The expression in C 14 is introduced by a quotation formula, וכתוב ("And it is written"). It occurs as an insertion in the middle of a quotation or paraphrase of Deut 30:1 which, in the words of Qimron, "represents the biblical source in an idiosyncratic form that is at the same time both abbreviated and supplied with explanatory additions that date the promise in Deuteronomy to the end of days."[23]

All occurrences of the phrase in the Qumran writings, with the exception of 1QSa 1:1, are found in the context of scriptural interpretation. When the scriptural quotation is introduced by a quotation formula, as in our text, the usual way to express the temporal relation to the passage quoted is indicated not by the preposition *bet* but by the preposition *lamed*, as in 4Q174 (Florilegium) 1–2 i 15: אשר כתוב בספר ישעיה הנביא לאחרית הימים ("as it is

---

21 A. Steudel, "אחרית הימים in the Texts from Qumran," *RevQ* 16/62 (1993) 225–46.

22 DJD X, 60. Qimron's translation is here misleading insofar as it does not respect the sizable lacuna of the manuscript and connects the word with the previous sentence: "'you will return unto Him with all your heart and with all your soul,' at the end [of time, so that you may live. . . .]"

23 DJD X, 59.

written in the book of Isaiah, the prophet, for the last days"). Even more important is the fact that this quotation of Deut 30:1 is preceded in C 12 by another quotation (ואף כתוב) from Deut 31:29, a biblical text in which the expression באחרית הימים appears with the usual meaning of "in the latter days" or "in the future." While it is true that the text of the quotation in MMT is abbreviated and in the singular rather than plural, and that our phrase is one of the expressions which is omitted, the quotation is clearly recognizable, as attested by the commentary in the *editio princeps*.[24] The proximity of the two quotations leads one to suspect that the expression is used in C 14 in its biblical sense and not in the typical eschatological sense it acquires in other Qumran writings.

This suspicion is strengthened by the fact that at the beginning of C 12 we also find the word וקדמוניות, translated by Qimron as "and former days," the exact opposite of אחרית הימים in the biblical sense. The closest parallel to this section of MMT is to be found in 4Q504 1–2 iii 12–14 (4QDibHam^{a}), a pre-Qumranic text which not only mentions Moses and the Prophets but also uses Deut 31:29: "which Moses wrote and your servants the prophets whom you sent, so that evil would overtake us in the last days."[25] In conclusion: a pre-Qumranic meaning for the expression in 4QMMT C 14 seems more likely.

What about the use of the phrase in C 21? It is difficult to get a precise grasp on the meaning of the sentence because in its present context it could be related either to the preceding sentence in the past tense, שבאוו ("which have come"), or to the next sentence in the future tense, שישובו ("which will come"). The word הוא in this phrase is also ambiguous since it can be read either as the verb היה ("to be") or as a pronoun. Relating the phrase to the preceding sentence the resulting translation could read: "We know that some of the blessings and the curses as written in the book of Moses have come, and this is the אחרית הימים." This would mean that the writers of the document have understood that some of the future blessings and curses announced by Moses in Deut 31:29 had already happened in the history of Israel. The times of Solomon and the exile as well as their own days could be identified with this future. The writers will have concluded, by a pesher-like interpretation, that they were living in the

24 DJD X, 59.

25 DJD VII, 141–42.

אחרית הימים. In this interpretation the expression will not have the eschatological connotations current in the Qumran writings, but could be considered an incipient form of the thought that would develop later in the exegetical writings of the Qumran group. As Steudel notes, in the Qumran writings אחרית הימים also refers on some occasions to events of the past, at least from the point of view of the writer. The Qumran community certainly thinks that אחרית הימים includes its own present, since its members thought they were living in the last days.[26]

In the second possible interpretation, the phrase would be linked to the following sentence, which could then be translated: "And the אחרית הימים is when in Israel they will return to the Law," or, if the reconstruction and interpretation of Qimron discussed above is to be preferred, "when they will return to Israel forever." The expression in this case is disconnected from the blessings and curses that have already occurred. The אחרית הימים refers to the future, as in many of the Qumranic uses of the expression (either with the verb in the future tense or as a participle with future meaning), but the eschatological character of the period so designated depends on the nature of the anticipated events.

It could be argued that the final return to Israel, in Qimron's reading, could permit such an eschalogical meaning, but that is far from certain. The immediate context with the mention of גלות ("exile") would point to a return from the exile rather than to the eschatological return to Zion.[27] The return to the law in my own interpretation could also arguably be constructed in a similar way; after all we know that a necessary condition for becoming a member of the Qumran group באחרית הימים was precisely to "undertake a binding oath to return to the Law of Moses."[28] But since we do not know exactly from this text who it is in Israel that will return to the law, we cannot be sure of the eschatological content of the phrase.

Although the expression could represent in both interpretations the first stage of an idea which in its more developed form is characteristic of the ideology of the Qumran group, much as the

---

[26] Steudel, "אחרית הימים," 229–30.

[27] I do not think Qimron is assuming that the subject of the verb is the blessings and the curses, as he seems to suggest for the next phrase, "and not be cancelled," DJD X, 61.

[28] 1QS 5:8; CD 15:9,12; 16:1,4.

incipient dualism of MMT C 29 could be viewed as a predecessor to the radical dualism we know from other Qumranic writings, the concrete meaning of the expression in MMT favors a pre-Qumranic setting for this composition over the more fully-developed sectarian context.

III

In the section entitled "Specifically Qumranic Juridical Expressions," Qimron lists the term מעשים; he apparently considers it a synonym of דברים, as meaning "laws" or "precepts":

> In MMT laws are not called halakhot, מצוות and the like, but rather מעשים (B 2) and מעשי התורה (C27). . . . It is only from the Second Temple period and onwards, however, that we find widespread use of the plural מעשים as a term specially designating the laws or commandments of the Bible. The term מעשים in this sense is also found in some other Qumranic works (4Q174, 1–2 i 7, 1QS 6:18. . .).[29]

For Qimron this meaning of the word is significant because it belongs to the "expressions which are confined to the Qumran sect."[30] The implication is clear. If this meaning of the expression is typical of the writings of the Qumran group, then the composition in which it appears originates from the same source. I have some difficulties with this argument.

Qimron's explanation of the meaning of the word, in my opinion, not only disagrees with its usage in other Qumran writings, but is not even defensible on the basis of the manner in which it is employed in MMT. In the *Graphic Concordance of the Dead Sea Scrolls* more than 130 texts are listed in which the word is used.[31] Of all these occurrences Qimron has been able to detect only two in which this particular meaning of the word would be attested. In all other occurrences the word clearly carries the traditional meaning of "works," "deeds" or the like. If, therefore, this peculiar meaning of the word as "laws" or "precepts" were really characteristic of a Qumranic setting, we should expect a more frequent use of it in those writings. Furthermore, when

[29] DJD X, 139.

[30] DJD X, 138.

[31] J. H. Charlesworth, *Graphic Concordance to the Dead Sea Scrolls* (Tübingen: J. C. B. Mohr [Paul Siebeck]/Louisville: Westminster John Knox, 1991) 407–408.

we look carefully to the two texts Qimron adduces as proof for this meaning, neither one qualifies.

4Q174 (Florilegium) 1–2 i 7 is simply the result of a wrong reading of the manuscript by Allegro,[32] already queried by Strugnell in 1970,[33] corrected by George Brooke in 1985[34] and definitively discarded by the palaeographic analysis of Puech in 1993[35] and by Kuhn in 1994.[36] Allegro read תורה in his text, but the correct reading is, without doubt, מעשי תודה ("works of thanksgiving").

The second text Qimron quotes is 1QS 6:18. Here the reading ומעשיו בתורה is clear, but the meaning of "laws" or "precepts" in this case is impossible. The text is describing the procedure for joining the community. The candidate, to whom all the third person pronouns refer, in 6:14 is first examined לשכלו ולמעשיו ("with regard to his insight and his deeds"); in 6:17 after one year he is examined again לרוחו ומעשו ("concerning his spirit and his work"); and then, after he has completed a year within the community,[37] comes the final examination לפי שכלו ומעשיו בתורה ("with regard to his insight and his works according to the law"). The strict parallel with the preceding lines requires that the usage in 6:18 have the same meaning. As in the other cases, it is the insight and the deeds of the aspirant member which are examined to see if they are according to the law and not the precepts or commandments of the law itself.

Qimron apparently senses the problem which the presence of the preposition *bet* poses to his interpretation and has tried to resolve it by

---

32 J. M. Allegro, DJD V, 53.

33 J. Strugnell, "Notes en marge du Volume V des 'Discoveries in the Judaean Desert of Jordan'," *RevQ* 7 (1967–69) 221.

34 G. J. Brooke, *Exegesis at Qumran: 4QFlorilegium in its Jewish Context* (JSOTSup 29; Sheffield: JSOT Press, 1985), 108.

35 E. Puech, *La croyance des Esséniens en la vie future: Immortalité, résurrection, vie eternelle? Histoire d'une croyance dans le judaïsme ancien* (Etudes Bibliques 22; Paris: Gabalda, 1993) 2.578.

36 H.-W. Kuhn, "Die Bedeutung der Qumrantexte für das Verständnis des Galaterbriefes aus dem Münchener Projekt: Qumran und das Neue Testament," *New Qumran Texts and Studies: Proceedings of the First Meeting of the International Organization for Qumran Studies, Paris 1992* (ed. G. J. Brooke with F. García Martínez; STDJ 15; Leiden: E. J. Brill, 1994) 205–206, pl. 9.

37 Or "a year perfectly" as reads 4QS^{b}. See *The Dead Sea Scrolls. Hebrew, Aramaic, and Greek Texts with English Translations. Volume 1: Rule of the Community and Related Documents* (ed. J. H. Charlesworth; Tübingen: J. C. B. Mohr [Paul Siebeck]/Louisville: Westminster John Knox, 1994) 64–65.

pointing out, rightly, that in some cases מעשים and מעשים בתורה are equivalent within a manuscript (as in 1QS 5:21, 23) and interchangeable in different manuscripts of the same work (e.g., 1QS and 4QS^{d}).[38] But the logical conclusion of this observation is not that מעשים means laws or commandments of the Bible, but that the "works" or "deeds" in question are indeed works according to the law. Anyway, the real problem for the interpretation of Qimron in all these cases, as in 1QS 6:18, is that the personal pronoun attached to the word excludes the possibility of connecting it with the term "Torah" so that it means "commandments" or "precepts" of the Law. It rather refers to "his" or "their" works. In no other Qumranic text, therefore, is to be found the peculiar meaning given by Qimron to its use in MMT. Is this new meaning required by the context of this document?

The term appears three times in MMT, once in the halakhic section at B 2 and twice in the hortatory section at C 23 and 27, the latter the place from which the current title of the composition has been taken. The best way to understand it is to begin with the second occurrence which appears in the fragment whose position is disputed. The text of MMT C 23 exhorts the addressee, whoever it may be, to remember the kings of Israel and to understand מעשיהם ("their deeds"). The personal pronominal suffix makes it clear that the meaning of the word here must be precisely the same as in the Qumran texts just mentioned, a conclusion confirmed by the continuation of the text, which in the best Old Testament tradition asserts that the retribution follows the works which are done: "Whoever among them feared [God and observed the l]aw was delivered from troubles." This conclusion has already been drawn by Qimron who translates in this case: "Think of the kings of Israel and contemplate their deeds."[39]

In 4QMMT C 27, however, Qimron translates מעשי התורה as "some of the precepts of the Torah," but nothing in the text itself demands that we give the word this new meaning. The theme of retribution is repeated in the preceding line, this time applied to David who is also delivered from his troubles because he has been a pious man. Then in a new sentence which introduces the conclusion of the document, the phrase under discussion summarizes the contents of the entire document with the purpose of exhorting the

---

38 DJD X, 139, n. 43.

39 DJD X, 61.

addressee to follow the examples that have been mentioned. If he follows the practices expounded in the legal section he (and his people) will also be rewarded. "We have written to you some of the works of the law" then becomes a perfect summary of MMT: a collection of some of the practices, of the works, which according to the prescriptions of the law should be done in order to be rewarded. In this way, as indicated in the last line, "you will be doing what is upright and good before Him."

In spite of the fragmentary context the same meaning applies, in my opinion, to the first occurrence of the word in the introduction to the legal section at MMT B 2. Qimron again considers it a synonym of דברינו and translates: "These are some of our rulings [. . .] which are [some of the rulings according to the] precepts (of the Torah) in accordance with. . . ."[40] But here also the normal meaning of "works," "deeds" or "practices" would suffice. The following rulings represent the works prescribed in the Law. The remainder of the legal section shows the manner in which the author(s) of the document intend that they be put into practice and followed.

The first interpreter, as far as I am aware, to understand מעשי התורה in this way and to react to its translation as "precepts of the law" was Robert Eisenman, who wrote in 1991:

> They translate it as "Some precepts of the Torah", but, as should be clear from the underlying Hebrew, it deals with "acts" or "works of the Law", a not unknown theme in this period, and where my approach is concerned, a highly significant one.[41]

His reasons for qualifying מעשי התורה as "unclean acts of the Torah" or "unclean works of the Torah" elude me. But he was certainly right in opposing the translation "precepts of the Torah."

We can conclude that the Qumranic setting postulated by Qimron for this phrase does not seem well-founded. The phrase is completely neutral and therefore perfectly compatible with either a pre-Qumranic, Qumranic or post-Qumranic setting for the composition. Its relationship with the well-known New Testament phrase is a subject outside the scope of this paper.[42]

---

[40] DJD X, 47.

[41] R. Eisenman, "A Response to Schiffman on MMT," *Qumran Cave 4 and MMT. Special Report* (ed. Z. J. Kapera; Kraków: Enigma, 1991) 96.

[42] See John Kampen's paper in this collection for a brief discussion.

Conclusion

Of the two phrases discussed in this paper, one points to a pre-Qumranic setting for the composition and the other does not demand a Qumranic setting at all. It is my hope that this rather modest conclusion can be of some help in determining the proper placement of the disputed fragment from 4Q398. In its limited way, it shows that there are no compelling reasons to maintain Qimron's ordering of the fragments if the material indications noted by Strugnell prove after further analysis to be true. The immediate context definitely favours the ordering of the fragments presented by Qimron in the Composite Text, but the location favored by Strugnell also provides a perfectly reasonable text within a pre-Qumranic context, closely related to the later Qumran group.

My argument with Strugnell is that I do not think the order in which we read the fragments in question matters that much. At least I was not able to discover any shocking difference, perhaps because I am convinced that MMT as a whole is better understood as coming from the parent group of the Qumran community. This pre-Qumranic group had already adopted the calendar, followed the halakhah we know from other Qumran compositions and started to develop some of the characteristic theological ideas we know in a much more developed form from the same Qumranic compositions. I already espoused this view in the context of my development of the Groningen Hypothesis.[43]

Qimron and Strugnell, in spite of their quarrels, have jointly given birth to a very healthy child. For that we will always be thankful. The child is not a letter, is not Qumranic and talks about the works that should be done according to the Law. But this child remains one of the most fascinating documents of the Second Temple period and now that it has escaped the custody of both caring fathers will keep us very busy for a long, long time.

---

43 Which considers MMT (and 11QTemple) as "works of the formative period, presenting a vision still not so clearly differentiated from the Essenism which is its ultimate source but containing indications of future developments and offering an already characteristic halakha," F. García Martínez and A. S. van der Woude, "A 'Groningen' Hypothesis of Qumran Origins and Early History," *RevQ* 14/56 (1990) 525. See also F. García Martínez, "Qumran Origins and Early History: A Groningen Hypothesis," *Folia Orientalia* 25 (1988) 122.

The Employment and Interpretation of Scripture in 4QMMT: Preliminary Observations[1]

MOSHE J. BERNSTEIN
Yeshiva University
New York, NY

I. Introduction

One of the few universally agreed upon characteristics of Qumran literature is its bibliocentricity, the crucial role which Hebrew Scripture plays as source and model for the themes, language and subject matter of the various kinds of documents from the Dead Sea caves. In the course of our surveying a "new" Qumran text like 4QMMT, one of our first tasks must therefore be to examine its relationship to Hebrew Scripture. Such a study should ideally be as multifaceted as possible, including issues of language and vocabulary, style, exegesis, and, probably, theology as well. This kind of analysis is particularly important in the evaluation of a legal document, which 4QMMT at least in part is, because it may give us particular insight into the ways in which Scripture and halakhah were related for its author or authors.

Although "biblical interpretation at Qumran" has been the subject of more than a few studies, careful examination of the themes of these books and articles shows that most of the treatments of this question have dealt with non-legal texts.[2] It is particularly premature, therefore,

---

1 Thanks are due to my co-editor, Professor John Kampen, and to Professor Lawrence H. Schiffman for commenting on an earlier version of this paper.

2 G. Vermes, "Biblical Interpretation at Qumran," *Eretz Israel* 20 (1989) 190, nn. 1–9, furnishes a substantial list of earlier treatments of Qumran biblical exegesis which serves as the foundation for the following: F. F. Bruce, *Biblical Exegesis in the Qumran Texts* (Grand Rapids: Eerdmans, 1959); O. Betz, *Offenbarung und Schriftforschung in der Qumransekte* (Tübingen: Mohr [Siebeck], 1960); G. Vermes,

to engage in comparative analysis before we have studied carefully the employment of Scripture within a legal text like 4QMMT. There is no reason to assume that 4QMMT, presumably composed early in the Qumran sect's history, must adhere to the same exegetical methodology as other legal material deriving from the group. The focus of this paper therefore is 4QMMT alone, and not the comparative interpretation of Scripture in Qumranic halakhah. If our independent examination of 4QMMT indicates that there is some shared practice with other texts, our cautious approach will have been vindicated.

Virtually any study of 4QMMT will find its starting point in the recently published edition by Qimron and Strugnell, and this one is no exception. We must always keep in mind, however, as we work from the composite text which they reconstructed, that many questions still remain regarding individual readings of the text and the integration of the six fragmentary manuscripts.[3] Theories about the legal system of the authors, about their attitude to Scripture and halakhah, as well as the identity of their opponents, have an effect on both the reconstruction and interpretation of the fragments. Here, too, I have attempted, as far as possible, to pursue the study of Scripture and its interpretation in 4QMMT with as few preconceptions as I could. At

---

Scripture and Tradition in Judaism (Leiden: Brill, 1973); id., *Post-Biblical Jewish Studies* (Leiden: Brill, 1975); id., "Biblical Proof-Texts in Qumran Literature," *JSS* 34 (1989) 493–508; E. Slomovic, "Toward an Understanding of the Exegesis in the Dead Sea Scrolls," *RevQ* 7 (1969–71) 3–15; D. Patte, *Early Jewish Hermeneutic in Palestine* (Missoula: Scholars, 1975); M. P. Horgan, *Pesharim: Qumran Interpretations of Biblical Books* (Washington, D.C.: Catholic Biblical Association, 1979); H. Gabrion, "L'interprétation de l'Ecriture dans la littérature de Qumran," *ANRW* 19.1 (Berlin: Walter de Gruyter, 1979) 779–848; G. J. Brooke, *Exegesis at Qumran: 4QFlorilegium in its Jewish Context* (Sheffield: JSOT Press, 1985); D. Dimant, "Qumran Sectarian Writings," *Jewish Writings of the Second Temple Period* (ed. M. E. Stone; Philadelphia: Fortress, 1984) 503–514; M. Fishbane, "Use, Authority and Interpretation of Mikra at Qumran," *Mikra: Text, Translation, Reading and Interpretation of the Hebrew Bible in Ancient Judaism and Early Christianity* (ed. M. J. Mulder; Minneapolis: Fortress, 1990) 339–377; J. Milgrom, "The Qumran Cult: Its Exegetical Principles," *Temple Scroll Studies* (ed. G. J. Brooke; Sheffield: JSOT Press, 1990) 165–180; id., "The Scriptural Foundations and Deviations in the Laws of Purity of the Temple Scroll," *Archaeology and History in the Dead Sea Scrolls* (ed. L. H. Schiffman; Sheffield: JSOT Press, 1990) 83–99.

[3] In my discussion of the text below, I rely on the composite text except where I specify otherwise. The only text bracketed in my citations will be material not found, according to the editors, in any of the manuscripts. This mode of citation differs from that of the editors in the composite text, and the citations in this paper therefore will look different from their presentation in the composite text.

times, the lack of a theoretical construct has left me unable to answer many questions with any degree of certainty, but I prefer, at this early stage of our study of 4QMMT, to distinguish clearly between what we know, however tenuously, and what we do not know. Some of my hesitation with regard to the work of Qimron and Strugnell is due to my insistence on extrapolating as little as possible from the text at this time. In a few cases, I shall suggest readings or reconstructions of the text which differ from those of Qimron and Strugnell.

II. Editorial Presumptions About the Role of Scripture in 4QMMT

In describing 4QMMT Qimron asserts that "MMT, however (unlike the Sadducean Book of Decrees), does allude to the biblical source of most of its halakhot."[4] He claims further

> In most of the halakhot there are allusions to the biblical passages on which the particular halakha is based. Some words from each biblical parallel occur in the halakha of MMT (sometimes in a grammatical form different from that of the source).[5]

For Qimron, this familiarity with the sources of the halakhot helps to elucidate them even when the text is damaged. But it is not yet clear to me that even scriptural allusions can clarify all of the difficulties in the phraseology of the halakhot in a fragmentary text.[6]

Qimron concludes his brief summary of the formulation of the halakhot by writing, "In fact, MMT actually consists of certain precepts of the Pentateuch as understood by the sectarians."[7] This in fact is true

---

[4] DJD X, 132. This is not the place to discuss Qimron's apparent acceptance of the rabbinic description of the Sadducean ספר גזרתא. The first interpretation in the scholion to Megillat Taʿanit for the fourth of Tammuz (ed. H. Lichtenstein, *HUCA* 8–9 [1931–32] 331) describes it as a Sadducee list of capital punishments, which does not cite biblical authority. I simply raise the question whether we are to rely on a comparatively late rabbinic source for the nature of this lost and enigmatic document. In light of the presumed Sadducee preference, according to rabbinic tradition, for literalist readings of Scripture, the scholion is at least a little bit puzzling, and Qimron's reliance on it is perhaps misplaced.

[5] *Ibid.*, 136.

[6] Qimron himself writes, DJD X, 133, n. 23, "It should be noted that MMT deals with the observance of the commandments, not with the manner in which they are deduced; it makes only passing reference to such fundamental questions." Even if this statement is not taken to be at variance with those quoted immediately above, it certainly de-emphasizes the relationship of the laws in 4QMMT to Scripture.

[7] DJD X, 136. Is there an echo of מקצת מעשי התורה in "certain precepts of the Pentateuch"?

of some of MMT, but not of all of it. There are laws in MMT which seemingly have no scriptural source. We should not strive too hard to make the possibly Sadducean authors of MMT the kind of "Scripture only" figures which rabbinic Judaism attempted to make of them. For example, the laws in B 49–54 forbidding entry into the Temple for certain groups and B 55–58 regarding the impurity of poured liquids show no signs of scriptural derivation in 4QMMT.[8] Once it becomes clear that some of the laws in MMT do not derive from the interpretation of biblical verses, another aspect of the document becomes more perplexing. Although the dispute between the author of the document and his opponents does not revolve solely around scriptural interpretation, we can see no distinction in the arrangement of this text between disputes which are scripturally-oriented and those which are not. In other words, the basis of the dispute does not at first glance affect the literary structure of 4QMMT. This matter will not be touched upon in our subsequent discussion, and we merely point it out as an area which demands further study from the perspectives of the structure of 4QMMT and of the nature of the disputes between the author and his opponents.

III. Biblical Language and Style

When I mentioned the topic of this paper to a number of my graduate students in advance of the AJS meetings, one of them looked at me quizzically. She had studied some of 4QMMT as an undergraduate when it circulated only in *samizdat* copies, and wondered whether there was any Scripture or scriptural interpretation in it at all. Her questioning glance was not out of place. Despite the fact that we are all familiar with the fairly accurate truism mentioned above that the literature of Qumran is heavily scripturally-oriented, it is noteworthy, for our purposes, to recall that 4QMMT was once titled 4QMishnique, presumably on the basis of language as well as content.[9]

---

[8] L. H. Schiffman, "The Prohibition of the Skins of Animals in the *Temple Scroll* and *Miqṣat Maʿaseh Ha-Torah*," *Proceedings of the Tenth World Congress of Jewish Studies: Division A* (Jerusalem: World Union of Jewish Studies, 1990) 193, writes, citing Y. Yadin, *The Temple Scroll* (Jerusalem: Israel Exploration Society, 1983) 1.309, concerning 11QT 47:7–15, which presents material partially parallel to 4QMMT B 18–23: "The attempt to suggest a biblical derivation for this law is highly unsuccessful." Schiffman prefers to see the law as deriving from "legal argumentation." I believe that the same is true of B 18–23 despite the law of Lev 11:39–40.

[9] J. T. Milik, "Le travail d'édition des manuscrits du Désert de Juda," *Volume du*

Even fairly recently, John Strugnell described MMT as being "written in a form of proto-Mishnaic Hebrew, not in Qumran's typical biblicizing Hebrew."[10]

Qimron's thorough linguistic survey and analysis of 4QMMT makes it eminently clear that, despite such initial perceptions, the language of MMT owes a good deal to biblical Hebrew. Identifying the nature of this debt, however, will present us with a significant, although not unusual, analytical difficulty. In its style 4QMMT resembles neither 11QTemple which is formulated in the mode of legal material from the Hebrew Bible nor other Qumran legal texts such as CD and its Cave 4 ancestors. The unusual "epistolary" genre of this text may be responsible for both the very different style of formulation of law in 4QMMT and its very different handling of the biblical text and idiom from that found in other Qumran legal material. We must ask ourselves whether the employment of scriptural language in the central legal portion of a work like MMT is to be understood as biblical exegesis in those passages where the law seems to be related to a biblical passage, or whether it is merely the stylistic employment or imitation of convenient terminology, without regard to the derivation of the law. A good illustration of this problem can be found in my treatment below of the text on sufferers from skin-disease.

Congrès, Strasbourg 1956 (*VTSup* 4; Leiden: Brill, 1957) 24: "deux pièces de papyrus appartenant à un ouvrage apocalyptique . . . ," and proceeds to cite language from section C of 4QMMT, including the words מקצת מעשי התורה. Cf. id., *Ten Years of Discovery in the Wilderness of Judaea* (tr. J. Strugnell; London: SCM, 1959) 130 regarding "two works found in several copies in Cave IV . . . which are written in a neo-classical Hebrew with features, however, proper to the Mishnaic dialect (such as the frequent use of the participle instead of the indicative and of the relative *š* instead of *ašer*)." He cites material from 4QMMT in his discussion of 3Q15 (Copper Scroll) in DJD III, 225, as "étude pseudépigraphique mishnique." In E. Qimron and J. Strugnell, "An Unpublished Halakhic Letter from Qumran," *Biblical Archaeology Today: Proceedings of the International Conference on Biblical Archaeology Jerusalem, April 1984* (Jerusalem: Israel Exploration Society, 1985) 405, we read, "The initial impression created by the language of MMT is that it differs from that of the other Dead Sea Scrolls, and is very similar to MH. However, a closer examination of the linguistic components proves that the similarity to MH is restricted to vocabulary and to the use of the particle ש, whereas in areas of grammar (spelling, phonology, morphology, and syntax) there is a very great similarity to the Hebrew of the other Dead Sea Scrolls." For Qimron's most recent position, cf. DJD X, Chapter 3, "The Language," 65–108, especially 3.7, "MMT's Language and its Relation to Other Types of Hebrew," 104–108.

[10] J. Strugnell, "The Qumran Scrolls: A Report on Work in Progress," *Jewish Civilization in the Hellenistic-Roman Period* (ed. S. Talmon; Sheffield: Sheffield Academic Press, 1991) 99.

Likewise, in attempting to restore lacunae in the text, when ought we to be guided by biblical formulae, and when should we allow for freer composition by the author? The description and analysis of biblical interpretation can thus be more elusive even than the search for biblical language. The fact that there is no comprehensive, or even large-scale, treatment of legal exegetical methodology at Qumran available for comparative purposes complicates the issue further.

This study will be limited to Sections B and C of MMT and, even then, we will deal with only some of the potential sub-topics of our topic. Concerning the subject of the utilization of biblical language in the scroll, and specifically its vocabulary, our study would add little to the presentation by Qimron in Chapter III of his edition.[11] Classifying the lexical elements into four groups, Qimron attempts to locate the language of 4QMMT amid biblical, Second Temple and mishnaic Hebrew. He notes that a certain amount of the vocabulary from biblical Hebrew which does not appear in later Hebrew is to be found in MMT; most of this vocabulary, however, does occur elsewhere at Qumran so that its appearance here is unsurprising. A few words such as בדד, which are not typical of Qumran literature, owe their presence in MMT to biblicizing contexts.[12] A question which we pose for future examination is: Why does the author of 4QMMT at times employ biblical vocabulary and at times deviate from it? Is the employment of biblical vocabulary in any way related to the particular law's being scripturally-based or not?

A good deal of scriptural imitation is evident in the idiom of MMT, like that of so many other Dead Sea Scrolls. At B 14, the language והסורף אותה והאוסף את אפרה והמזה את [מי] החטאת ("he who burns it, he who gathers its ashes, and he who sprinkles the [water of] purification"[13]) derives from expressions employed in Num 19:8, 10, 21. An expression like ולהיות יראים מהמקדש ("they should be reverential of the Sanctuary"; B 49) is clearly based on Lev 19:30 ומקדשי תיראו ("you shall revere my sanctuary"), and a phrase such

[11] DJD X, 65–108. Lexical elements are dealt with on pp. 83–101. This section should be supplemented by his article "Observations on the History of Early Hebrew (1000 B.C.E.–200 C.E.) in the Light of the Dead Sea Documents," *The Dead Sea Scrolls: Forty Years of Research* (eds. D. Dimant and U. Rappaport; Leiden/Jerusalem: Brill/Magnes, 1992) 349–361.

[12] DJD X, 84.

[13] Translations from 4QMMT are, as far as possible, my own. Occasional coincidence with Qimron and Strugnell's rendition was, however, unavoidable.

as ונשים]לוקחים [להיו]תם עצם אחת ("they take [wives in order to] become one bone"; B 40) derives from Gen 2:23–24 עצם מעצמי ובשר מבשרי . . . והיו לבשר אחד ("bone from my bone and flesh from my flesh . . . they shall be as one flesh"), with only a slight adjustment. In both of these cases, there is no interpretation of the underlying scriptural text which appears to be employed purely stylistically. In the "hortatory epilogue," the description of David as איש חסדים (C 25) is based on a complex of allusions in Scripture which associate David with the Hebrew root חסד, at times referring to his actions and at times to God's. Thus, 2 Sam 7:15 וחסדי לא יסור ממנו, Isa 55:3 ואכרתה לכם ברית עולם חסדי דוד הנאמנים, Ps 89:50 (cf. also 25, 29, 34) איה חסדיך הראשונים אדני נשבעת לדוד באמונתך, 2 Chron 6:42 זכרה לחסדי דויד עבדך. This is more than mere stylistics and probably represents the borrowing of a biblical theological frame of reference more than anything else.

Qimron writes that the concluding lines of 4QMMT (C31–32) ונחשבה לך לצדקה בעשותך הישר והטוב לפנו לטוב לך ולישראל ("it shall be reckoned for you as righteousness when you do that which is upright and good before Him, so that it be good for you and for Israel") are "perhaps influenced by Deut 6:24–25" לטוב לנו כל הימים לחיתנו כהיום הזה וצדקה תהיה לנו כי נשמר לעשות את כל המצוה הזאת לפני ה' אלהינו כאשר צונו. He refers further to Deut 12:28 למען ייטב לך ולבניך אחריך עד עולם כי תעשה הטוב והישר בעיני ה' אלהיך as the model for the phrase beginning בעשותך.[14] This passage indicates the difficulty with determining the biblical model for the language of a text like MMT. If Qimron is correct in his reference to Deut 6:24–25, then Deut 6:18 ועשית הישר והטוב בעיני ה' למען ייטב לך is more likely than Deut 12:28 to be the model for בעשותך הישר והטוב לפנו, since it is more proximate to the other passage which influences the context, and furthermore, since, uniquely in the Hebrew Bible, it shares with MMT the word order הישר והטוב. But there is no question that ונחשבה לך לצדקה is modeled either on Gen 15:6 והאמן בה' ויחשבה לו צדקה or Ps 106:31 ותחשב לו לצדקה.[15] I wonder

---

[14] Qimron, DJD X, 63.

[15] Qimron does not refer to these passages *ad loc.*, but alludes to them, p. 84, as well as the phrase ויתחשב לו לצדקה, deriving from Gen 15:6, which he cites from J. T. Milik's edition of the Copper Scroll (above, n. 9) 225. The text in which

whether the employment of Gen 15:6 in 4QMMT is not meant to convey an overtone of proper belief or of taking something on trust (והאמן), as well as proper practice.

IV. Scriptural Exegesis in Section B

A. Implicit Scriptural Exegesis

Turning to Scripture as the source for the law in 4QMMT, we begin with a passage like [כי לבני] הכוהנ[ים] ראוי להזהר בדבר הזה בשל שלוא י[היו] מסיא[י]ם את העם עוון ("[for] it is right [for the pr]iests to be careful in this matter so that they [should not] cause the people to b[e]ar guilt;" B 11–13), despite the fact that there is no citation formula present. Qimron notes correctly that MMT reads Lev 22:16 והשיאו אותם עון אשמה ("they shall cause them to bear the iniquity of guilt") as meaning that the priests shall cause the laymen to bear guilt. We must add to his observation that it is the following words in Lev 22:16 באכלם את קדשיהם ("when they eat their sacred food") which suggest to the interpreter that the subject of the biblical text is the proper time for eating sacrifices, which is the very point at issue in MMT. The phraseology of 4QMMT thus indicates an implicit interpretation of the biblical passage. The same may be true of B 72–74 ועל [טמאת נפש] האדם אנחנו אומרים שכול עצם ש[היא . . .] ושלמה כמשפט המת או החלל הוא ("and regarding the [impurity of a] human [corpse] we say that any bone w[hich is . . .] and whole has the law of the dead or the slain") where the equation of bone with dead or slain derives from, or is modeled on, Num 19:16 וכל אשר יגע על פני השדה בחלל חרב או במת או בעצם אדם or 19:18 הנגע בעצם או בחלל או במת.[16]

---

that phrase appears (4Q225 2 i 8 [psJub^a]) has just been published by James C. VanderKam in DJD XIII, 145 and Plate X, with the reading ותחשב לו צדקה. The first three letters are only partially preserved, but there is clearly no ל before צדקה.

[16] For discussion, see DJD X, 170–71. I believe that Qimron's restoration עצם ש[היא חסרה] is unlikely, since חסרה ושלמה is a very improbable combination (Qimron renders "[whether it] has flesh on it or [not]"). I should suggest, fairly unconfidently, עצם ש[היא מלאה] ושלמה ("a bone w[hich is complete] and whole"), implying that whereas flesh conveys impurity in very small quantity, a bone needs to be whole in order to do so. This exegesis, that only a complete bone is called a bone, would then compare only whole bones to the dead or slain.

The laws regarding fourth year produce and animal tithe ואף על מטעת עצי המאכל הנטע בארץ ישראל כראשית הוא לכוהנים ומעשר הבקר והצון לכוהנים הוא ("and also regarding the planting of food trees, that which is planted[17] in the land of Israel belongs like firstfruits to the priests; and the tithe of cattle and sheep belongs to the priests"; B 62–64) are obviously based on Lev 19:23–24 וכי תבאו אל הארץ ונטעתם כל עץ מאכל . . . ובשנה הרביעת יהיה כל פריו קדש הלולים לה' and 27:32 וכל מעשר בקר וצאן . . . העשירי יהיה קדש לה', respectively, although the scriptural foundations and exegesis are only inferential.[18] Only the terms עצי מאכל and מעשר הבקר והצון are biblical, as noted by Qimron, but the nature of the connection to Scripture is not difficult to extrapolate. In particular, the limitation of the law to planting in the land of Israel is based on the words אל הארץ in Lev 19:23, and the assignment to the priests derives from the expression "holy to the Lord" in both passages in Leviticus.[19] It is likely that the common assignment of these products to the priests, based on the identical exegesis of very similar verses, is what generates their juxtaposition in 4QMMT.

A passage like B 39–41 is difficult to characterize with regard to its relationship to the biblical text because of its fragmentary nature. Before the text of B 40 cited above which began ונשים לוקחים ("and they take wives"), but not immediately before it because there is clearly a gap in the text, we read in MMT [ועל העמו]ני והמואבי [ו]הממזר ופ[צוע הדכה וכרו]ת השפכת שהם באים בקהל ("[and regarding the Ammon]ite and Moabite [and] bastard and one cr[ushed in his genitals and cu]t in his member who enter the congregation"). This clearly refers to Deut 23:2–4 where a number of groups are prohibited from entry בקהל ה' ("into the Lord's assembly"). The context of 4QMMT implies furthermore that prohibited marriages are being

17 I read על מטעת עצי המאכל as a heading, with the law beginning with הנטע. I am not certain whether the latter is to be vocalized *niṭṭaʿ* (Niphal participle) or *neṭaʿ* (noun as in the mishnaic נטע רבעי).

18 Qimron, DJD X, 53, writes "Curiously enough, neither fruits nor the fourth year are explicitly mentioned in this halakhah, and the content can be deduced only from the linguistic allusions to Lev 19:23."

19 Qimron, DJD X, 164, lays out the linguistic resemblance between the biblical and Qumran texts. It is also possible that the language of Lev 19:25 "In the fifth year you shall eat its fruit" implies "but not before the fifth year!" See further Qimron's valuable comments, 164–166, on the relationship of these texts to other Second Temple legal sources.

discussed. So far the law does not appear to be one on which there could be dispute, as it merely restates the biblical injunctions agreed to by all Jewish groups at this time.

Qimron's reconstruction of B 41 adds the words ובאים למקדש ("and they enter the Sanctuary"), which could imply double exegesis of the idiom "to enter the assembly of the Lord," i.e., the prohibition of intermarriage as well as the injunction against entry into the Temple. Conceptually, this proceeds along the lines which are implied in 4Q174 (Florilegium)[20] 1–2 i 3–4 הואה הבית אשר לוא יבוא שמה [איש אשר בבשרו מום] עולם ועמוני ומואבי וממזר ובן נכר וגר עד עולם ("That is the house where no [one with a] permanent [defect in his body] or an Ammonite or Moabite or bastard or foreigner or proselyte may enter forever"). But since the only unrestored reference to the sanctuary in this context in MMT is B 49 ולהיות יראים מהמקדש, which is a bit distant, I am far from convinced by Qimron's restoration in line 41, despite the fact that it adds something to the biblical regulation which could be the subject of dispute between the author and his opponents.[21] The simple sense of MMT is that the subject under discussion is the law of marriage, not of the Temple.

B. Exegesis Including כתוב*-Formulas*

Let us turn to an examination of one of the most interesting "scriptural" features of 4QMMT, its employment of the citation-formula כתוב, which generally introduces direct quotations of Scripture elsewhere at Qumran and in rabbinic literature as well.[22]

---

20 I accept for the purpose of my analysis here the reading of Qimron, DJD X, 159, following Y. Yadin ("A Midrash on 2 Sam VII," *IEJ* 9 [1959] 96). For fuller discussion of other possible readings and an interpretation of this section of Florilegium, see G. J. Brooke, *Exegesis at Qumran* (above, n. 2), 86, 100–101, 227.

21 Qimron asserts, DJD X, 158, that Lam 1:10 כי ראתה גוים באו מקדשה אשר צויתה לא יבאו בקהל לך ("For she saw nations enter her Sanctuary whom You commanded shall not enter into Your assembly") understands the phrase "to enter into the assembly of the Lord" in Deuteronomy "as referring to entry into the sanctuary, while the rabbis explained it as referring to marriage with Jewish women." But the verse in Lamentations need not be reinterpreting Deuteronomy. It more likely presents an *a fortiori* argument: these nations are not permitted even to marry into the Israelite nation (and certainly not to enter the Temple), but they have now entered the Temple. If there is any reference in the lacuna of MMT to the prohibition against entering the Temple, it is likely to be based on the inference from the text in Lamentations.

22 Citation formulas at Qumran have been studied since the earliest period of

According to Qimron's index, the term כתוב appears in the manuscripts of 4QMMT six times in B and five times in C, to which the editors have added reconstructed occurrences (which I believe are superfluous) at B 10 and B 77.

B 27–28 reads [וע]ל שא כתוב [איש כי ישחט במחנה או ישחט] מחוץ למחנה שור וכשב ועז ("[*and re*]*garding that which is written* [should an individual slaughter in the camp or slaughter] outside the camp an ox, sheep or goat"). If reconstructed correctly, this text is a paraphrase of Lev 17:3 איש איש מבית ישראל אשר ישחט שור או כשב או עז במחנה או אשר ישחט מחוץ למחנה ("should any individual from the house of Israel slaughter an ox, sheep or goat in the camp or should he slaughter outside the camp"). The biblical text continues by imposing the penalty of *karet* for one who slaughters anywhere outside of the tabernacle. It is immediately clear that כתוב in MMT need not precede a quotation, but that paraphrase is to be considered כתוב as well.[23] This fact may be very important when we come across passages throughout Qumran literature which purport by

---

Dead Sea Scroll scholarship. The following is a selection from the literature: F. L. Horton, "Formulas of Introduction in the Qumran Literature," *RevQ* 7 (1969–71) 505–14; J. A. Fitzmyer, "The Use of Explicit Old Testament Quotations in Qumran Literature and in the NT," *Essays on the Semitic Background of the New Testament* (London: Geoffrey Chapman, 1971) 3–58; Horgan, *Pesharim* (above, n. 2), 239–44; Fishbane (above, n. 2), "Use of Citations and Citation Formulae," 347–356; D. Dimant, "The Hebrew Bible in the Dead Sea Scrolls: Torah Quotations in the Damascus Covenant," [Hebrew] *Sha'arei Talmon: Studies in the Bible, Qumran and the Ancient Near East Presented to Shemaryahu Talmon* (ed. M. Fishbane and E. Tov; Winona Lake: Eisenbrauns, 1992) 113*-122*; Vermes, "Proof-Texts" (above, n. 2); J. M. Baumgarten, "A 'Scriptural' Citation in 4Q Fragments of the Damascus Document," *JJS* 43 (1992) 95–98; M. J. Bernstein, "Introductory Formulas for Citation and Re-Citation of Biblical Verses in the Qumran Pesharim: Observations on a Pesher Technique," *DSD* 1 (1994) 30–70.

23 Qimron, DJD X, 140–41, writes of the use of כתוב, "This word is known in MH as a technical term introducing scriptural citations. In MMT it never introduces biblical verses. It sometimes precedes a description or paraphrase of a biblical verse" as at B 76–77, 66–67, and 70. "At B 38 it does not refer to any specific verse at all. It would therefore seem that כתוב is not intended to introduce a verbatim quotation from Scripture, but rather to introduce the statement which was derived from such a verse. This use of the word כתוב is distinctive of MMT, but כתוב (or אמר) followed by a paraphrase is also found in the Damascus Covenant." He cites as evidence L. Ginzberg, *An Unknown Jewish Sect* (New York: JTSA, 1976) 192–200 and Baumgarten "'Scriptural' Citation." That כתוב need not introduce a quotation in 4QMMT is clear; whether it can is another issue.

their introductory formulas to be biblical citations, but which are at variance with MT.[24] The introduction of non-citations by כתוב might at times explain such "variant" quotes.

The second occurrence of the citation formula כתוב comes at the end of a passage dealing with the slaughter and eating of a pregnant animal and its fetus (B 36–38).[25]

[ועל העברות א]נחנו חו[שבים שאין לזבוח א]ת האם ואת הולד ביום אחד
[... ועל] האוכל [אנח]נו חושבים שאיאכל את הולד
[שבמעי אמו לאחר שחיטתו ואתם יודעים שהו]א כן <u>והדבר כתוב עברה</u>

[And regarding pregnant animals w]e th[ink that one ought not to sacrifice] mother and child on one day. [. . . and regarding] one eating, [w]e think that the fetus [in its mother's innards] may be eaten [(only) after its slaughter and you know that it i]s so, *and the matter is written (about?) a pregnant one.*

The biblical verse on which these laws are based is, of course, Lev 22:28 ושור או שה אתו ואת בנו לא תשחטו ביום אחד. Regarding the biblical law prohibiting the slaughter of the parent animal together with its offspring, no Pharisee or other Second Temple Jew would have disagreed (putting aside the issue whether the prohibition pertains to male as well as female parents).

The uniqueness of the Qumran treatment, according to Qimron's restoration, is the association of Lev 22:28 with the prohibition against slaughtering a pregnant animal and the requirement to slaughter a fetus found alive in the womb of its dead mother.[26] This must be the

---

24 See the discussion in Baumgarten, "Scriptural Citation." I have discussed briefly the issue of non-MT citations (or paraphrases) introduced by כתוב in the pesharim in "Citation and Re-Citation," 53–54, nn. 67 and 70, and 57.

25 Qimron, DJD X, 158, assumes that the first half of the law refers only to sacrificial animals, based on the juxtaposition with B 35 which concludes א[י]נם שוחטים במקדש ("[they] do not slaughter in the sanctuary") and on the context of the related passage in the Temple Scroll which deals only with sacrifices. His arguments, however, are not completely compelling, as even he agrees that the second part refers to non-sacred slaughter. If the entire law deals with non-sacred slaughter, the restoration לזבוח ("to sacrifice") can be replaced by לשחוט ("to slaughter") without difficulty. See the brief discussion in L. H. Schiffman, "*Miqṣat Ma'aśeh Ha-Torah* and the *Temple Scroll*," *RevQ* 14 (1990) 448–451.

26 DJD X, 157. The law of not sacrificing pregnant animals is juxtaposed with the law of not sacrificing parent and child on the same day also in 11QTemple 52:5–7 which introduces to the context also the rule not to take the mother bird with its young.

subject of the dispute between the author of 4QMMT and his opponents. Granted the difficulty of restoring the gaps in this passage, how are we to understand "[and you know that i]t is so and the matter is written about a pregnant one"? The syntax of the Hebrew (underlined in the citation above) is very awkward, and there is certainly no obvious way of reading the biblical text which would imply that slaughtering pregnant animals is prohibited,[27] and it is even more difficult to infer from the text that a fetus found in a slaughtered animal must be slaughtered separately. The "argument" of MMT (if we may dignify it with that name) asserts, nevertheless, that this is the implication of Scripture. This appears to be the effect of the employment of the term כתוב based on Qimron's restoration of the preceding material. But so much of B 36–38 is reconstruction that a debate on the employment of כתוב cannot be grounded on hard facts.

The next two occurrences of כתוב are in the laws pertaining to skin-disease (צרעת) where the context is less fragmentary (B64–72).

ואף על הצרועים אנחנו
א[ומרים שלוא י]בואו   עם טהרת הקודש כי בדד
י]היו [מחוץ לבית וא]ף כתוב שמעת שיגלח וכבס [י]שב מחוץ
[לאוהלו שבעת י]מים ועתה בהיות טמאתם עמהם
הצ[רועים באים ע]ם טהרת הקודש לבית ואתם יודעים
[שעל השוגג שלוא יעשה את המצוה] ונעלה ממנו להביא
חטאת וע[ל העושה ביד רמה כת]וב שהואה בוזה ומגדף
[וכול עוד היות לה]מ[ה ט]מאות נ[גע] אין להאכילם מהקו[ד]שים
עד בוא השמש ביום השמיני

And also regarding those suffering skin-disease, we s[ay that they shall not e]nter with the sacred pure (food) but they shall be alone [outside the house.[28] *And i]t is also written* that from the time that he shaves and washes [he shall] remain outside of [his tent for seven d]ays. But now, while their impurity is upon them, those suf[fering skin-disease enter

---

27 One could claim that אתו ואת בנו could be expanded to include the pregnant animal and its fetus, but the masculine forms in the biblical text might argue against such an extension.

28 I translate here Qimron's text; for an alternative restoration, see below. Qimron, DJD X, p.55, renders "(and) outside any house." I believe that this is too strong a reading of a reconstituted text. It is more likely that it is to be translated as I have suggested. Likewise, the phrase in B 68 ע]ם טהרת הקודש לבית should be rendered, contra Qimron, with a definite article. The fundamental meaning of the passages, however, remains the same.

> wi]th sacred pure (food) into the house. And you know [that it is incumbent on one unintentionally not performing a commandment] from whom it is hidden to bring a sin-offering, whil[e regarding one who acts presumptuously *it is wr]itten* that he is a contemner and a blasphemer. [And as long as t]he[y have[29] the im]purity of d[isease], one should not allow them to eat of holy thin[gs] until sunset on the eighth day.

In this passage, we can see the biblical text which underlies the law more clearly. MMT juxtaposes a phrase from Lev 13:46 כל ימי אשר הנגע בו יטמא טמא הוא בדד ישב מחוץ למחנה מושבו ("all the days that the disease is upon him he shall remain impure; he is impure, *alone shall he remain, his residence is to be outside the camp*"[30]), paraphrased as בדד [י]היו [מחוץ לבית according to Qimron, with a paraphrase of Lev 14:8 וכבס המטהר את בגדיו וגלח את כל שערו ורחץ במים וטהר ואחר יבוא אל המחנה וישב מחוץ לאהלו שבעת ימים ("the one being cleansed shall wash his garment and shave all of his hair, wash his flesh in water and become pure; afterward he shall enter into the camp and he shall remain outside his tent for seven days"). The use of וכבס, with *vav* consecutive, in B 66 marks the citation as biblical even more clearly.

According to Qimron's restoration, the paraphrase of Lev 13:46 is purely stylistic, with the language of the biblical text which pertains to a leper during his full impurity taken (perhaps misleadingly to us) out of context.[31] The meaning of the Qumran text then must be that during the first stage of purification the leper may not enter houses. On the other hand, the contrast with ועתה בהיות טמאתם עמהם הצ[רועים באים ע[ם טהרת הקודש לבית ("But now, while their impurity is upon them, those suf[fering skin-disease enter wi]th sacred

---

29 I prefer something along the lines of this reading to Qimron's [ואף בהיות לה[מ]ה ("and also while they have") which creates more of a break from the previous line. My restoration might be said to resemble ועתה בהיות טמאתם עמהם of B 67.

30 Qimron, DJD X, p. 168, quite surprisingly, assumes that מחוץ למחנה מושבו which we translate "his residence is to be outside the camp," means "outside 'the camp of his dwelling,'" without noting that such a translation demands revocalizing the Hebrew text to read לְמַחֲנֵה as a construct where MT has the absolute form with definite article לַמַּחֲנֶה.

31 Qimron, DJD X, 169, writes, in defense of his restoration מחוץ לבית, "The passage is then no more than the heading to the polemic mentioned in the two lines that follow."

pure (food) into the house") shows how literally MMT takes מחוץ לאהלו in its paraphrase of Lev 14:8. It appears that MMT understands the reason for the biblical exclusion of the healing leper from his home to be his defilement of any pure food which is to be found therein.[32]

As the impetus for the restoration seems to be the invariable position of the editors that the author of MMT must be polemicizing on all points to which he alludes, a posture which I believe is open to question, the certainty with which the restoration is posited is also unsure. Accepting, nevertheless, a polemical motive for these lines, I suggest the following restoration and interpretation as a heuristic alternative: בדד יהיו [מחוץ לעיר ו]אף כתוב שמעת שיגלח וכבס [י]שב מחוץ [לביתו שבעת י]מים ("They shall be alone [outside *the city*. And] it is also written that from the time that he shaves and washes [h]e shall remain outside [*his house* for seven d]ays").[33] In this reading, both paraphrases of the biblical text are exegetical, rather than stylistic. The author of MMT believes that the correct interpretation of the biblical text is that those with skin-disease are to be kept out of cities (interpretation of biblical מחנה) and,

---

[32] This may be the simple sense of the biblical text, although rabbinic exegesis interprets אהלו as a euphemism for אשתו, and bars the *meṣoraʿ* from sexual intercourse. Cf. J. Milgrom, *Leviticus 1–16: A New Translation with Introduction and Commentary* (Anchor Bible 3; New York: Doubleday, 1991) 842–43, who cites this passage in 4QMMT as proof of his interpretation of the biblical passage.

[33] The first part of this restoration is equivalent to the reconstruction with למחנה which Qimron proposes and rejects, DJD X, 168–169, on the grounds that "this solution seems forced and hardly fits the continuation, which concerns the isolation of the healed leper." I think that the reading and interpretation suggested here is not subject to Qimron's objections. Qimron, DJD X, 169, n. 170, claims that his reconstruction מחוץ לבית is supported by 4QToh^{a} (4Q274) 1 i 1–2 בדד לכל הטמאים ישב ורחוק מן הטהרה שתים עשרה אמה בדברו אליו ומערב צפון לכול בית מושב ישב רחוק כמדה הזות ("Apart from all the unclean shall he remain, and twelve cubits distant from the purity when speaking with him. And he shall remain northwest of every residence by that distance." Complete text and translation in J. Milgrom, "4QTohora^{a}: An Unpublished Qumran Text on Purities," *Time To Prepare the Way in the Wilderness: Papers on the Qumran Scrolls by Fellows of the Institute for Advanced Studies of the Hebrew University, Jerusalem, 1989–90* [ed. D. Dimant and L. H. Schiffman; Leiden: Brill, 1995] 60–61 and J. M. Baumgarten, "The Laws About Fluxes in 4QTohora^{a} [4Q274]," *ibid.*, 1–3.) If Qimron and Milgrom are correct contra Baumgarten (and I think that they are), that this passage refers to the *meṣoraʿ*, the cited text may simply be the definition of מחוץ למחנה of the biblical text, or of my reconstructed מחוץ לעיר.

furthermore, that during the seven-day purification period they are to be kept from their homes (biblical אהלו). The polemic of the sectarian author against his opponents ועתה בהיות טמאתם עמהם הצ[רועים באים ע]ם טהרת הקודש לבית applies to both aspects of the treatment of skin-disease sufferers; they are not kept out of all cities during their impurity and they are not barred from their homes during the first stage of purification.[34]

Because of the apparent reference in B 70 to Num 15:30–31 את ה' הוא מגדף ונכרתה . . . כי דבר ה' בזה ואת מצותו הפר, Qimron restores the missing portion of B 69 שעל השוגג שלוא יעשה את המצוה to refer to the unintentional violation of the commandments as implied in Num 15:27 (with the extant continuation apparently based on Lev 5:2), and the missing portion of B 70 on the basis of Num 15:30 והנפש אשר תעשה ביד רמה.[35] If it were not for the appearance of the citation formula כתוב followed by language reminiscent of Num 15:30–31, I should have thought that the resemblances to the biblical text were stylistic and not exegetical. In any event, the contextual employment of the biblical verse is difficult to understand; it appears to interrupt the laws of צרעת which continue in B 71–72. Why in the middle of the critique of his opponents' practices in regulating skin-disease does the author of MMT cast a more general aspersion against them? Qimron, sensitive to this problem, writes,

> Here MMT draws the attention of the addressees to the fact that the opponents of the sect, in allowing the lepers to touch pure food before

---

[34] It is also plausible that not every section of every law cited by the author of 4QMMT needs to be cited for polemic reasons. Thus even if we deny Qimron's assertion (DJD X, 169) that B 64–66 is only a heading, it is possible that the term אנחנו אומרים ("we say") introduces the whole section which consists of two laws, even though MMT disagrees with its opponents only in the second law, where the opponents are accused of allowing those still in a state of impurity to enter houses which may contain pure food.

[35] DJD X, 54. In the chapter on the halakhah, DJD X, 169, Qimron writes, "We believe that ונעלה ממנו should be compared to ונעלם ממנו in Lev 4:13–14, 5:1–4, and that the words בוזה ומגדף should be compared to בזה and גדף in Num 15:27–31."

> completing the last stage of their purification, are intentionally transgressing. In such a way they are despising God.[36]

If he is correct, the biblical text is not being employed only for stylistic reasons, but for its halakhic context as well. Perhaps, while accepting Qimron's reconstruction of B 70, we should restore the first half of B 69 on the basis of Lev 5:2 or 5:3, including a reference to טומאה ("impurity") which is a theme of those verses, although I do not have a specific reconstruction to recommend. The flow of the argument in the text then would be that even one who violates the laws of purity unintentionally must bring a sin-offering and that wilful violation is to be treated even more severely.

B 76 and 77 have two certain occurrences of the כתוב formula, and another is restored by Qimron in B 77. Regarding immorality practiced by the people, MMT writes והמה ב[ני זרע] קדש משכתוב קודש ישראל ("and they are ch[ildren of] holy [seed] *as it is written, 'holy is Israel'*"). Qimron asserts that "כתוב can hardly introduce a quotation of Jer 2:3. It states rather that Israel is holy according to the Scripture."[37] Nevertheless, I believe that what we have here is a two-word biblical citation which affirms the sanctity of Israel. When a quotation is inexact, we may surely characterize it as a paraphrase, but there is no reason to claim that כתוב cannot introduce verbatim citation in MMT, even though that is not its primary function.

The text continues (B 76–79)[38] ועל בה[מתו הטה]ורה כתוב שלוא לרבעה כלאים ועל לבו[שו שלוא] יהיה שעטנז ושלוא לזרוע שדו וכ[רמו כלאי]ם בגלל שהמה קדושים ובני אהרון ק[דושי קדושים] ("and regarding his cl[ean ani]mal *it is written* that he not breed it in mixed species, and regarding [his] garment [that it not] be mixed stuff, and that he not sow his field or his vin[eyard with mi]xed types because they are holy and the sons of Aaron are m[ost holy]"). These are clearly allusions to the biblical laws regarding the mixture of diverse kinds in different contexts found in Lev 19:19

---

36 DJD X, 169.

37 Qimron, DJD X, 55.

38 We reject Qimron's restoration ועל לבוש[ו כתוב שלוא] יהיה שעטנז ("and regarding his ga[rment it is written that] it shall [not] be mixed stuff"), preferring the single formula כתוב to introduce all three laws. Qimron, DJD X, 56, points out that ושלוא לזרוע is an independent clause; this comment becomes unnecessary without the second כתוב. The omission of כתוב makes the line lengths relatively equal as well.

בהמתך לא תרביע כלאים שדך לא תזרע כלאים ובגד כלאים שעטנז לא יעלה עליך with the reference to vineyards coming from Deut 22:9.

The author of MMT employs them to castigate his opponents for permitting "mixed" marriages, whether between priests and non-priests, as Qimron believes, or between Jews and non-Jews, according to Baumgarten.[39] They are allusions, not citations, although they are introduced by כתוב. Qimron has difficulty discerning the biblical source of the sectarian custom as he understands it, the prohibition of marriage between priests and non-priests. Despite the fact that I cannot agree with any of the texts which he takes to prove his point,[40] I think that his reading may be preferable to Baumgarten's and that we have here another piece of Second Temple evidence for endogamous marriage among priests. But since, in my opinion, not everything in MMT needs to have a scriptural basis, I am not as concerned as Qimron about the apparent lack of a scriptural link for this law.

It should be clear that my perception of the function, and even the presence, of Scripture in the legal portion of MMT differs from its characterization by Qimron as cited at the beginning of this paper. Although some of the language of 4QMMT is biblical and some of its contents are manifestly the product of scriptural interpretation, much of MMT cannot be said to indicate the scriptural exegesis of its authors. Too many passages are too far removed from the biblical text to make such an assertion. Whether this apparent independence from Scripture is a product of the unusual genre of 4QMMT, as we suggested above, or whether our very sense of the scriptural orientation of most Qumran halakhah is itself an exaggeration, will require further investigation.

V. Scripture in Section C, "The Hortatory Epilogue"

When we turn to the third, non-legal, section of MMT, called "the hortatory epilogue" by the editors, the language of the document seems to become more biblical. I am not convinced that Section C begins with the fragmentary remains of MS d which are labeled C 1–7, but suspect that those lines are actually the conclusion of the halakhic

---

39 Qimron, DJD X, 171–172; Baumgarten's view (from personal communication) is cited on 171, n. 178a.

40 DJD X, 172–74.

section which the editors label B. The references to ועל הנשי[ם ("And regarding the women;" C 4) and והזנות ("and the fornication;" C6) could very well follow a section on immorality or sexual transgressions of various sorts which would naturally follow the concluding section of B (75–82) which was just discussed above.

The first citation in C 5–7 is [. . . בגלל] החמס והזנות אבד[ו הרבה] מקומות [ואף] כתו[ב בספר מושה ולו[א תביא תועבה א[ל ביתכה כי] התועבה שנואה היאה ("... [Because of] violence and immorality [many places][41] were destroy[ed]. [It is also] *writt[en* in the book of Moses], 'You shall n[ot] bring an abomination in[to your house' for] the abomination is hated"). Once again, I restore the latter portion as a quotation of Deut 7:26, while Qimron reads it as a paraphrase, שלוא תביא תועבה. This citation would be a fitting conclusion to the halakhic section, with the epilogue beginning with [ואתם יודעים ש]פרשנו מרוב העו[ם] ("[You know that] we have separated from the multitude of the peop[le]"). The word שנואה ("hated") is seen by Qimron as an interpretation of the biblical תועבה ("abomination"),[42] but it is far more likely in my view that we have here another harmonistic reading of two scriptural texts. Deut 12:31, in the context of idolatry, reads כי כל תועבת ה׳ אשר שנא עשו לאלהיהם ("for every *abomination of the Lord which he hates* they did for their gods"). 4QMMT is using Deut 12:31, which contains both תועבה and שנא, to explain or comment upon the word תועבה in Deut 7:26. The possible employment or imitation of Deut 12:2 in C 5–6 also may aid in indicating the biblical context of these lines.

C 11 has an enigmatic ובספר כתוב attested in two manuscripts, although there is no trace of the subsequent text to be reconstructed. But its presence, followed by that of the two citation terms in C 12, signifies that we are in a more heavily Scripture-based atmosphere than we saw in B. C 12–16 reads

ואף כתוב שת[סור] מהד[ר]ך וקרתך הרעה וכתוב
והיא כי
[יבו]א עליך [כו]ל הדבר[ים] האלה באחרית הימים הברכה

---

41 I do not see Qimron's reading [מקצת] מקומות ("some places"). If the source for the text is Deut 12:2 אבד תאבדון את כל המקומות, as Qimron, DJD X, 58, also holds, I think that the reconstruction הרבה corresponds to the biblical כל better than מקצת does.

42 Qimron, DJD X, 58.

והקללא [והשיבות]ה אל ל[בב]ך ושבתה אלו בכל לבבך
וב[כו]ל נפש[ך]באחרית[ ]

> And it is also written that you will [turn away] from the p[at]h and evil will befall you. And it is written, . . . "It shall be when [al]l these thin[gs] c[ome] upon you in the end of days, the blessings [and] the curse, [you shall bring (it) ba]ck to your he[ar]t and you shall return to him with all your heart and with [al]l [your] soul" . . . in the end. . . .

The first "citation" derives from Deut 31:29 כי ידעתי אחרי מותי כי השחת תשחתון וסרתם מן הדרך אשר צויתי אתכם וקראת אתכם הרעה באחרית הימים כי תעשו את הרע בעיני ה' להכעיסו במעשה ידיכם ("For I know that after my death you shall certainly become corrupt and *turn from the path* which I commanded you, *and evil shall befall you* in the end of days when you do what is evil in the eyes of the Lord to anger Him with your handiwork"). The author of 4QMMT has paraphrased the biblical texts and shifted to the singular from the plural original. MMT continues with a longer selection based on Deut 30:1–2 והיה כי יבאו עליך כל הדברים האלה הברכה והקללה אשר נתתי לפניך והשבת אל לבבך בכל הגוים אשר הדיחך ה' אלהיך שמה. ושבת עד ה' אלהיך ושמעת בקלו ככל אשר אנכי מצוך היום אתה ובניך בכל לבבך ובכל נפשך ("*It shall be when all these things come upon you, the blessing and the curse* which I have set before you, *then you shall return to your heart* amid all the nations where the Lord your God has thrust you. *And you shall return to the Lord your God* and heed his voice in accord with everything which I command you today, you and your children, *with all your heart and with all your soul*"). The words באחרית הימים ("at the end of days"), which do not occur in those verses, probably derive from Deut 31:29 which was cited just above.[43]

It is clear that the author of MMT understands the content of 31:29, the misfortune which will befall the people in the end of days, to be the same as the curse of 30:1. Thus that text also can be located at the end of days. The further reference in C 20–21 ואנחנו מכירים שבאוו מקצת הברכות והקללות שכתוב בס[פר מו]שה וזה הוא

43 Florentino García Martínez also notices this phenomenon in his paper in this volume. Qimron refers to this phrase (DJD X, 55) as "an addition to MT." It should also be noted, however, that Deut 4:30 בצר לך ומצאוך כל הדברים האלה באחרית הימים ושבת עד ה' אלהיך ושמעת בקלו could have had an impact on the formulation.

אחרית הימים שישובו בישר[אל] לת[ורה] ("we recognize that some of the blessings and curses which is [sic] written in the bo[ok of Mo]ses have come, and this is the end of days when they will return in Isr[ael] to the T[orah]") is also based on the integration of Deut 30:1–2 and 31:29.[44] The continuation of C 16, according to Qimron's translation of the composite text, is "at the end [of time so that you may live . . . .]," but there is no text, extant or restored beyond [ ]וח[[ ]באחרית which appears in the composite text facing that rendering.[45] It appears that Qimron is restoring something along the lines of באחרית [העת] וח[יית].[46] This seems to echo Deut 30:16 וחיית ורבית וברכך ה' אלהיך בארץ אשר אתה בא שמה לרשתה thereby keeping the focus of this part of section C at the end of Deuteronomy.

Finally, the Bible plays a further role in section C in addition to the citations from its text. At the beginning of the exhortation (C 10–11), in an extremely broken passage, the author of MMT advises his addressee . . . שתבין בספר מושה [ו]בספר[י הנ]ביאים ובדוי[ד במעשי] דור ודור ("that you ponder the book of Moses [and] the book[s of the pr]ophets and Davi[d . . . the deeds of] every generation"), implying that proper analysis of biblical history will show him the error of his ways.[47] After the paraphrases from the latter chapters of Deuteronomy just examined, there follows a historiography of the Bible which asserts that the blessings and curses alluded to in the Pentateuch have already been partially fulfilled in the

---

44 This is true whether we translate וזה הוא אחרית הימים to mean "this is" or "this was." Qimron's reference (DJD X, 61) to "the term אחרית הימים refer[ring] to the days of Saul" in 4Q252 1 iv 1–2 is based on a common misunderstanding of that passage. I believe that I have shown convincingly in "4Q252: From Re-written Bible to Biblical Commentary," *JJS* 45 (1994) 15–16 and n. 51 that the reference in that text must be to the eschaton. In our MMT passage, אחרית הימים is not to be translated "at the end of days," but "the end of days" as García Martínez also points out in his paper. Like García Martínez and others, I restore the final word as לתורה and not לתמיד.

45 DJD X, 60–61.

46 Qimron, DJD X, 37, in his readings of 4Q398, MS e, restores העת without traces (cf. C 30 באחרית העת).

47 Although Qimron restores מעשי after 4QD[e] ובהבינכם במעשי דור ודור ("and when you contemplate the deeds of every generation"), perhaps we ought to follow the biblical model of Deut 32:7 בינו שנות דור ודור and read שנות דור ודור.

time from Solomon and Jeroboam through the exile of Zedekiah.[48] The author of MMT believes that אחרית הימים ("the end of days") is now here, and entreats his addressee to contemplate further the history of the kings of Israel. It is clear that מלכי ישראל ("kings of Israel") is not employed, as it often is in the Bible, in contrast to מלכי יהודה ("the kings of Judah") since the reference is to positive lessons which can be learned from them, and since David is included among them. It is possible that the author of 4QMMT is here following the model of the Chronicler who seems to use the term מלכי ישראל of Judean kings in such passsages as 2 Chr 28:27, 33:18 and 35:18. The adoption of Chronicles as a model by 4QMMT is worthy of further consideration.

VI. Concluding Remarks

Scholarship is just beginning to scratch the surface of this fragmentary document. In this examination, we have begun to probe the employment of Scripture in MMT, and, at this point, we still have more questions than answers. In the legal section, we need to know whether MMT is exegetically Scripture-based or whether the laws are at times more loosely related to the Bible as in certain aspects of rabbinic *Torah she-be'al peh* ("Oral Law"). Some of the more difficult and fragmentary laws, whose relationship to Scripture we did not discuss above (e.g., B 5–8 and 9–11), require further study and analysis from this perspective. The hortatory epilogue, in particular, demands further analysis of its approach to and use of biblical history, as well as a full comparison with CD/4QD and the many other Qumran texts which employ the rewriting of biblical history as a part of their theological framework. There is a need, for example, to determine whether the attitude of the Qumran authors to biblical history remained constant, or whether it underwent development as the group developed its unique identity. We have not touched on the significance of 4QMMT for the question of biblical canon.[49] Finally,

---

48 I am inclined to agree with Qimron and Kister against Strugnell regarding the placement of the crucial fragment C 18–24 at this point in the document. I suggest as a possible reading in C 18 [הבר]כות שבא[ו]ו ב[ימי דויד ו]בימי שלומוה בן דויד ("[the bles]sings which ca[m]e in [the days of David and] in the days of Solomon son of David.")

49 Qimron, for example, DJD X, 59, considers C 10 בספר מושה [ו]בספר[י הנ]ביאים ובדויד ("in the book of Moses [and] in the book[s of the p]rophets

suffice it to say that, although the employment of Scripture is not the fundamental issue in the interpretation of MMT, very close attention will have to be paid to the presence and absence of scriptural interpretation in order to achieve full comprehension of this important text from both exegetical and theological perspectives.

---

and in Davi[d]") as "a significant piece of evidence for the history of the tripartite division of the Canon." In remarks on the historical setting of MMT, DJD X, 111–112, he expands on that comment. The spacing of the surviving words on the three fragments which make up this line is extremely uncertain, as Qimron marks in the text. I find it surprising that the author of MMT would refer even to the book of Psalms as דויד; we certainly should have expected ספר דויד or the like (e.g., in 11QMelch ii 9–10 we read כאשר כתוב עליו בשירי דויד ["as it is written about him in the songs of David"]). As for the third part of a tripartite canon, I remain unconvinced.

4QMMT and the History of the Hasmonean Period[1]

HANAN ESHEL
Bar-Ilan University
Ramat Gan, Israel

Some of the scrolls found at Qumran mention other compositions which have yet to be identified. Examples include: ספר ההגי ("The Book of Hagi"); ספר התורה החתום ("The Sealed Book of the Torah"); ספר התורה השנית ("The Book of the Second Torah"); and החוק והתורה אשר שלח אליו ("the Law and the Torah which he [the Teacher of Righteousness] sent to him [the Wicked Priest]").[2] Because so many manuscripts found at Qumran lack titles, it is possible that some of these unidentified compositions may have been preserved among them. In this paper I would like to examine the possibility, suggested by J. Strugnell and E. Qimron, that "the Law and the Torah" mentioned in 4QpPs^{a} is Miqṣat Maʿaśe Ha-Torah (MMT),[3] and to discuss the historical background of MMT in the light of two of the biblical commentaries (pesharim) found at Qumran.[4]

---

[1] I would like to dedicate this article to Professor John Strugnell in appreciation of his scholarship and collegiality.

[2] "The Book of Hagi" is mentioned in CD 10:4–6; 13:2–3; 14:6–8 and 1QSa 1:6–8; "The Sealed Book of the Torah" is mentioned in CD 5:1–5; "The Book of the Second Torah" is mentioned in 4Q177 (Catena A) 2 14; and "the Law and the Torah which he [the Teacher of Righteousness] sent to him [the Wicked Priest]" is mentioned in 4QpPs^{a}.

[3] See DJD X, 120 and J. Strugnell, "MMT: Second Thoughts on a Forthcoming Edition," *The Community of the Renewed Covenant* (eds. E. Ulrich and J. VanderKam; Notre Dame: University of Notre Dame Press, 1994) 70–73.

[4] Although 1QpHab and 4QpPs^{a} were composed in the first century BCE, I assume that their authors knew what the circumstances were in the time of the Teacher of Righteousness, and that we can therefore use those pesharim in order to understand the historical situation of the second century BCE.

In 4QpPs^a we find the following commentary to Ps 37:32–33:[5]

צופה רשע לצדיק ומבקש [להמיתו יה]וה [לוא יעזבנו בידו ו]ל[וא י]רשיענו
בהשפטו פשרו על [הכו]הן הרשע אשר צ[פה למור]ה הצד[ק ובקש]
להמיתו [על דבר החו]ק והתורה אשר שלח אליו

> "The wicked watches for the righteous, seeking to [put him to death. The Lo]rd [will not abandon him (the righteous) to his (the wicked's) power, he will not let] him be condemned in judgment."
> Its interpretation concerns the Wicked Pr[iest] who sp[ied on the Teac]her of Righteousn[ess and tried] to put him to death [because of the la]w and the Torah which he had sent to him . . .

Since the publication of this pesher, scholars have speculated about "the Law and the Torah" that were sent by the Teacher of Righteousness to the Wicked Priest. Y. Yadin, for example, suggested that the document so described might be the Temple Scroll.[6] It is possible, of course, that in the future a composition may be discovered which will explicitly identify itself as "the Law and the Torah" sent by the Teacher of Righteousness to the Wicked Priest. Until then, however, of all the documents found at Qumran, MMT emerges as the most likely candidate to be identified with "the Law and the Torah" mentioned in 4QpPs^a.[7]

At the end of MMT we read (C 26–32):[8]

---

5 4Q171 1–10 iv 7–9; see J. M. Allegro, "Further Light on the History of the Qumran Sect," *JBL* 75 (1956) 94; id., DJD V, 45 and pl. XVII. Some of the readings and the restorations of this text in the *editio princeps* are incorrect; see J. Strugnell, "Notes en marge du volume V des 'Discoveries in the Judaean Desert of Jordan'," *RevQ* 7 (1970) 216; M. P. Horgan, *Pesharim: Qumran Interpretations of Biblical Books* (CBQ Monograph Series 8; Washington, DC: Catholic Biblical Association, 1979) "Texts," 55 [references to "Horgan, 'Texts'" are to the separately paginated pamphlet containing the Hebrew texts of the pesharim which accompanies her commentary]; Y. Yadin, *The Temple Scroll* (3 vols.; Jerusalem: Israel Exploration Society, 1983) 1.396. My reading and reconstruction are based on DJD X, 120.

6 Yadin, *The Temple Scroll*, 1.396. Yadin offered this identification before MMT was known. Now that we have this text, it seems much more likely than the Temple Scroll to be the "Law and the Torah" written by the Teacher of Righteousness to the Wicked Priest. See DJD X, 120, n. 24.

7 The terms חוק ("Law") and תורה ("Torah") appear separately in MMT. חוק is mentioned in B 52 (DJD, X, 52), in relation to judgments regarding purity regulations, which are a significant part of MMT. The term Torah is used in the description of this composition: "and we have indeed written you some of the precepts of the Torah" (see the following quote from the end of MMT).

8 DJD X, 62–63. I have adapted the translations of Qimron and Strugnell in places.

ואף אנחנו כתבנו אליך
מקצת מעשי התורה שחשבנו לטוב לך ולעמך שר[א]ינו
עמך ערמה ומדע תורה הבן בכל אלה ובקש מלפנו שיתקן
את עצתך והרחיק ממך מחשבת רעה ועצת בליעל
בשל שתשמח באחרית העת במצאך מקצת דברינו כן
ונחשבה לך לצדקה בעשותך הישר והטוב לפנו לטוב לך
ולישראל

. . . and we have indeed written you some of the precepts of the Torah according to our decision, for your welfare and the welfare of your people. For we have s[e]en (that) you have wisdom and knowledge of the Torah. Consider all these things and ask Him (God) that He reform your plan and remove from you the plots of wickedness and the advice of Belial, so that you may rejoice at the end of time, finding that some of our words are correct. And this will be counted to you as righteousness, when you will be doing what is upright and good before Him (God), for your own welfare and for (the welfare) of Israel.

Some other parts of MMT are also, like this passage, written in the form of a direct address, leading some to believe that the document was a letter, directed explicitly to a specific individual. However, even if we conclude that MMT was not an actual letter, and that this work was attributed to the Teacher of Righteousness but written by someone else,[9] we can still maintain that if MMT is indeed the text mentioned in 4QpPs[a], then the author of this pesher and his readers assumed that this text was composed by the Teacher of Righteousness. For our purposes, their perception is more important than the reality. From the fact that six copies of MMT were found at Qumran, we can infer that members of the Qumran sect studied this text as a document of some significance.

At the end of the section from 4QpPs[a] quoted earlier, it is stated that the Wicked Priest tried to kill the Teacher of Righteousness. In 1QpHab, in the commentary on Hab 2:15, there is a more specific description of an incident which resembles this one:[10]

הוי משקה רעיהו מספח
חמתו אף שכר למען הבט אל מועדיהם

9 Strugnell, "Second Thoughts," 72, emphasizes that the author of MMT always writes in the plural in order to avoid the impression that this composition was written by one individual.

10 1QpHab 11:2–8. W. H. Brownlee, "The Habakkuk Commentary," *The Dead Sea Scrolls of St. Mark's Monastery I* (ed. M. Burrows; New Haven: The American School of Oriental Research, 1950) pl. LXIII; Horgan, "Texts," 8.

פשרו על הכוהן הרשע אשר
רדף אחר מורה הצדק לבלעו בכעס
חמתו אבית גלותו ובקץ מועד מנוחת
יום הכפורים הופיע אליהם לבלעם
ולכשילם ביום צום שבת מנוחתם . . .

> . . . "Woe to him who makes his neighbor drink to intoxication, indeed, as he pours out his wrath, in order to look upon their feasts." Its interpretation concerns the Wicked Priest, who pursued the Teacher of Righteousness—to swallow him up with the force of his wrath—at his place of exile. And at the time of the festival of the repose of the Day of Atonement, he appeared to them to swallow them up and to make them stumble on their fast day, a restful Sabbath.

The description offered here hints that the Wicked Priest attacked the Teacher of Righteousness and his followers because of something that had to do with the calendar, and specifically with the correct day on which to observe the Day of Atonement. Since the high priest would be busy at the Temple in Jerusalem on the Day of Atonement, no high priest could leave Jerusalem on this holy day and go to a "place of exile." Accordingly, it seems from the details provided by 1QpHab that the Wicked Priest and the Teacher of Righteousness disagreed about when to observe the Day of Atonement.[11] Significantly, one copy of MMT ($4QMMT^a$= 4Q394) starts with the calendar, perhaps indicating that one dispute between the author of MMT and the addressee was about calendaric issues.[12]

Also significant for understanding the historical background of MMT is another passage from 1QpHab. In a comment on Hab 2:5–6 we read:[13]

---

11 S. Talmon, "Yom Hakkippurim in the Habakkuk Scroll," *Biblica* 32 (1951) 549–563.

12 DJD X, 7–9. Strugnell raises doubts whether the calendar was originally part of MMT, because, of the two manuscripts which preserve the beginning of the composition, only one has the calendar (see Strugnell, "Second Thoughts," 61–62). The fact that the calendar was copied on the same parchment, together with MMT (in 4Q394) shows that at least one scribe thought that the calendar was connected to this composition. If MMT was copied in order to be studied by the members of the sect, one can understand why the calendar was not included in 4Q395 (DJD X, 203). Since MMT was important for studying halakhic disputes and not the calendar, the calendar might not have been copied in some of the manuscripts. For a different view, see L. H. Schiffman's essay in this collection.

13 1QpHab 8:3–13. Brownlee, *Scrolls of St. Mark's Monastery*, pl. LVIII; Horgan, "Texts," 6.

ואף כיא הון יבגוד גבר יהיר ולוא
ינוה אשר הרחיב כשאול נפשו והוא כמות לוא ישבע
ויאספו אלו כול הגוים ויקבצו אלו כול העמים
הלוא כולם משל עליו ישאו ומליצי חידות לו
ויומרו הוי המרבה ולוא לו עד מתי יכביד עלו
עבטט פשרו על הכוהן הרשע אשר
נקרא על שם האמת בתחלת עומדו וכאשר משל
בישראל רם לבו ויעזוב את אל ויבגוד בחוקים בעבור
הון ויגזול ויקבוץ הון אנשי חמס אשר מרדו באל
והון עמים לקח לוסיף עליו עון אשמה ודרכי
ת[ו]עבות פעל בכול נדת טמאה

". . . And moreover, wealth betrays an arrogant man, and gives (him) no respite, which (the wealth) has made (the man's) gullet as wide as Sheol and as insatiable as Death. All the nations are gathered about him, and assembled about him are all the peoples. Surely all these shall utter a satire against him, a pointed epigram concerning him. They shall say: 'Woe to him who piles up what is not his! How much longer will he make even heavier his load of indebtedness?'" Its interpretation concerns the Wicked Priest, who was called by the true name at the beginning of his public life, but when he ruled over Israel he became arrogant, abandoned God, and betrayed the laws for the sake of wealth. He stole and amassed the wealth of the men of violence who had rebelled against God, and he took the wealth of peoples to add to himself guilty sin. And abominable ways he practiced with every sort of unclean impurity . . .

From this passage, we learn that at the beginning the Wicked Priest "was called by the true name," which seems to be an idiom for following the path of righteousness; only later, when he ruled over Israel, did he abandon God and start to do evil. The verses in Habakkuk do not speak about a man who performed good deeds in his early days and abandoned God later on. Because there is no scriptural basis for describing the Wicked Priest as one who underwent a change of heart from good to evil, we must assume that historical circumstances underlie this description.[14] Furthermore, because the author of 1QpHab wrote that the Wicked Priest tried to kill the

---

14 Reading this pesher we are puzzled as to why such an interpretation of the Habakkuk verses was offered. The author of 1QpHab understood יבגוד ("betray") as pointing to someone who changed his way from good to evil, but the easy interpretation was to understand this as speaking about the הון ("wealth"), and to suggest that because the rulers of Judea collected wealth, the nations gathered about them and made their indebtedness heavier. Such an interpretation fits the way the authors of the pesharim worked.

Teacher of Righteousness, he would be unlikely to portray the Wicked Priest as good in any way unless he wanted to explain something to his readers. I believe that this author and his audience studied MMT (which was written decades earlier) and therefore the author of 1QpHab was forced to account for the respectful tone of address in MMT by explaining the initial circumstances under which the Wicked Priest and the Teacher of Righteousness had once been on reasonable terms.

In another part of 4QpPs^a, in a comment on Ps 37:14–15, we find that the Teacher of Righteousness was opposed by two groups:[15]

חרב פתחו רשעים וידרוכו קשתם לפיל עני ואביון
ולטבוח ישרי דרך חרבם תבוא בלבם וקשתותיהם תשברנה
פשרו על רשעי אפרים ומנשה אשר יבקשו לשלוח יד
בכוהן ובאנשי עצתו...

> . . . "The wicked drew their sword and bent their bow to bring down the lowly and needy, to slaughter upright men. Their swords shall pierce their own hearts, and their bows shall be broken." Its interpretation concerns the wicked ones of Ephraim and Manasseh, who will seek to lay their hands on the priest and on his advisers . . .

Here the author of 4QpPs^a speaks about the wicked people of Ephraim and Manasseh who tried to harm the Teacher of Righteousness.[16] In 4QpNah, Ephraim is identified as the Pharisees and Manasseh as the Sadducees.[17] It seems that the author of 4QpPs^a used these terms in a similar way in describing how the two groups opposed the Teacher of Righteousness.[18]

---

15 4QpPs^a 1–10 ii 15–18 (DJD V, 43–44; Horgan, "Texts," 53 [16–19]).

16 Although the Teacher of Righteousness is not mentioned in this commentary, we shall identify "the priest" (הכוהן) with the Teacher of Righteousness, because in 4QpPs^a the phrase הכוהן מורה ה[צדק] appears (1–10 iii 15; see the bibliography in notes 36 and 37 below).

17 The scholars who suggested such identifications are: J. D. Amusin, "Ephraim et Manassé dans le Péshèr de Nahum," *RevQ* 4 (1963) 386–396; A. Dupont-Sommer, "Le Commentaire de Nahum découvert près de la Mer Morte (4Q p Nah): Traduction et notes," *Semitica* 13 (1963) 55–88; Y. Yadin, "Pesher Nahum (4Q pNahum) Reconsidered," *IEJ* 21 (1971) 2, esp. n. 8; Horgan, *Pesharim*, 8, 161; D. Flusser, "Pharisäer, Sadduzäer und Essener im Pescher Nahum," *Qumran: Wege der Forschung* (eds. K. E. Grözinger et al.; Darmstadt: Wissenschaftliche Buchgesellschaft, 1981) 121–166; D. R. Schwartz, "To Join Oneself to the House of Judah," *RevQ* 10 (1981) 440, n. 5.

18 There is no reason to understand Ephraim and Manasseh as referring to one group. Ephraim and Manasseh are not mentioned in Psalm 37, so the author of

In a famous passage from MMT we read (C 7–10):[19]

[ואתם יודעים ש]פרשנו מרוב הע[ם]
[ו]מהתערב בדברים האלה ומלבוא ע[מהם]לגב אלה ואתם י[ודעים שלוא]
[י]מצא בידנו מעל ושקר ורעה כי על [אלה א]נחנו נותנים א[ת לבנו ואף]
[כתב]נו אליכה שתבין בספר מושה [ו]בספר[י הנ]ביאים ובדוי[ד]

> . . . [And you know that] we have separated ourselves from the multitude of the people [. . . and] from being involved with these matters and from participating with [them] in these things. And you [know that no] sacrilege or deceit or evil can be [f]ound in our hand (i.e. in us) since to [these things] we give [our attention. And] we have [written] to you so that you should learn (carefully) the book of Moses and the book[s of the Pro]phets and (the writings of) Davi[d] . . .

One can discern three groups in this passage: 1) the 'we' group of the author, 2) the 'you' group of the addressee, and 3) the multitude of the people (רוב העם).[20] This section of MMT is intended to establish the credentials of the 'we' group, or the addressors, and influence the 'you' group, or the addressees, to regard them favorably. Accordingly, the sender would not write: "You know that we left your group for these reasons," because such a statement might alienate the addressee further. Both grammatically and rhetorically the 'you' group, the target of persuasion, indicates a group distinct from רוב העם.

The phrase רוב העם can indicate "the majority of the people" or "a significant part of the people."[21] In either case, it seems to refer to a

---

the pesher did not name them because of the biblical verse. He mentioned only Ephraim in 1–10 i 24 (Horgan, "Texts," 52). Therefore it seems that the author of 4QpPs^{a} used the terms Ephraim and Manasseh to refer to two separate groups, like the author of 4QpNah.

19 DJD X, 58–59. Qimron and Strugnell believe the reason that the author of MMT and his group separated themselves from the multitude of the people was the halakhot, the precepts of the Torah that are specified in MMT, and therefore they reconstructed at the end of C 7 ומכול טמאתם ("and from all their impurity"), but, as we will see, I have doubts whether the 'we' group separated themselves from the multitude of the people because of those reasons, and therefore other reconstructions should be considered.

20 See DJD X, 114–115, where Qimron and Strugnell associate רוב העם with לך ולעמך ("to you and your people"), and thus the followers of the addressee. But, as we will see, there are reasons to distinguish between the followers of the addressee and רוב העם, who were probably a third group. See the article of D. R. Schwartz in this volume.

21 D. Flusser suggested that the phrase רוב העם in this passage of MMT should

third group which includes a large number of people, in contradistinction to the smaller 'you' group and 'we' group. Thus this section refers to a time when the addressee was not the leader of the majority of the people although he had a group of followers.[22] It also testifies that the perception of three divisions among Israel existed at the time MMT was written. It seems that the 'you' group would later solidify into the Pharisees and רוב העם was following the priests that later led the Sadducean party (Ephraim and Manasseh of 4QpPs[a]).[23]

I would like to suggest that the author of MMT and his group separated themselves from the multitude of the people not because of the halakhot, the precepts of the Torah, that were specified in MMT. Rather, they separated themselves for other reasons. In C 9 the author of MMT emphasized that his group has nothing to do with מעל ושקר ורעה ("sacrilege or deceit or evil").[24] It appears that there were

---

be understood as הרבים mentioned in the other sectarian compositions; see D. Flusser, "Some of the Precepts of the Torah from Qumran (4QMMT) and the Benediction Against the Heretics," [Hebrew] *Tarbiz* 61 (1992) 366; on the meaning of הרבים in the sectarian literature as the sectarian assembly, see J. Licht, *The Rule Scroll—A Scroll from the Wilderness of Judaea* [Hebrew] (Jerusalem: Bialik Institute, 1965) 109–110. Based on the content of MMT, however, I see no reason why we should not understand this phrase as "the majority of the people" or as "a significant part of the people."

22 Qimron and Strugnell, DJD X, 115, 117, suggest that the addressee was already the leader of the majority of Israel when MMT was "sent" to him. In light of 1QpHab, they also assume, 118, that MMT was addressed to the Wicked Priest at the beginning of his political life before "he ruled over Israel and became arrogant." Qimron and Strugnell understand וכאשר משל of 1QpHab as "while he ruled" (and not "when he ruled"). They think that the Wicked Priest abandoned God after a period when he ruled over Israel. I believe that it was his act of taking the high priesthood (i.e., ruling over Israel) that caused the Qumran sect to criticize the Wicked Priest. Therefore, my understanding of this passage in MMT is that either the Wicked Priest was not ruling over the majority of Israel, or that he had just been appointed as a high priest when MMT was addressed to him.

23 According to Josephus, there were three groups of learned people in the religious and political life of Judea at the end of the Second Temple period. Nevertheless, the people of Judea were actually split into at least four groups: three 'philosophies' (Josephus' term) whose followers were known as Pharisees, Sadducees and Essenes, and the majority of the people, supposedly unlearned (known as עם הארץ in later rabbinic literature), who did not observe purity laws. This section of MMT indicates that when this text was composed this majority followed the Hellenized priests, i.e., the ancestors of the Sadducees.

24 Although Qimron and Strugnell translate מעל as "treachery," מעל in Lev 5:15 is misappropriation of the property of the temple, and this is the meaning of the word in the Mishnah (*meʿilah*). This accusation fits the priests of Jerusalem and not the Pharisees. Thanks are due to Professor J. Kugel for this suggestion.

people who were accused of those sins and I assume that this description alludes to the multitude of the people. In other words, the author of MMT had a debate with the addressee about how to interpret the law, but he and his group left the majority of Israel because of other reasons that probably had to do with the hellenization of Jerusalem.

There is a long-standing debate among scholars about the identification of the Wicked Priest. Most scholars have followed G. Vermes and J. T. Milik and identified the Wicked Priest as Jonathan son of Mattathias, the high priest during the years 152–142 BCE.[25] Others have identified him as Jonathan's brother Simon, who ruled between 142–135 BCE.[26] Still others, especially Israeli scholars, have preferred to identify him as Alexander Jannaeus, the king of Judea in the years 103–76 BCE.[27]

Everyone, however, who has written about the halakhah of MMT has agreed that the halakhah of the addressee was Pharisaic.[28] This conclusion is based on the two well-known examples of המוצקות ("the liquid streams"), mentioned also in *m. Yad*, and of שריפת הפרה ("the burning of the Red Heifer"), mentioned also in *m. Para*.[29] In light of these examples we may conclude that the addressee of this letter was probably a Pharisee.

---

25 G. Vermes, *Discoveries in the Judean Desert* (New York: Desclée, 1956) 89–97; J. T. Milik, *Ten Years of Discovery in the Wilderness of Judaea* (tr. J. Strugnell; Studies in Biblical Theology 26; London/Naperville, IL: SCM/Allenson, 1959) 74–87; G. Jeremias, *Der Lehrer der Gerechtigkeit* (Göttingen: Vandenhoeck & Ruprecht, 1963); and see the bibliography mentioned in n. 36 below.

26 F. M. Cross, *The Ancient Library of Qumran and Modern Biblical Studies* (Garden City, NY: Doubleday, 1961) 141–156.

27 See J. van der Ploeg, *The Excavations at Qumran* (London/New York/Toronto: Longmans Green and Co., 1958) 59–62; Yadin, "Pesher Nahum," 12; Flusser, "Pharisäer, Sadduzäer und Essener," 143; B. Nitzan, *Pesher Habakkuk: A Scroll from the Wilderness of Judaea (1QpHab)* [Hebrew] (Jerusalem: Bialik Institute, 1986) 132–135.

28 Qimron and Strugnell, DJD X, 110–111, 175–177; Y. Sussmann, "The History of the Halakha and the Dead Sea Scrolls: Preliminary Talmudic Observations on *Miqṣat Maʿaśe ha-Torah* (4QMMT)," *ibid.*, 186–190; L. H. Schiffman, "The New Halakhic Letter (4QMMT) and the Origins of the Dead Sea Sect," *BA* 53 (1990) 69; J. M. Baumgarten, "Sadducean Elements in Qumran Law," *The Community of the Renewed Covenant* (eds. E. Ulrich and J. C. VanderKam; Notre Dame: University of Notre Dame Press, 1994) 29–30.

29 Sussman ("History of the Halakha," 189–190) suggested that other disputes that are mentioned in MMT are also alluded to in rabbinic literature. But cf. Yaakov Elman's essay in this volume.

If we assume that the addressee of the letter was a Pharisee and that MMT is "the Law and the Torah" sent from the Teacher of Righteousness to the Wicked Priest mentioned in 4QpPs^{a}, then we cannot identify the Wicked Priest with Alexander Jannaeus who was a Sadducee.[30]

In addition, the passage from MMT just quoted reflects a situation when the people of Judea were divided into three groups, and a significant part of the people were following neither the author of MMT nor the addressee. These people were probably following the priests of Jerusalem.[31] However, from the end of MMT we know that the addressee did have some influence on the people of Israel, since it is specified that this composition was sent to him "for his welfare and for the welfare of Israel."[32]

In light of the evidence from the sectarian writings, it seems that we should adopt Vermes and Milik's suggestion and identify the Wicked Priest as Jonathan.[33] Following the description of 1QpHab, we might consider the possibility that MMT is referring to the situation in Judea in the period around 152 BCE. In 161 BCE Jonathan became the political leader of those who followed his brother (Judah) on the battlefield. They were not willing to admit that the Hasmonean revolt had failed. Jonathan gained more and more influence after 159 BCE, until in 152 BCE he took the high priesthood from the unknown priest who had held this position in the years 159–152 BCE. "The beginning

---

[30] In addition to this argument, two descriptions in 1QpHab (8:13–9:2; 9:9–12) of the way the Wicked Priest died fit the murder of Jonathan by Tryphon (1 Macc 12:39–13:25) and not the death of Alexander Jannaeus, who died as a result of an illness on the battlefield (Josephus, *J.W.* 1§106, *Ant.* 13§398–404). On Simon, see n. 33 below.

[31] See D. R. Schwartz' article in this volume.

[32] See the first quotation of MMT (C 26–32) cited above. It seems that the phrase לטוב לך ולישראל ("for your own welfare and for [the welfare of] Israel") does not attest that the addressee was the leader of Israel, but rather that it will be for the benefit of Israel if he will accept the laws of MMT. Qimron and Strugnell, DJD X, 117, and Schiffman, "The New Halakhic," 67, pointed out that comparing the addressee to Solomon and other kings of Israel in lines 18–20 in part C of MMT (DJD X, 60–61) proves that the addressee was an important leader.

[33] The suggestion to identify the Wicked Priest as Simon is based on 4QTest (see Cross, *The Ancient Library of Qumran*, 141–156). But as I have tried to demonstrate elsewhere, 4QTest does not have anything to do with the Wicked Priest. It speaks about John Hyrcanus and not about Simon; see H. Eshel, "The Historical Background of the Pesher Interpreting Joshua's Curse on the Rebuilder of Jericho," *RevQ* 15 (1992) 411–429.

of his public life before he ruled over Israel"—as we read above in 1QpHab—probably alludes to the years when Jonathan was in Michmash "where he began to judge the people" (1 Macc 9:56–73). At that point Jonathan had some influence over Israel, especially over people who lived outside Jerusalem and were not from priestly families, while a significant part of the people of Judea still followed the Hellenized priests of Jerusalem.[34] It seems reasonable to assume that even after Jonathan became the high priest, the Hellenized priests of Jerusalem had a significant influence over the people of Judea. MMT refers to the situation immediately after Jonathan became the high priest in Jerusalem or just before this event, when Jonathan was still in Michmash.[35] In either case, when this composition was written, the opponents of the Hellenistic priests had already realized that the leadership of that priestly group was temporary and would not last long, and that it was likely that Jonathan would be the next high priest. Therefore, the author of MMT included laws that dealt with the purity of the Temple in his composition.

The passage from MMT under discussion which testifies that a significant part of the people of Judea were not following the author or the addressee of this composition, seems to contradict the assumption held by some that the Teacher of Righteousness was the high priest between 159–152 BCE.[36] This assumption is based on the fact that the Teacher of Righteousness is called in the pesharim הכהן ("the priest"). Some scholars have suggested that during the Second

---

34 It is important to note that when we read Pesher Nahum which describes the situation in Judea in the middle of the first century BCE, the situation is completely different. Then the majority of the people were the followers of Ephraim (the Pharisees) and they are called פתאי אפרים ("simple of Ephraim") (4QpNah 3–4 iii 5); Jerusalem is called עיר אפרים ("the city of Ephraim") (3–4 ii 2). Flusser suggested that the situation described in 4QpNah, i.e., where the Pharisees were leading the majority of the people, was due to the policy of Shlomzion; see Flusser, "Pharisäer, Sadduzäer und Essener," 149.

35 I would like to emphasize that I am not suggesting that MMT was sent from Qumran to Jonathan sitting in Michmash or in Jerusalem, since I do not think that the sect was in Qumran at such an early date, and I am not sure that MMT was a real letter. I do think that the people who later studied MMT in Qumran knew what the situation had been during the time of the Teacher of Righteousness and the early days of the Wicked Priest.

36 H. Stegemann, *Die Entstehung der Qumrangemeinde* (Bonn: privately published, 1971); J. Murphy-O'Connor, "The Essenes and their History," *RB* 81 (1974) 215–244; id., "Demetrius I and the Teacher of Righteousness," *RB* 83 (1976) 400–420; id., "The Essenes in Palestine," *BA* 40 (1977) 100–124.

Temple period "the priest," with an article, always meant the high priest. It is possible, however, that an important priest like the Teacher of Righteousness was called by his followers "the priest," even though he never served as the high priest.[37] My reading of MMT in light of the pesharim indicates that most of the people of Judea were following neither the Teacher of Righteousness nor the Wicked Priest in the years before the Wicked Priest became the high priest. It is reasonable to assume that during this period the multitude of the people were following a high priest who was then heading the Temple of Jerusalem.[38]

In this paper, I have argued that MMT is the "Law and the Torah" mentioned in 4QpPs[a]. Although this hypothesis cannot be proven, the nature and language of MMT point strongly in this direction. Taken in conjunction with the evidence of the pesharim, MMT supports the idea that the Wicked Priest should be identified as Jonathan and that MMT was composed around 152 BCE. The precipitating cause of the Qumran sect's split from the Temple cult was a quarrel not with Jonathan and the Pharisaic movement, but rather with the Hellenized priesthood in charge of the Temple until 152 BCE. The troubles between the Qumran sect and the Pharisees began only later when they arrived at their irremediable break resulting from the debate about the calendar. MMT was written at the beginning of Jonathan's rise to power. It reflects the sect's notion that it shared with Jonathan and the Pharisees some fundamental assumptions about the biblical

---

[37] For the evidence on the use of הכהן in the Second Temple period, see M. Wise, "The Teacher of Righteousness and the High Priest of the Intersacerdotium: Two Approaches," *RevQ* 14 (1990) 589–602. Although Wise did not deal with the most important evidence, the coin of Yohanan HKHN [see: D. Barag, "A Silver coin of Yohanan the High Priest and the Coinage of Judea in the Fourth Century B.C.," *Israel Numismatic Journal* 9 (1986–1987) 4–21], it seems to me that his conclusion that "the priest" is not necessarily the high priest is correct. Wise's second approach, in which he tried to identify the Teacher of Righteousness as the author of the Temple Scroll and as the high priest in the years 159–152 BCE, is baseless.

[38] Note the difficulties which J. Murphy-O'Connor ("The Essenes," 230–232; "Essenes in Palestine," 117–118), encounters when he tries to explain how after three Hellenized high priests (Jason, Menelaus and Alcimus), the Teacher of Righteousness, who was by Murphy-O'Connor's definition a radical conservative, was elected as the high priest. There is no doubt, however, that the Teacher of Righteousness came from the other end of the priestly spectrum from the Hellenized priests. If my understanding of MMT is correct, after the death of Alcimus in 159 BCE another Hellenized priest served as high priest until Jonathan took over in 152 BCE.

laws and their interpretation. Jonathan shattered this illusion when he continued to follow the Pharisaic concept of the law and did not accept the calendar and the more rigorous halakhah of the Teacher of Righteousness. By the mid-first century BCE the sect viewed both Pharisees and Sadduccees with equal enmity. I hope that by comparing MMT to the pesharim found at Qumran I have succeeded in shedding some light on the way the members of the Qumran sect in later years understood MMT.[39]

---

[39] This article was written while I was a Harry Starr Fellow at Harvard University. I would like to thank the Center for Jewish Studies at Harvard University and the Fulbright Fellowship for their support during that year, and Professor L. H. Schiffman for inviting me to lecture on MMT at the Annual Conference of the Association for Jewish Studies. Thanks are also due to Dr. Ellen Birnbaum and to Mrs. Ruth Clements for their important comments and for improving the English style of this article.

MMT, Josephus and the Pharisees

DANIEL R. SCHWARTZ
Hebrew University
Jerusalem, Israel

The impact of the Dead Sea Scrolls upon the study of the Pharisees has been indirect, intense, and ironic. It has been indirect, for the term "Pharisee" does not appear, so far, in any of the Scrolls, so all inferences about allusions to them are based to some extent upon other knowledge about them. Thus, for example, it is Josephus' information (*J.W.* 1 §97; *Ant.* 13 §380) which allows us to deduce that the דורשי החלקות executed by the כפיר החרון of Pesher Nahum were Pharisees executed by Alexander Jannaeus, just as it is the rabbinic usage of the terms *talmud* and *seyyag* which gives us, as Prof. Schiffman and others have argued, the confidence to see in some Qumran texts allusions to Pharisaic scholarship and legislation.[1] But the Scrolls' impact has been intense, for there is a large number of such Qumran texts which, however indirectly, bear on the Pharisees, their laws, their history and their opponents, and there is, as always, a great deal of scholarly interest in these topics.[2] Finally, the impact of the Dead Sea Scrolls upon the study of the Pharisees has been ironic, as we shall now detail, however briefly.

The irony lies in the way such new texts as MMT have widely been taken as reason to return scholarship on the Pharisees, at the end of

---

1 See L. H. Schiffman, "Pharisees and Sadducees in *Pesher Nahum*," *Minhah le-Nahum: Biblical and Other Studies Presented to Nahum M. Sarna in Honour of his 70th Birthday* (JSOTSup 154; ed. M. Brettler and M. Fishbane; Sheffield: Sheffield Academic Press, 1993) 272–290; id., *Reclaiming the Dead Sea Scrolls* (Philadelphia/Jerusalem: Jewish Publication Society, 1994) 249–250.

2 For recent scholarship on the Pharisees see the works cited in n. 18 below. Earlier literature is surveyed and criticized by J. Neusner, *The Rabbinic Traditions About the Pharisees Before 70* (3 vols.; Leiden: Brill, 1971) 3.320–368. In conjunction with the Scrolls, see the essays by L. H. Schiffman and J. C. VanderKam in *Understanding the Dead Sea Scrolls* (ed. H. Shanks; New York: Random House, 1992).

the twentieth century, to about where it was a hundred years ago. We refer to two major assumptions. A hundred years ago most Jewish and non-Jewish scholars believed that, as Josephus explicitly reports (esp. *Ant.* 13 §§288, 298, 401–402; 18 §15) and as various statements in the New Testament and rabbinic evidence also indicate, Pharisaism was the dominant variety of Judaism during the Second Temple period. Moreover, they held, by and large, that Pharisaism of the Second Temple period, before the destruction of that temple in 70 CE, was largely identical with rabbinic Judaism of the post-Destruction era. There was little debate on either issue. Such debates as there were had to do only with the question, was Pharisaic-rabbinic Judaism fairly characterized by works such as Schürer's chapter on "Life Under the Law"? Studies such as Schürer's built on a gospel picture of the Pharisees as petty casuists, illustrated by legal details cited from the Mishnah which were taken to display a religion with little feeling or higher values.[3] In the first decades of the twentieth century, scholars such as Montefiore, Strack and Billerbeck made available a much broader picture of rabbinic literature. The arguments of Jewish scholars, and of such prominent supporters as R. Travers Herford and George Foot Moore, carried the day; rabbinic Judaism was seen as a real and many-sided religion, wherein morals and ethics played serious and sincere roles.[4] But the two basic assumptions, that the rabbis were

[3] For some major handbooks and debates, see E. Schürer, *Geschichte des jüdischen Volkes im Zeitalter Jesu Christi* (4th ed.; Leipzig: Hinrichs, 1907) 2.456–475, 545–579; W. Bousset, *Die Religion des Judentums im neutestamentlichen Zeitalter* (Berlin: Reuther & Reichard, 1903), esp. 163–168; J. Wellhausen, *Israelitische und jüdische Geschichte* (7th ed.; Berlin: Reimer, 1914) 282–284; I. Abrahams, "Professor Schürer on Life Under the Jewish Law," *JQR* o.s. 11 (1899) 626–642; F. Perles, *Bousset's Religion des Judentums im neutestamentlichen Zeitalter kritisch untersucht* (Berlin: Peiser, 1903); and W. Bousset, *Volksfrömmigkeit und Schriftgelehrtentum: Antwort auf Herrn Perles' Kritik meiner 'Religion des Judentums im N.T. Zeitalter'* (Berlin: Reuther & Reichard, 1903). See also F. S. Perles, "Felix Perles, 1874–1933," *Leo Baeck Institute Year Book* 26 (1981) 171–178 and, in general, K. Hoheisel, *Das antike Judentum in christlicher Sicht* (Studies in Oriental Religions 2; Wiesbaden: Harrassowitz, 1978) 7–60 ("Das traditionelle 'Spätjudentumsbild'").

[4] An important turning-point was Moore's long and critical review of "Christian Writers on Judaism," *HTR* 14 (1921) 197–254. On the rehabilitating scholarship on the Pharisees in the early twentieth century in general, see the review composed on the eve of the changes to be described in the next paragraph: R. Marcus, "The Pharisees in the Light of Modern Scholarship," *JR* 32 (1952) 158–164; note also M. J. Cook, "Jesus and the Pharisees: The Problem as it Stands Today," *JES* 15 (1978) 442–443.

Pharisees and that the Pharisees dominated Judaism of the Second Temple period, remained largely untouched.

Along came the 1940s and '50s and the Dead Sea Scrolls, and the scholarly world learned that during the period supposedly dominated by the Pharisees there was at least one other group which maintained itself for centuries and produced a manifold literature. Possibly due to the impact of Cold War understandings of the nature of propaganda, it was easy to infer that Josephus' statements about Pharisaic dominance, and those of the New Testament and the rabbis, were untrue. Already in 1956, the late Morton Smith posited, in his seminal study of "Palestinian Judaism in the First Century,"[5] that Josephus was merely propagandizing for the sect which, *when he was writing the Antiquities in the nineties,* dominated the Jewish scene; the Pharisees did not dominate the scene before the Destruction of the Temple, the period of which Josephus wrote. Similarly, in his *Jesus the Magician*[6] Smith would later argue, along with other scholars (see below), that Pharisaic prominence in the Gospels too was anachronistic, reflecting the post-Destruction period when the Gospels were composed and not the days of Jesus which they purport to describe. As for rabbinic literature, the rabbis' claims that the Pharisees dominated the scene, and that from their court in the Temple "law went out unto all of Israel," as the Mishnah puts it (*Sanh.* 11:2), are no more than to be expected from any party which claims "the people is with us and always has been"—and worthy of no more credence.

These arguments by Smith, which boil down to a neutralization of the main evidence for Pharisaic hegemony during the Second Temple period, were taken up, expanded and popularized by a host of scholars, especially Jacob Neusner.[7] The latter was also instrumental in undermining the other major assumption of the earlier consensus, that not much changed between the Pharisees of the Temple period and the rabbis of the post-Destruction period. On the contrary, in

---

5 In *Israel: Its Role in Civilization* (ed. M. Davis; New York: Harper & Brothers, 1956) esp. 74–78.

6 (London: Gollancz, 1978) esp. 153–157. On Smith's general agenda, see D. R. Schwartz, *Studies in the Jewish Background of Christianity* (WUNT 60; Tübingen: Mohr [Siebeck], 1992) 140–141.

7 Neusner first published an essay on Josephus' Pharisees in 1972; its most recent version (?) is "Josephus' Pharisees: A Complete Repertoire," *Josephus, Judaism, and Christianity* (eds. L. H. Feldman & G. Hata; Detroit: Wayne State Univ. Press, 1987) 274–292.

study after study he, along with his students and others, argued and demonstrated that a great deal changed in the generations after the Destruction of the Temple, and that it is irresponsible to use later rabbinic texts *tout cour* as evidence for Pharisaism of the first century or earlier.[8]

This was, naturally, gobbled up very willingly by New Testament scholars who had been told by Moore *et al.* that they must become experts in a very daunting literature in Hebrew and Aramaic. Now they were told that rabbinic literature has its own history and reflects the times and places in which it was produced. Since it was produced later than the New Testament period, it need not be mastered by those who wish to study that period and its literature.

In addition to the Qumran discoveries, two other factors contributed to the emerging portrait of a variegated first-century Judaism. The first factor was the Holocaust, which had a dual impact. First, for some Christians it delegitimated anti-Semitism,[9] thereby making it necessary for Christian scholarship to deal with the implications of Jesus' attacks upon the Pharisees in the gospels. Two methods in particular emerged. On the one hand, many scholars began to draw a firm line between Jesus and the gospel writers, emphasizing that especially Matthew (the main culprit—chapter 23!) had a special anti-Pharisaic animus which was not characteristic of Jesus. Not only gospel narratives which display the Pharisees in a negative light, but even Jesus' attacks upon them, are turned into mere *Gemeindebildungen*, not authentic words of Jesus.[10] Others, borrowing a

[8] E.g., Neusner's "The Use of the Later Rabbinic Evidence for the Study of First-Century Pharisaism" and "The Use . . . of Paul," which appeared in *Approaches to Ancient Judaism* (BJS 1,9; ed. W. S. Green; Chico: Scholars Press, 1978–1980) 1.43–63 and 2.215–228, respectively.

[9] For other aspects of the Holocaust's impact on Christian scholarship concerning the first century, including the reinterpretation of Rom 13:1–2, the making of Jesus into a rebel, and the enhancement of the significance of Romans 9–11 in the Pauline corpus, see Schwartz, *Studies*, 130–134.

[10] This point of view, already urged by D. W. Riddle, *Jesus and the Pharisees* (Chicago: Univ. of Chicago Press, 1928), especially took root after the Holocaust. See *inter alia* E. Haenchen, "Matthäus 23," *ZTK* 48 (1951) 59–63 (id., *Gott und Mensch* [Tübingen: Mohr (Siebeck), 1965] 50–54); T. F. Glasson, "Anti-Pharisaism in St. Matthew," *JQR* 51 (1960/61) 316–320; and, eventually, S. van Tilborg, *The Jewish Leaders in Matthew* (Leiden: Brill, 1972) (which includes what R. H. Gundry, *JBL* 92 [1973] 138, called "a piece of ecumenical overcomment for our time, [in which] van Tilborg absolves the Jewish leaders, particularly the Pharisees, of Matthew's charges and absolves the Christian Matthew of making anything but

leaf from those who grapple with "the Jews" in the Fourth Gospel, argued that the Pharisees attacked were not, in any case, the mainstream of Judaism, but rather some particular limited group.[11] These arguments dovetailed beautifully with Smith's thesis, for the former means that the Pharisees (= rabbis) dominated the Jewish scene after the Destruction and the latter—that the earlier scene was much more complex than previously assumed.

Second, the Holocaust also had an impact upon Jews dealing with our issue. Realizing that things could never be the same in the wake of such a massive catastrophe, Jewish scholars found it more difficult to assume that the destruction of the Second Temple was not a major watershed in Jewish history. That is, they too became more willing to assume that the post-70 situation was significantly different from the pre-70 situation. In this connection, we may note that the explicit and implicit comparison of the Holocaust to the Destruction of the Second Temple is widespread in Jewish historiography and its implications deserve further study.[12]

The other factor contributing to a reappraisal of first-century Jewish history was the foundation of the State of Israel, an innovation

---

stylized [as opposed to personal] charges") and D. E. Garland, *The Intention of Matthew 23* (NovTSup 52; Leiden: Brill, 1979). This line of research led directly to Smith's above-mentioned study. For protests against the *verharmlosen* of Gospel attacks on the Pharisees by disassociation of them from Jesus, see, among others, H. Merkel, "Jesus und die Pharisäer," *NTS* 14 (1967/68) 194–208, and B. Lindars, "Jesus and the Pharisees," *Donum Gentilicium: New Testament Studies in Honour of David Daube* (ed. E. Bammel, C. K. Barrett and W. D. Davies; Oxford: Clarendon, 1978) 51–63.

11 For a survey of such views, see Cook, "Jesus and the Pharisees," 454–455. As he indicates, this approach has been especially popular with Jewish writers. See also R. A. Wild, "The Encounter between Pharisaic and Christian Judaism: Some Early Gospel Evidence," *NovT* 27 (1985) 105–124; Wild disarms Gospel attacks upon the Pharisees by portraying them as internal debates between close colleagues. A related line of research is that which portrayed Matthew himself as a scribe and, hence, colleague of the Pharisees, explaining the animus as a result of proximity. See, for example, J. Schwark, "Matthäus der Schriftgelehrte und Josephus der Priester: Ein Vergleich," *Theokratia* 2 (1970–72 [*Festgabe für H. Rengstorf*]) 138–140, where additional bibliography is cited.

12 For some cases in point, see B. M. Bokser, "Rabbinic Responses to Catastrophe," *PAAJR* 50 (1983) esp. 60–61; J. Neusner, "Judaism in a Time of Crisis," *Judaism* 21 (1972) esp. 326–327, with the response of S. J. D. Cohen, "Jacob Neusner, Mishnah, and Counter-Rabbinics: A Review Essay," *Conservative Judaism* 37/1 (Fall 1983) esp. 50, 57–58; and my "On Abraham Schalit, Herod, Josephus, the Holocaust, Horst R. Moehring, and the Study of Ancient Jewish History," *Jewish History* 2/2 (Fall 1987) 10–13.

which represented a reassertion of Jewish unity and a claim for hegemony in the Jewish world, in a way and to a degree without precedent during the nineteen centuries since the Destruction of the Second Temple. Obviously, Jews used to having no central institutions may be put out at the notion of there being some such;[13] and one way of dealing with this is to argue that, even in the good old days when the Temple stood, pluralism was characteristic of the Jewish world. This agenda figures prominently in modern Jewish scholarship on the Pharisees, competition with Israel combining with older trends to combat Orthodoxy[14]—and a reconstruction such as Smith's, which has first-century Palestine "swarming" with sects, is very congenial.[15]

Since the late 1970s a reaction to this development has been underway, and now MMT has been invoked in defense of that reaction. First, the 1977 publication of the Temple Scroll showed that the Qumran sect, whether as author or as preserver and copyist of that text, was interested in the nitty-gritty of Jewish law. Other legal texts which circulated and were published in the 1980s and '90s, of which MMT and halakhic fragments of the Damascus Document are the prime examples, establish the same point. By demonstrating that even this highly spiritualized branch of Judaism in the Second Temple period was so concerned about law and its details, that the people who produced and preserved the *Hodayot* cared a great deal about ritual purity and the like, these texts lent renewed probability to the notion that Pharisaic Judaism shared similar concerns. In that case later rabbinic literature, which shows such legal interests, might not be so far from the Pharisaism of the Second Temple period. Second, the specific contents of some of these texts jibe well with what we read in rabbinic literature. Here, I refer to the fact that in some cases, as has often been noted, the Qumran writer adopts legal positions which the rabbis attribute to the Sadducees while they themselves, the rabbis,

---

13 For a case of such resentment, see Schwartz, *Studies*, 121, n. 25.

14 On the role of Pharisees in anti-Orthodox Jewish polemics, see Schwartz, *Studies*, 66–80.

15 In this connection, note S. Schwartz's qualification of his comment that Smith's reconstruction of the place of first-century Pharisaism was generally accepted: "at least north and west of the Litani River" (*AJSRev* 19 [1994] 84). As a matter of fact, the generalization that Israeli scholars generally rejected Smith's basic thesis is not easily justified, but Schwartz's statement does reflect a correct perception of what is at stake here.

agree with the contrary views held by the Pharisees.[16] Whether this means the Qumran sect was or began Sadducean, or whether it means only that Sadducees and Qumranites shared certain legal views which differed from those of the Pharisees, these texts certainly lend a new confidence to our use of rabbinic literature for the study of Second Temple period sects.[17]

But what of our major question: Did the Pharisees dominate the scene? Here, two developments are relevant. First, concerning Josephus, the Smith-Neusner case was undermined by the demonstration that several of Josephus' passages which speak of Pharisaic dominance bemoan it and denounce the Pharisees; so, for example, *Ant.* 13 §§288, 401–402. These passages may not be explained away as Josephus' propaganda on the Pharisee's behalf, as Smith had suggested. Whether they are source-critically seen as Nicolaus of Damascus' hostile views of a party which opposed his patron Herod, or whether, as Steve Mason has argued, they reflect Josephus' own views, they cannot simply be discounted and ignored.[18] It should also be emphasized, however, that whether it is Josephus or Nicolaus who is

---

16 For this important point, see J. M. Baumgarten, "The Pharisaic-Sadducean Controversies About Purity and the Qumran Texts," *JJS* 31 (1980) 157–170; Y. Sussmann, "The History of the Halakha and the Dead Sea Scrolls," DJD X, esp. 187–191; and essays by Baumgarten and by Schiffman in *Jewish Civilization in the Hellenistic-Roman Period* (JSPSup 10; ed. S. Talmon; Sheffield: Sheffield Academic Press, 1991).

17 For an impressive example of such confidence, see now A. I. Baumgarten, "Josephus on Essene Sacrifice," *JJS* 45 (1994) 181, n. 44, following J. M. Baumgarten, "A New Qumran Substitute for the Divine Name and Mishnah Sukkah 4.5," *JQR* 83 (1992) 5, where further literature is cited; see also, for example, the latter's "Halakhic Polemics in New Fragments from Qumran Cave 4," *Biblical Archaeology Today* (ed. Janet Amitai; Jerusalem: Israel Exploration Society, 1985) 397, and L. H. Schiffman, "From Temple to Torah: Rabbinic Judaism in Light of the Dead Sea Scrolls," *Shofar* 10/2 (Winter, 1992) 2–15.

18 For the first view, see my "Josephus and Nicolaus on the Pharisees," *JSJ* 14 (1983) 157–171; for the latter, S. Mason, *Flavius Josephus on the Pharisees* (SPB 39; Leiden: Brill, 1991). For these debates in general, see id., "Josephus on the Pharisees Reconsidered: A Critique of Smith/Neusner," *SR* 17 (1988) 455–469; D. Goodblatt, "The Place of the Pharisees in First Century Judaism: The State of the Debate," *JSJ* 20 (1989) 12–30; A. I. Baumgarten, "Rivkin and Neusner on the Pharisees," in *Law in Religious Communities in the Roman Period* (ed. P. Richardson; Studies in Christianity and Judaism 4; Waterloo, Ontario: Wilfrid Laurier Univ. Press, 1991) 109–26; K. G. C. Newport, "The Pharisees in Judaism Prior to A.D. 70," *AUSS* 29 (1991) 127–137; D. S. Williams, "Morton Smith on the Pharisees in Josephus," *JQR* 84 (1993) 29–42; and S. Schwartz's review of Mason's 1991 volume (above, n. 15).

the hostile observer of the Pharisees, the critique does not necessarily make the claims true. Nicolaus and Josephus could complain about Pharisaic control even if the Pharisees were not dominant, just as whoever wants to can always claim that Jews control all the banks and newspapers. Hence, this development of Josephan scholarship does not really affect the question of the Pharisees' relative influence, and Smith's position could remain untouched.[19]

The other development now thought to undermine Smith's theory is 4QMMT. As early as 1984 it became known that MMT, which upholds some legal positions shared by the Mishnah's Sadducees and contrary to those of the Pharisees, concludes with the statement that "we have separated ourselves from רוב העם"—which in the first published accounts of this text was rendered "the majority of the people."[20] The obvious conclusion was that the Pharisees, with whom MMT's halakhah disagrees, are the majority of the people. Thus, MMT has been taken to clinch the case that legalism was at the heart of Second Temple period religion, that rabbinic literature is reliable for the study of Second Temple period Pharisaism, and that that Pharisaism—"hypercritical" Josephan scholarship notwithstanding (see n. 21)—was the dominant version of Judaism during the Second Temple period. But although the dossier of texts has changed, these are the characteristic positions held during the opening years of this century. Hence the irony mentioned at the outset of this essay: the discovery of sectarian literature has led to a restoration of orthodoxy. The triumphalism in some quarters is quite evident.

Determining the proper impact of a new text on a body of knowledge and theory is never simple. As Thomas S. Kuhn showed in his *The Structure of Scientific Revolutions*, scholars have to choose between absorbing new data into preexisting theories or letting the

---

19 I emphasize this, because occasionally my "Josephus and Nicolaus" has been taken to contradict Smith's reconstruction. In fact, it does not; it deals only with the use of Josephus' evidence. As I emphasize (p. 165), Smith's case for the variety of Judaisms in first-century Judaism is indeed quite convincing: ". . . so convincing, in fact, that it is not in need of legitimization; [t]he question is, whether Josephus made such a claim as is attributed to him [by Smith], or whether his testimony on the Pharisees is to be explained otherwise."

20 So, *inter alia*, E. Qimron and J. Strugnell, "An Unpublished Halakhic Letter from Qumran," *Israel Museum Journal* 4 (Spring 1985) 10, and "An Unpublished Halakhic Letter from Qumran," *Biblical Archaeology Today*, 402; Z. J. Kapera, "An Anonymously Received Pre-Publication of the 4 Q MMT," *Qumran Chronicle* 2 (December, 1990) 7.

new data dictate a new theory.[21] In the present case, where we are faced with the possibility that this new text from Qumran might upset conclusions based on Josephan studies, I would sound three words of caution, based on the text of MMT as we now see it in the magnificent edition by Qimron and Strugnell. One, a minor point, has to do with translation. The crucial passage in MMT says that "and you (plural) know that we separated ourselves from רוב העם." As stated above, the original articles about the document rendered רוב as "majority." In the final official publication, however, the translation is "multitude"; a note explains that "multitude" is the biblical meaning and that there is no certain Qumran evidence for using it in its mishnaic sense, "majority."[22] From our point of view, then, even if it were the case that this passage associates רוב העם with the Pharisees, it would support Josephus' claims somewhat less clearly than has been thought. But this is a minor point.

Our two main caveats may best be understood against the background of the following passage in the new MMT volume:

> The erroneous halakhic traditions of the 'they' group in section B were in all probability the same traditions that provoked the separation from the רוב העם in section C. The detailed discussion in our halakhic chapter will identify much of the halakhah of the 'they' group with that of the Pharisees; it is interesting to note that we find a similar early association of the Pharisee group with the רוב העם attested also by Josephus, at a time which, we will shortly suggest, is about as early as MMT.[23]

While we have no quarrel with the first half of the middle sentence in the above quote, nor with the early Hasmonean date to which, shortly later, the editors assign MMT,[24] we would take issue with the opening sentence and with the closing reference to Josephus.

Our first caveat has to do with the structure and interpretation of MMT. We make two observations. First, all, or almost all, of the laws

---

21 Thomas S. Kuhn, *The Structure of Scientific Revolutions* (Chicago: University of Chicago Press, 1962).

On this general problem, cf. D. R. Schwartz, "On Some Papyri and Josephus' Sources and Chronology for the Persian Period," *JSJ* 21 (1990) 175; see p. 181 on the rejection of "hypercritical" Josephan scholarship due to an epigraphical discovery.

22 4QMMT C 7. See DJD X, 58, n. 7.

23 Qimron and Strugnell, DJD X, 115; in a footnote they cite *Ant.* 18 §15.

24 DJD X, 121.

dealt with in Section B of MMT have to do with the Temple cult and the priesthood. They hardly serve to reflect popular practice; they rather represent only what is done in the most centralized institution of Judaism, that is, *the one most easily supervised by the government* and, hence, most subject to change with shifts in power. Second, the passage about the "multitude of the people" does not appear in connection with the laws disputed by the sectarians and their opponents. It does not come in Section B, the long list of things about which "we say X," implying that the opponents or some undefined "they" say anti-X. Rather, it appears in the conciliatory concluding section of the document, which the editors render as follows:

> And concerning the women [. . . the malice] and the treachery [. . .] for in these [. . . because of] malice and the fornication [some] places were destroyed. [And it is] written [in the book of Moses] that you should [not] bring any abomination [into your home, since] abomination is a hateful thing. [And you know that] we have separated ourselves from the multitude of the people [and from all their impurity] and from being involved with these matters and from participating with [them] in these things. And you [know that no] treachery or deceit or evil can be found in our hand (i.e., in us), since for [these things] we give . . . .[25]

In this passage, the author claims that "we" have separated from the multitude of Israel because the latter is involved in crimes of fornication (זנות) and crimes of מעל—instead of "treachery" we prefer the more literal translation "misappropriation of holy property."[26] This passage is very reminiscent of columns 3–5 of the Damascus Document. There we read of a group which separated itself from the establishment, claiming that its opponents, like Eli's sons in 1 Sam 2:22, were polluting the sanctuary through iniquities with women.[27] In even closer parallel to Eli's sons (1 Sam 2:12–17), crimes with Temple property are added in MMT to the iniquities with women. But Eli's sons were prototypical wicked priests,[28] just as, most probably, those

---

[25] 4QMMT C 4–9; DJD X, 59.

[26] See B. Bokser, "*Maʿal* and Blessings Over Food," *JBL* 100 (1981) 561–562.

[27] For this understanding of the allusions of CD here, pointed up especially by the use of בית נאמן (CD 3:19/1 Sam 2:35) and להשתפח (CD 4:11/1 Sam 2:36 [ספחני]), as well as by the reference to Zadok (CD 4:1/1 Kgs 2:27!), see my "'To Join Oneself to the House of Judah' (Damascus Document IV,11)," *RevQ* 10 (1979–81) 435–446.

[28] See also *b. Pesaḥ.* 57a, where "depart from here, sons of Eli" is the heading for a group of four plaints which the Temple Court itself is said to have made against wicked priests of the late Second Temple period; for the interpretation of this text,

who sinned with sacrifices and women in *Pss. Sol.* 8:11–12 were also priests. Correspondingly, note that Pesher Habakkuk specifically and repeatedly attacks the Wicked Priest, and the "last priests of Jerusalem," for being involved in מעל and חמס.[29] The writer of MMT says that "you" (plural), the recipients, know that "we" separated ourselves from the multitude of the people, for the latter are involved in such terrible crimes. Given the conciliatory tone of this section calling upon the addressees to study the Torah diligently and see if it does not conform to the laws espoused by the writer,[30] it is unthinkable, to my mind, that the author would use such language of his addressees and their behavior. To accuse someone of זנות, מעל and חמס is not the same as to list one's arguments with him on points of legal detail. Rather, the author of MMT is telling his addressees, with whom he has various legal arguments, that—as opposed to "the multitude of the people"—they and he are all serious in their religion. The point of the statement that the writer and his community have "separated themselves" from the multitude of the people is to prove their religious sincerity. By so doing, it supplies a reason for the addressees to take seriously the call to reconsider their positions considering the enumerated legal issues. Indeed, the use of פרשנו ("we separated ourselves") indicates that the writers have done just what the Pharisaic addressees too have done, and it is quite difficult to imagine that the writer could have used this verb without intending a positive comparison to the Pharisees (פרושים).[31]

Thus, the situation reflected by MMT is as follows. Section B, the main, halakhic, part of the text is addressed to a group denoted by the second person plural, which the writer assumes to be interested in the details of Jewish law; Section C, however, is addressed to a ruler of the Jewish people. The writer expects the group he is addressing to accept

see D. R. Schwartz, "KATA TOYTON TON KAIPON: Josephus' Source on Agrippa II," *JQR* 72 (1981/82) 263–266. See also: M. Beer, "The Sons of Eli in Rabbinic Legend," *Bar-Ilan* 14–15 (1977) 79–93 (Hebrew, with English summary).

29 1QpHab 1:6; 8:11 [?]; 9:3–9; 11:17–12:10.

30 Note the characterization of MMT's "somewhat friendly" attitude toward the addressees' leader in DJD X, 118 and of the "relatively eirenic" (sic) relationship between the "we" group and the "you" group (p. 121).

31 On the general tendency of sectarians to take pride in their separateness, see in connection with our text A. Baumgarten, "Qumran and Jewish Sectarianism during the Second Temple Period," *The Scrolls of the Judaean Desert: Forty Years of Research* (ed. M. Broshi et al.; Jerusalem: Bialik Institute and Israel Exploration Society, 1992) 142–143 (in Hebrew).

his own sincerity and that of the group he represents—after all, they separated themselves from the multitude because they take their religion seriously. Therefore, he expects them to consider seriously the legal positions defended in the letter. As for the ruler, he similarly is reminded of examples from Israel's biblical past and exhorted to heed the Law properly. What is the relationship of these two parts of the letter? The simplest answer, it appears, is that the group addressed is in close alliance with the ruler.

Josephus allows us to fit this perspective into a historical framework. From him we learn that there was opposition to the Hasmonean high priests; the last Zadokite high priest, Onias III or IV, opened up a competing temple in Egypt in which priests of his own *genos* were to serve.[32] This allows us to infer that the Sadducees, who appear in the days of Jonathan, the first Hasmonean (non-Zadokite) high priest, a group whose very name is derived from "Zadok," were also a legitimist party that opposed the Hasmonean high priests because they were not Zadokite.[33] Perhaps they had other reasons as well. Josephus makes it clear that the Pharisees are the party in power when he reports that midway through the Hasmonean period, under John Hyrcanus I, a rupture developed between the Hasmoneans and

---

32 *Ant.* 12 §§387–388; 13 §§62–73; *J.W.* 7 §§423–432; *Ant.* 13 §63. On this temple and its founder see, most recently, F. Parente, "Onias III'(sic) Death and the Founding of the Temple of Leontopolis," *Josephus and the History of the Greco-Roman Period: Essays in Memory of Morton Smith* (eds. F. Parente and J. Sievers; Leiden: E. J. Brill, 1994) 69–98.

33 *Ant.* 13 §§171–173. On this theme, see my "Josephus and Nicolaus," 161–162 and "Two Aspects of a Priestly View of Descent at Qumran," *Archaeology and History in the Dead Sea Scrolls: The New York University Conference in Memory of Yigael Yadin* (JSPSup 8; ed. L. H. Schiffman; Sheffield: Sheffield Academic Press, 1990) 158–65 (unfortunately, due to an oversight the latter paper was published from uncorrected galleys; the publisher subsequently supplied me with a corrected version, and I will be happy to supply copies to interested parties). On *Ant.* 13 §§171–173 see now S. Goranson, "Posidonius, Strabo and Marcus Vipsanius Agrippa as Sources on Essenes," *JJS* 45 (1994) 295. His suggestion that Josephus is based here on a connected account of the Jews in Strabo's lost history, which opened with an account of the Jewish sects, is unargued and, it seems, unlikely, for most of the passages on the Jews in Strabo's history, such as we know it (from Josephus' *Antiquities* 13–14), appeared in the context of Hellenistic and Roman history, not in a connected account of Jewish history. See M. Stern, *Greek and Latin Authors on Jews and Judaism* (3 vols.; Jerusalem: Israel Academy of Sciences and Humanities, 1974–1984) 1, nos. 99–108. Strabo's connected account of the Jews comes in his *Geographica* 16.2.34–36 (Stern, no. 115).

the Pharisees; until then the Hasmonean ruler had been their disciple.[34]

If, then, MMT was written by a Qumran spokesman early in the Hasmonean period, it amounts to a call upon the party in power and its ruler to revise the laws of the Temple and priesthood in line with the positions of the Qumran community. The text would indicate that the Hasmoneans and their Pharisaic backers had introduced various changes into the Temple cult—something which has long been suspected, for example, with regard to the calendar in use. Our text would not indicate that the majority of the people followed the Pharisees, even in the Hasmonean period, and certainly not—and here is our last caveat—in any later period after the Hasmoneans changed sides and moved the Sadducees into power, or later yet, when Herod silenced the Sanhedrin, ruled without a coalition and appointed foreign nobodies to the high-priesthood.[35] MMT says something about the ruling party in the days of the Hasmoneans—no more, no less. It is difficult to see how that could impact upon conclusions, on other grounds, as to whether or not Josephus' statements about Pharisaic hegemony, in the late first century, are to be accepted.[36] This difficulty applies doubly with regard to *Ant.* 18 §15, cited by Qimron and Strugnell in the inset passage above, for it not only was written in the first century, but also appears in a first-century context.[37]

We can go a little further. Who is that so-called "multitude of the people," viewed here as sinful, from whom the writer and his community have separated themselves? If they are not the Pharisees, the recipients, nor the Qumran Essenes, who wrote the letter, then they may be the Sadducees—the Temple establishment of the pre-

---

[34] *Ant.* 13 §§288–298. Rabbinic tradition (*b. Qidd.* 66a) places the break under Hyrcanus' son, Alexander Jannaeus. The discrepancy is immaterial here.

[35] See M. Stern, "Social and Political Realignments in Herodian Judaea," *The Jerusalem Cathedra* (3 vols.; ed. L. I. Levine; Jerusalem: Izhak ben Zvi/Detroit: Wayne State University Press, 1981–83), 2.44–45, 49–55.

[36] By way of comparison, note that this lecture was originally given in November 1994, shortly after national elections created a Republican majority in both houses of the U. S. Congress, thus reversing the situation which had obtained for decades. What would we think of future historians who use mid-1994 evidence on the composition of that Congress in order to reconstruct the same of even one year later, or vice versa?

[37] This is not to say that Josephus' statements in earlier contexts, such as *Ant.* 13 §§288, 298, are any more applicable to them.

Hasmonean period. Indeed, the identification of this body as the Temple priesthood is supported by the usage of the priestly term מעל and the implicit comparison to the sons of Eli. Thus, the writer of MMT is indicating to his Pharisaic addressees that he, although of the priestly camp, is sincere in his religion: after all, he and his community separated themselves from the multitude of bad priests. In other words, we have here a Qumran text of the early Hasmonean period in which the writer attempts to justify his group's sincerity by saying, "don't mix us up with other priests, we separated ourselves from them," i.e., in the previous period when they ran the Temple and the whole show. Read this way MMT dovetails nicely with the first column of the Damascus Document. There too we read of the sect beginning as an opposition party in the pre-Hasmonean period, in which case the opposition must have been to the Zadokite establishment.

In conclusion, MMT shows us a view of three major groups, termed "us," "you" and "them." It indicates that the Pharisees were in power subsequent to a priestly group. This fits what we know of the pre-Hasmonean period, when the Zadokite priesthood ran the Jerusalem establishment (see Ben Sira 50 and 51:12ix!), and of the early Hasmonean period, when the Pharisees formed part of the ruling Hasmonean coalition. Just as the sectarian author of Pesher Nahum sees two major groups, Ephraim and Manasseh, corresponding to the Pharisees and Sadducees, and just as the Gospels apparently show us another sect viewing its competitors as being of mainly two varieties,[38] so too MMT shows us a Jewish world divided mainly into three camps: Qumranites, Pharisees and a Temple establishment which we associate, generally, with the Sadducees. But MMT says nothing about any later period such as that of the New Testament and Josephus, the era addressed in Smith's "Palestinian Judaism in the First Century." Nor does MMT tell us anything about any broad popular support for the Pharisees and their version of Judaism. Concerning the Pharisees, MMT shows us only that they were in the ruling coalition in the early Hasmonean period. But we already knew that from Josephus.

---

[38] On Pesher Nahum and "scribes and Pharisees," see Schwartz, *Studies*, 101. To the literature concerning Pesher Nahum listed there, n. 64, add Schiffman, "Pharisees and Sadducees."

The Place of 4QMMT in the Corpus of Qumran Manuscripts

LAWRENCE H. SCHIFFMAN
New York University
New York, NY

4Q *Miqṣat Maʿaśe Ha-Torah* (MMT, or the "Halakhic Letter") is a composite of six fragmentary manuscripts which have been arranged in a composite text by Elisha Qimron, based on the work he and John Strugnell did together on this text.[1] The composite reconstruction of this text is, as Qimron asserts, a matter of scholarly judgment. Nevertheless, the overall structure of the document, as suggested by their research, seems to be clear and will be taken as the starting point for this discussion.

The composite text may be divided into three parts: (A) the calendar at the beginning, (B) the list of laws, and (C) the homiletical conclusion.[2] The suggestion that MMT is originally two documents rather than one,[3] we find unacceptable, since two manuscripts (MSS d and e) definitely contain elements of both the legal and homiletical sections of the text.[4] Each of the three sections which make up MMT

---

[1] E. Qimron and J. Strugnell, DJD X, 44–57. See the earlier articles, E. Qimron and J. Strugnell, "An Unpublished Halakhic Letter from Qumran," *Biblical Archaeology Today* (ed. J. Amitai; Jerusalem: Israel Exploration Society, 1984) 400–407, and (a different article by the same name) *Israel Museum Journal* 4 (1985) 9–12.

[2] Cf. DJD X, 109–11.

[3] R. Eisenman and M. Wise, *The Dead Sea Scrolls Uncovered* (Shaftesbury, Rockport, Brisbane: Element, 1992) 182, 196. For the controversy regarding this book, see the section entitled, "Ethics of Publication of the Dead Sea Scrolls: Panel Discussion," *Methods of Investigation of the Dead Sea Scrolls and the Khirbet Qumran Site, Present Realities and Future Prospects* (eds. M. O. Wise et al.; Annals of the New York Academy of Sciences 722; New York: The New York Academy of Sciences, 1994) 455–97 and F. García Martínez, "Notas al margen de *The Dead Sea Scrolls Uncovered*," *RevQ* 16 (1993) 123–50.

[4] DJD X, 25–8, 34–7.

can be studied with regard to its links with other elements of the Qumran corpus. This analysis will better enable us to understand the document as a whole and its evidence for the history of the Qumran sect and the Judaism of the time.

A. The Calendar

From the earliest discussions of 4QMMT, after its announcement (or better: debut) at the 1984 conference on biblical archaeology in Jerusalem,[5] it was already clear that the relationship of the calendar to the text that followed was a matter of question from a literary point of view. The calendar's conclusion is found in MS a (4Q394 3–7 i), which is immediately followed, on the same fragment, by the introductory sentence to the list of laws and then by the laws themselves.[6] The editors, in the series *Discoveries in the Judaean Desert*, placed another fragment (4Q394 1–2 i-v) above it, and restored much of the calendar from parallel Qumran calendrical texts, on which we will have more to say below. This fragment, however, seems out of place since it sets out the calendar in five columns, while the concluding section, that found in the fragment containing the beginning of the legal section, is written in the normal way across the entire column. For this and other reasons, it has recently been suggested that this five-columned fragment should be detached from MMT and that the text be restored in such a way that it would be written across the page. In any case, we would have to reckon with the presence of the very same calendar text.[7]

That the calendar is indeed to be restored above the legal section, and that the calendar to be restored is indeed the so-called sectarian calendar, can be shown from the final words of this section:

---

5 See the description of that event in L. H. Schiffman, *Reclaiming the Dead Sea Scrolls* (Philadelphia: Jewish Publication Society, 1994) xvii-xviii.

6 See DJD X, 7–8, 109–10, and the photograph on pl. II.

7 The hesitations about the present join and reconstruction are engendered by the unlikely scribal technique involved in having five columns of calendrical material on the top of a column (a page) followed by full width columns below. Such an approach is not impossible, but certainly is very unlikely in light of what we know of the Qumran corpus. For such irreguarly shaped columns, see the Jonathan Prayer (4Q448), in E. Eshel, H. Eshel, and A. Yardeni, "A Qumran Composition Containing Part of Ps. 154 and a Prayer for the Welfare of King Jonathan and his Kingdom," *IEJ* 42 (1992) 200.

[. . . The twenty-eighth day of it (i.e. the twelfth month)] is a Sabbath. To it (the twelfth month), after [the] Sab[bath, Sunday and Monday, a day is to be ad]ded. And the year is complete[8]—three hundred and si[xty-four] days.[9]

The 364 day calendar is, of course, the calendar known from various Qumran texts, such as the so-called Mishmarot detailing the priestly courses and the *Temple Scroll*, as well as previously known pseudepigrapha also found at Qumran—Jubilees and Enoch.[10] Regardless of whether 4Q394 1–2 i-v is to be joined to the beginning of MMT or which restorations are to be accepted, such a calendar certainly was copied at the beginning of MMT.

In the Qimron-Strugnell reconstruction,[11] the calendar mentions, in addition to the solar months, the specific extra day added after three months of thirty days at the equinoxes and solstices, as well as the 91–day quarter which is the basic division of the year.[12] Further, it also mentions the wine festival on the third day of the fifth month and the oil festival on the 22nd of the sixth month, as well as the festival of the wood offering starting on the twenty-third of the same month. All these are among the extra festivals associated with the solar calendar in the *Temple Scroll*.[13]

From the beginning there has been a question as to whether this calendar is to be considered integral to the text of MMT or not. It ends in MS a (4Q394 3–7 i line 3=composite text A 21) after the first word of the line, and the rest of the line is blank. The text begins the halakhic section on the next line with the incipit, "These are some of

[8] Cf. *Jub.* 6:30 for a similar expression.

[9] Adapted from DJD X, 45.

[10] For a brief survey of the calendar issue, see Schiffman, *Reclaiming*, 301–5 and bibliography on 443. See also S. Talmon, *The World of Qumran from Within* (Jerusalem: Magnes Press, 1989) 147–85.

[11] DJD X, 44.

[12] The mention of a Day of Remembrance on the first day of the fourth month indicates that the ritual sequence of this calendar differed from that of the *Temple Scroll* which celebrated only the first days of the first and seventh months. The Days of Remembrance are a regular feature of 4QMishmarot[a] and 4QMishmarot[b] as well as of the calendar text known as 4QS[e]. In addition, they are known from *Jub.* 6:23–29; see L. H. Schiffman, "The Sacrificial System of the *Temple Scroll* and the Book of Jubilees," *SBLSP 1985* (ed. K. H. Richards; Atlanta: Scholars Press, 1985) 228–9.

[13] See Y. Yadin, *The Temple Scroll* (Jerusalem: Israel Exploration Society, 1983) 1.116–9.

our rulings" (אלה מקצת דברינו . . . [line 4=composite text B 1]), and the laws follow. Since the substance of this incipit returns towards the end of the homiletical section (C 26–27) which contains similar wording (ואף אנחנו כתבנו אליך מקצת מעשי התורה), it seems certain that the legal and homiletical section are to be considered as one unit. But it appears to us most likely that the calendar at the beginning of MMT was placed there by a scribe who copied (as far as can be known only in one MS) the sectarian calendar immediately before the so-called halakhic letter or treatise.[14]

This assumption is strengthened by the fact that this calendar is clearly a separate literary unit which, even if it were part of the MMT text, must have been imported whole cloth into the text. The very same calendar lies behind a text termed 4QCalendarA-B.[15] Since this calendar existed separately, and since a calendar was also attached to one of the manuscripts of the *Rule of the Community* from cave 4 (4QS^{e}),[16] it is apparent that this calendrical list was not composed by the author of the MMT text. This calendar must therefore be considered extraneous to the original composition.

This view is supported by an examination of the legal and homiletical sections (B and C) of MMT. (Here comes an argument from silence.) Surprisingly, calendar issues are never referred to in either of these sections, and none of the additional festivals or characteristics of the Qumran calendrical system are mentioned at all in the text of MMT proper. One would certainly have expected these to be mentioned in a document giving the legal reasons for the

---

14 This same position is taken by Strugnell in an appendix to DJD X, 203, also published in J. Strugnell, "MMT: Second Thoughts on a Forthcoming Edition," *The Community of the Renewed Covenant, The Notre Dame Symposium on the Dead Sea Scrolls* (eds. E. Ulrich and J. VanderKam; Notre Dame: University of Notre Dame Press, 1994) 61–2. Strugnell further argues that it is most likely that this calendar was not part of MS b (4Q395) because "enough uninscribed leather is preserved before Section B to make it highly probable that no text ever stood before it." This comment is difficult to understand from the photo reproduced as Plate III, at the bottom, unless he is referring to the blank space to the right of the text as being too wide for a columnar margin.

15 See the preliminary edition according to the readings of J. T. Milik from the Preliminary Concordance, in B. Z. Wacholder and M. G. Abegg, *A Preliminary Edition of the Unpublished Dead Sea Scrolls, The Hebrew and Aramaic Texts from Cave Four* (Washington, DC: Biblical Archaeology Society, 1991) 1.60–76.

16 A preliminary edition, based on the readings of J. T. Milik as recorded in the Preliminary Concordance, appears in Wacholder-Abegg, 1.96–101.

foundation of the sect, and that, in our view, is the purpose of MMT.[17] Indeed, it may very well be that the scribe copied the calendar before MMT precisely because calendrical issues were to him determinative and he could not imagine that they were not a factor in the initial schism. But in so doing, he actually added an issue to the document which had never been discussed in the original treatise.[18]

The decision of this scribe to integrate the calendar into MMT was not all that unreasonable in light of the situation in the *Temple Scroll.* Like MMT, this scroll reflects the Sadducean trend in Jewish law.[19] In our view it is made up of Sadducean sources, yet redacted by someone who was either a member of, or close to, the Qumran sect.[20] In rewriting the Torah so as to include his opinions on Jewish law, the author/redactor incorporated a pre-existent source known to scholars as the Festival Calendar.[21] This source recapitulated the festival calendar of Numbers 28–29 while at the same time integrating material from Leviticus 23 and other sources. In the process, the author of this source wove in elements of the calendar known to us as the sectarian calendar, including the special festivals outlined in that text in detail—the same as those mentioned in MMT. While it was possible to deny that this was indeed the sectarian calendar previous to

---

17 See L. H. Schiffman, "The New *Halakhic Letter* (4QMMT) and the Origins of the Dead Sea Sect," *BA* 53 (1990) 64–73; id., *Reclaiming*, 83–9.

18 Strugnell, DJD X, 203 and "MMT: Second Thoughts," 62 prefers to see it as prefixed for non-controversialist or non-polemical reasons.

19 See the important article of Y. Sussmann, "The History of Halakha and the Dead Sea Scrolls—Preliminary Observations on *Miqṣat Maʿaśe Ha-Torah* (4QMMT)" [Hebrew] *Tarbiz* 59 (1990) 11–76. An English version of the body of this article and some of the notes appears in DJD X, 179–202. The first to realize the Sadducean halakhic tendencies of 4QMMT, when only a short passage from it was known, was J. M. Baumgarten, "The Pharisaic-Sadducean Controversies about Purity and the Qumran Texts," *JJS* 31 (1980) 157–70. Attention was called to Sadducean elements in the *Temple Scroll* by M. R. Lehmann, "The Temple Scroll as a Source for Sectarian Halakhah," *RevQ* 9 (1977–8) 579–87.

20 See L. H. Schiffman, "The *Temple Scroll* and the Status of its Law: The Status of the Question," *Community of the Renewed Covenant,* 46–8.

21 On the sources of the *Temple Scroll,* see A. M. Wilson and L. Wills, "Literary Sources of the Temple Scroll," *HTR* 75 (1982) 275–88. On the Festival Calendar, see Y. Yadin, *The Temple Scroll* (Jerusalem: Israel Exploration Society, 1983) 1.89–142. He did not, however deal with this as a separate source, only as a literary unit. This source was described in detail in M. O. Wise, *A Critical Study of the Temple Scroll from Qumran Cave 11* (Studies in Ancient Oriental Civilization 49; Chicago: The Oriental Institute of the University of Chicago, 1990) 129–54. See also Schiffman, "Sacrificial System," 217–33.

the availability of all the calendrical scrolls,[22] such a claim is no longer likely, and we must view the calendar of the *Temple Scroll* as identical to that prefaced to MMT by the scribe of MS a or some previous compiler.

Since the legal regulations of MMT are similar in some cases to those of the *Temple Scroll*, there is little reason to be surprised that a scribe would similarly assume that the calendar of the sectarians was to be associated with MMT as it was with the *Temple Scroll*.

B. The Legal Section

1. *Temple Scroll*

In a previous paper we investigated in detail those laws in MMT which were paralleled in the *Temple Scroll*.[23] In order to clarify this important aspect of the relationship of MMT to the Qumran corpus, we summarize these parallels here.

The *Temple Scroll* (11QT 20:11–13) requires that *šelamim* sacrifices (gift-offerings) be eaten by sunset on the very same day that they are offered. This law is paralleled by MMT B 9–13 where it is stated that the meal offering of the *šelamim* is to be offered on the very same day. The opponents of the group are said to have left it over to the next day. We can assume that the meal offerings and the actual meat of the sacrifices had the very same time restrictions. This MMT passage is clearly a reference to the same view as that of the *Temple Scroll* that the offering must be eaten by sunset, as opposed to the Pharisaic-Rabbinic view which allowed it to be eaten until dawn, with the proviso of the tannaim that it be eaten if possible by midnight.[24] In any case, these two texts share the requirement that it be eaten before sunset.[25]

---

22 As maintained by B. A. Levine, "The *Temple Scroll*: Aspects of its Historical Provenance and Literary Character, " *BASOR* 232 (1978) 7–11; id., "A Further Look at the *Moᶜadim* of the *Temple Scroll*," *Archaeology and History in the Dead Sea Scrolls, The New York University Conference in Memory of Yigael Yadin* (ed. L. H. Schiffman; JSPSup 8; JSOT/ASOR Monographs 2; Sheffield: JSOT Press, 1990) 53–66.

23 L. H. Schiffman, "*Miqṣat Maᶜaśeh Ha-Torah* and the *Temple Scroll*," *RevQ* 14 (1990) 435–57. To this material, cf. now the analysis of Qimron in DJD X, 148–77 which Strugnell and he had been kind enough to make available to me already in 1984, and that of Sussman, DJD X, 187–91.

24 *M. Ber.* 1:1; cf. *m. Zebaḥ.* 6:1.

25 DJD X, 150–2; Schiffman, "*Miqṣat*," 436–8.

Both texts, in a variety of laws, reject the policy of the Pharisees and later tannaim[26] who allow the *ṭevul yom*, one who has immersed but not yet completed the sunset of his last day of purification, to eat pure food.[27] The Sadducees, as known from elsewhere, followed by MMT and the *Temple Scroll* in a variety of passages, rejected this possibility, insisting on waiting for sunset. The *Temple Scroll* expresses this view in 11QT 45:9–10 regarding immersion of one impure from seminal emission who must complete the entire third day through sunset before being permitted to eat of pure food.[28] Regarding purification from the impurity of the dead, 11QT 49:19–29 insists on completion of the last day of the seven-day purification period.[29] In 11QT 51:2–5 those who come into contact with the impure creeping things (*šeraṣim*) are also impure until after sunset.

The same view is expressed in MMT B 13–17 in regard to those who are involved in the offering of the red heifer who must be entirely pure after completing their period of purification at the setting of the sun.[30] As hinted in the polemic of MMT, the Pharisaic-Rabbinic tradition disagreed radically. The "elders of Israel" supposedly went so far as to purposely render the priest who would burn the offering impure so as to make him a *ṭevul yom*. The view of MMT is identified explicitly in the Mishnah as Sadducean.[31] We will see below that the *Zadokite Fragments* also agree with MMT and the *Temple Scroll* in this regard.

11QT 47:7–15 prohibits bringing hides of animals slaughtered outside the Temple precincts into the temenos.[32] Only the skins of animals slaughtered in Temple rituals may be used to store food in the

---

26 Cf. *m. Neg.* 14:3; *Sipra* ʾEmor chap. 4:8.

27 See Qimron and Strugnell, DJD X, 153–4; Schiffman, *Miqṣat*, 438–42; Baumgarten, "Pharisaic-Sadducean Controversies," 157–61; and L. H. Schiffman, "Pharisaic and Sadducean Halakhah in Light of the Dead Sea Scrolls, The Case of Ṭevul Yom," *DSD* 1 (1994) 285–99, where I deal with the full range of applications of this Sadducean principle in Qumran texts.

28 Cf. Yadin, *Temple Scroll*, 1.288–9.

29 Cf. L. H. Schiffman, "The Impurity of the Dead in the *Temple Scroll*," *Archaeology and History*, 146–8.

30 This same requirement may be referred to in 4Q276–7 (Ṭohorot B^{b} and B^{c}) which requires that the sprinkling be done by a priest who is pure of all impurities. See the transcription in Eisenman-Wise, *Scrolls Uncovered* 211, and Wacholder and Abegg (1995) 3.85–87.

31 *M. Para* 3:7.

32 Cf. Yadin, *Temple Scroll*, 1.308–11; Schiffman, "*Miqṣat*," 442–8.

Temple. This law is paralleled by MMT B 18–23 which prohibits bringing into the Temple containers made of hides of animals slaughtered outside. The *Temple Scroll* includes in this prohibition also bones (and hooves as well), and this is made explicit in MMT B 21–23 (according to an almost certain restoration) which also prohibits bringing bone vessels into the sanctuary.[33]

11QT 52:5–7 prohibits the slaughter of pregnant animals, making use of the language of Deut 22:6–7 to make clear that it is considered like taking the mother and its young at the same time. MMT B 36–38 shares the same prohibition, but instead derives the law from Lev 22:28. The polemical language shows that this was contrary to the Pharisaic-Rabbinic view which, as we know from later sources, permitted the slaughter of pregnant animals.[34] It took the prohibition on slaughtering an animal and its child, stated in the masculine in Lev 22:28, as referring only to the slaughter of a mother and its young on the same day, not to the prohibition on slaughtering pregnant animals.[35]

The *Temple Scroll* (11QT 60:2–4) indicates that various offerings are to be allotted to the priests. These include wave offerings, first born, tithe animals, all sacred donations, and "fruit offerings of praise," that is, fourth year produce. Some of these elements, namely the fourth year produce and the cattle and sheep tithes, are also assigned to the priests by MMT B 57–59.[36] In this case the *Temple Scroll* and MMT are in agreement, but we must remember that there are more elements in the *Temple Scroll* list than in that of MMT, indicating that these passages are not literarily dependent one on the other, but rather are related only in terms of representing the same halakhic tradition.

The final area we will mention is the use of the term "camps" to denote the various levels of sanctity of Jerusalem and the Temple complex. The Torah contains various regulations regarding the

---

33 Cf. DJD X, 154–6; Schiffman, "*Miqṣat,*" 442–8; Yadin, *Temple Scroll,* 1.308–11.

34 See *m. Ḥul.* 4:5 where the opinion of Rabbi Meir that "he is obligated for (violation of) the prohibition against slaughtering an animal and its young" refers only to his view that one must slaughter a fully mature embryo which survives its mother's ritual slaughter. In such a case, in the view of Rabbi Meir, it is forbidden to slaughter the embryo on the same day as its mother. The anonymous Mishnah does not require slaughter of the mature fetus and so the issue is not raised by the other sages.

35 DJD X, 157–8; Schiffman, "*Miqṣat,*" 448–51; Yadin, *Temple Scroll,* 1.320–14.

36 DJD X, 164–6; Schiffman, "*Miqṣat,*" 452–6.

"camp" of the Israelites in the wilderness. The *Temple Scroll* made use of these passages to derive the levels of sanctity of the three courts of the Temple city—the inner court, containing the Temple, the middle and outer courts. In this respect the scroll followed the same scheme as is found in tannaitic sources which interpreted the biblical passages as referring to the camp of the divine presence, containing the Tabernacle; the camp of the Levites, including the residence of Moses and the priests; and the camp of Israel in which the rest of the people dwelled.[37] For the *Temple Scroll*, this set of camps, concentrically arranged, constituted the Temple complex, which a visionary architect designed in imitation of the Tabernacle and desert camp which it represented.[38]

MMT seems to take a somewhat different attitude, although some interpreters have sought to harmonize the two texts.[39] MMT alludes to the camps twice. As restored by Strugnell and Qimron, MMT B 29–31 states polemically that the authors think that the sanctuary is equivalent to the tabernacle of the desert period, and that the camp is Jerusalem, and outside that camp is the camp of the cities. This means that the text accepts a three camp notion, with the entire Temple as the inner camp, the city of Jerusalem as the middle camp, and the entire settled area of the cities as the camp of Israel.[40] Such a pattern is indeed similar to the three camps of the wilderness, but differs in some respects from the view of the *Temple Scroll*. In B 60–62 we hear that Jerusalem is the most important of the camps of Israel and it is termed the camp of holiness. This clearly refers to the same concept, describing the middle camp which the text of MMT already asserted was Jerusalem.

Here again we see commonality between MMT and the *Temple Scroll*, but the same basic concept is found in tannaitic thought. At the same time, MMT and the *Temple Scroll* differ in significant respects in

---

37 *T. Kelim B.Qam.* 1:12; *Sipre Num.* Naso 1.

38 See L. H. Schiffman, "Exclusion from the Sanctuary and the City of the Sanctuary in the *Temple Scroll*," *HAR* 9 (1985) 308–9; id., "Architecture and Law: The Temple and its Courtyards in the *Temple Scroll*," *From Ancient Israel to Modern Judaism: Intellect in Quest of Understanding, Essays in Honor of Marvin Fox* (eds. J. Neusner, E. S. Frerichs, and N. M. Sarna; BJS 159; Atlanta: Scholars Press, 1989) 1.267–84.

39 DJD X, 144–5; and the remark of Y. Yadin, in "Discussion," *Biblical Archaeology Today*, 429.

40 Cf. DJD X, 142–6.

the way this concept is applied. Indeed, this difference may result from the utopian character of the *Temple Scroll* as opposed to MMT which deals with the halakhic system of the author's own day, expressing the views of the Sadducean-Zadokite priests.

2. Zadokite Fragments

The links between MMT and the *Zadokite Fragments* are also close. The *Zadokite Fragments,* initially discovered by S. Schechter in the Cairo genizah,[41] were found subsequently in ten Qumran manuscripts.[42] It is certainly the case that the halakhic tradition behind the *Zadokite Fragments* is the same as that of the Qumran sect, even if they represent the members of the sect living in scattered groups ("camps") throughout the country. Here also we see some examples of agreement with MMT.

4Q266 (4QD[a]) 9 ii 1–4 provides that a woman who is impure from a non-menstrual flow of blood must wait "until sunset on the eighth day" to be considered pure. This law, based on Lev 15:25–30, presumes the rejection of the concept of *ṭevul yom* which we consider to be a "smoking gun" indication of the Sadducean approach to Jewish law.[43]

It is most probable that the fragmentary reference in 4Q266 (4QD[a]) 13 4–5, mentioning planting in the third year and sanctification in some other year,[44] originally paralleled the requirement of MMT B 62–3 that the fruit of the fourth year be given to the priests like *terumah,* as opposed to the Pharisaic-Rabbinic view that it should

---

[41] His initial publication is *Documents of Jewish Sectaries: Fragments of a Zadokite Work* (Cambridge: Cambridge University Press, 1910; repr. with Prolegomenon by J. A. Fitzmyer; New York: Ktav, 1970).

[42] The transcriptions of the cave 4 fragments by J. T. Milik for the Preliminary Concordance were published in reconstructed form in Wacholder-Abegg, 1.1–59. We have provided manuscript numbers (e.g. 4Q266) for these texts as well as letters (e.g. 4QD[a]), since the letter sigla have been changed over the years. The letters used to designate the manuscripts in Wacholder-Abegg are superseded by those in E. Tov, with S. J. Pfann, *The Dead Sea Scrolls on Microfiche, Companion Volume* (Leiden: E. J. Brill, 1993) 38. A full edition is being prepared by J. M. Baumgarten. For the other Qumran manuscripts, see Schiffman, *Reclaiming the Dead Sea Scrolls,* 469. On the legal material in these texts see J. M. Baumgarten, "The Laws of the *Damascus Document* in Current Research," *The Damascus Document Reconsidered* (ed. M. Broshi; Jerusalem: Israel Exploration Society, 1992) 51–62 and L. H. Schiffman, "New Halakhic Texts from Qumran," *Hebrew Studies* 34 (1993) 21–33.

[43] Schiffman, "Pharisaic and Sadducean Halakhah," 296–8.

[44] The text most likely referred to planting in the third year of the Sabbatical cycle which would result in sanctification of the fruits (the fourth year produce) in year six.

be eaten by the owner in the precincts of Jerusalem.[45] This same prescription, as already mentioned, is found also in the *Temple Scroll.*

As part of a list of those forbidden from entering "into the midst of the congregation," CD 15:15–17=4Q266 (4QD[a]) 17 i 6–9=4Q270 (4QD[e]) 10 ii 7–9 (restored) includes "one who is weak of the eyes so that he cannot see" as well as one who is deaf.[46] This passage may be compared with the prohibition in MMT of the blind and deaf from contact with the "sacred food" or from entering the Temple precincts, depending on how the passage is interpreted.[47] We should also note that the *Temple Scroll* (11QT 45:12–14) prohibits the blind from entering the Temple city, in our view equivalent to the temenos, the Temple precincts.[48]

While MMT and the *Zadokite Fragments* do have in common the exclusion of these two categories, the blind and deaf, we need to recognize that each occurs in a long list of disqualified individuals of which the other categories are not equivalent. If these laws were truly identical, we would expect the lists to be the same in their entirety. When we bear in mind that the *Temple Scroll* excludes only the blind and the *Rule of the Congregation* excludes an entirely different, though overlapping list from the community of the end of days (1QSa 2:3–11),[49] we recognize that these texts share a trend of interpretation, but that they are not identical in their approach.

It appears that MMT and the *Zadokite Fragments* include the identical prescription regarding the comparison of some kind of illegal marriage with the laws of forbidden mixtures (*kilʾayim*). 4Q271 (4QD[f]) 1 i 9–11=4Q270 (4QD[e]) 5:15–16=4Q269 (4QD[d]) 9:2–3 prohibits giving a girl in marriage to one who is inappropriate (לאשר לוא הוכן לה). Such a match is then compared to forbidden mixtures of either plowing animals or threads, in a passage making use

---

45 *Sipre Num.* 6; *Sipra* Qedoshim parashah 3:8.

46 Cf. L. H. Schiffman, *The Eschatological Community of the Dead Sea Scrolls, A Study of the Rule of the Congregation* (SBLMS 38; Atlanta: Scholars Press, 1989) 44–9. This passage, then not known in its original Hebrew, is discussed on 47–8.

47 See DJD X, 160–61.

48 See Schiffman, "Exclusion," 309–11 and Yadin, *Temple Scroll,* 1.289–91. Yadin, however, interprets the Temple City to encompass the entire city of Jerusalem. A table comparing exclusion of various classes from the Temple according to MMT and the *Temple Scroll* is provided in *DJD* X, 146.

49 See the detailed discussion in Schiffman, *Eschatological Community,* 37–52. The exclusion of various classes from the army and military camp is taken up there as well.

of the language of Scripture (Deut 22:10–11). But here there is no specific information on the nature of the inappropriateness of the match. In MMT B 75–82 (the end of the preserved portion of the legal section), we find what must be the exact same law, although it remains difficult to understand. This passage begins by referring to "*zenut* ('sexual immorality') that is performed among the people" which is compared to violation of the laws of forbidden mixtures (all varieties are listed here). From the continuation it seems clear that this is an offense of the priests about whom it is said that "you know that some of the priests and the people are mixing, and they mingle and defile the holy seed . . . ." The editors take this to refer to priests marrying Israelites which they claim this document prohibits.[50] Another view that they cite suggests that it refers to marriage with non-Jews.[51] Whatever the correct interpretation of this law, it is most probably the same prescription as that of the *Zadokite Fragments* and the restoration of that passage will have to be attempted in light of this law in MMT.

4Q271 (4QD^{f}) 1 ii 8=4Q269 (4QD^{d}) 10:3–4=4Q270 (4QD^{e}) 7:20 clearly refers to a prohibition on accepting sacrifices from non-Jews. The continuation also prohibits the reuse by Jews of metals from which non-Jews have made idols. The prohibition on acceptance of sacrifices from non-Jews is paralleled in MMT B 8–9 which castigates the sect's opponents for accepting such sacrifices.[52] Indeed, it is well known that Pharisaic-Rabbinic law does permit the acceptance of such offerings.[53] This is certainly another example of a law common to MMT and the *Zadokite Fragments.*

The continuation of this same passage (4Q271 [4QD^{f}] 1 ii 8–11=4Q269 [4QD^{d}] 10:4–6=4Q270 [4QD^{e}] 7:20–21) refers to the prohibition of bringing to the Temple hide, cloth or any vessel which is susceptible to impurity, unless it has been purified appropriately. This passage may relate to issues raised as well in MMT, although we

---

50 DJD X, 171–5.

51 The view of J. M. Baumgarten as reported in DJD X, 171 n. 178a.

52 See DJD X, 149–50. This issue was a matter of controversy at the beginning of the Jewish revolt against Rome in 66–73 BCE. The pro-revolt forces argued that such sacrifices were forbidden, while the anti-revolt group argued that it was permitted. See Josephus, *J.W.* 2 §409–21 and the echoes of this event in *b. Git.* 56a. See also I. Knohl, "The Acceptance of Sacrifices from Gentiles," [Hebrew] *Tarbiz* 48 (1978–79) 341–5 for later echoes of the controversy over whether to accept sacrifices from non-Jews.

53 See *b. Ḥul.* 5a and L. H. Schiffman, *Who Was a Jew? Rabbinic and Halakhic Perspectives on the Jewish Christian Schism* (Hoboken: Ktav, 1985) 49.

cannot be certain. MMT B 18–20 refers to the prohibition of bringing certain skins of animals or vessels made of them into the Temple precincts. This law has been related to that of the *Temple Scroll* prohibiting skins slaughtered outside from being brought into the Temple, as discussed above. If these passages relate to the same issues, then the *Zadokite Fragments* recognize the possibility of purification where MMT and the *Temple Scroll* do not, since for these latter texts the issue is the need for sacral slaughter, not ritual impurity. On the other hand, it is possible that the two laws are unrelated, one dealing with problems of impurity and the other dealing with problems of slaughtering and hides not slaughtered sacrificially.

4Q270 (4QD^{e}) 9 ii 6–9 lists a variety of offerings which are to go to the priests. These include, among others, the tithe from the herd (cattle) and flock (sheep and goats). The tithe animals are specifically mentioned in a parallel law in MMT B 63–64 which states that they are to go to the priests, as is clear from line 6, despite the disconnected and fragmentary nature of the passage.[54] The longer list of gifts is paralleled in the *Temple Scroll* (11QT 60:2–5), where numerous items are listed. But the Pharisaic-Rabbinic tradition rules that these animals are to be offered in the Temple, the blood sprinkled, and the meat eaten by the owners.[55] The view of the *Zadokite Fragments* and MMT is also followed in some apocryphal texts as well.[56] But we should note again that the various lists—the *Zadokite Fragments*, MMT and the *Temple Scroll*—are sufficiently different in formulation that we cannot assert literary dependence, only that they belong to the same school of legal thought.

The final example was also already encountered in our discussion of the *Temple Scroll*. 4Q270 (4QD^{e}) 9 ii 14–15 refers to the prohibition of slaughtering a pregnant animal, whether a domestic animal (*behemah*) or beast (*ḥayyah*). MMT B 36 contains the same prohibition, explained as a violation of the Torah's requirement that a mother and child not be slaughtered on the same day.

The large number of parallels between MMT and the *Zadokite Fragments* leads one to conclude that there would have been a much larger number of parallels if the entire text of both documents had

---

54 DJD X, 165–6.

55 *M. Zebaḥ* 5:8; cf. *t. Zebaḥ* 6:18; *baraita* in *b. Pesaḥ*. 64b, *b. Pesaḥ*. 37a and 56a; *Sipre Num.* 118; *Sipre Deut.* 78.

56 Jub. 13:25–6; Tob. 1:6; cf. Schiffman, "*Miqṣat*," 453 and nn. 87–90.

survived. In any case, the extant parallels can only be attributed to the common halakhic substratum of the Sadducean tradition, which was opposed in the cases we cited to the Pharisaic-Rabbinic approach.

3. Florilegium

Also to be compared to MMT is 4Q174 (*Florilegium*) 1–2 i 3–4. This text, a series of eschatological explanations of biblical verses, alludes to the prohibition on entrance into the Temple in the end of days by an Ammonite, Moabite, *mamzer*,[57] foreigner, or proselyte or their descendants forever.[58] Here the phrase "to enter the congregation" in Deut 23:2–9 is taken as referring to entrance into the Temple, whereas these prohibitions were understood as referring to marriage in the Pharisaic-Rabbinic tradition.[59] The *Temple Scroll* also takes this expression as referring to entrance into the Temple, as noted above. In any case, MMT B 39–49 takes this as referring to *both* entrance into the Temple and marriage.[60] Further, while the lists share the Ammonite, Moabite, and *mamzer*, the proselyte and foreigner are not mentioned in the MMT passage, and the two forms of genital injuries mentioned in Deuteronomy are not mentioned in the *Florilegium*, even though they appear in MMT. This indicates again that although we deal with a common halakhic trend, there is no literary dependence in the legal traditions we are evaluating.

C. The Homiletical Section

In the final section, the authors of MMT attempt to sway their opponents with arguments of a homiletical nature. This is the section which I have argued is addressed primarily to the ruler, the Hasmonean high priest.[61] My view is conditioned by the shift in this section from the plural form for the addressee found in the halakhic section (although the text is usually restored), to the singular. My argument was that the plural addressee referred to the authors'

---

[57] Defined by the halakhic tradition as the Jewish offspring of a forbidden marriage whose ancestry disqualified him or her from marriage with free, hereditary Jews of the classes priest, Levite or Israelite.

[58] Cf. G. J. Brooke, *Exegesis at Qumran, 4QFlorilegium in its Jewish Context* (JSOTSup 29; Sheffield: JSOT Press, 1985) 100–102.

[59] *Sipre Deut.* 246–249.

[60] Qimron and Strugnell, DJD X, 158–60. But cf. the article of M. J. Bernstein in this collection, pp. 37–38.

[61] Schiffman, "New *Halakhic Letter*," 64–73; id., *Reclaiming*, 83–9.

erstwhile Sadducean colleagues who had remained in the Temple, while the singular section at the end referred to the ruler who is compared with the kings of Israel in the First Temple period.

This section, beginning with C 10, "And we have written to you (sing.)," is essentially a Deuteronomic rebuke passage, aimed not at the people (a collective you plural), but at an individual. This section is introduced by the explicit reference to the tripartite canon (C 10–11).[62] A passage woven together out of Deut 31:29 and 30:1–3 comes next, followed by the statement that some of these blessings and curses came true in First Temple times and that others are now coming to be in the time of the authors. The example of the First Temple kings is invoked to influence the ruler to follow the ways of the Torah, as understood by the writers, presumably referring to the twenty-two legal rulings they have presented above in the legal section.

What we have, then, is a kind of royal *tokaḥah,* to which there is only one parallel I know of, at the end of the Law of the King of the *Temple Scroll* (11QT 59). The Law of the King is a separate document, one of the sources which make up the scroll.[63] Its veiled allusion to the kidnap and murder of Jonathan the Hasmonean (11QT 57:9–11),[64] as well as its sustained polemic against the order of the day in Hasmonean times, make it certain that this source was composed no earlier than the reign of John Hyrcanus (134–104 BCE).[65]

After presenting various laws regarding the king and his conduct of the affairs of state and the military, 11QT 58:21 concludes with an allusion to the king succeeding in all his ways if he will "go forth (to battle) according to the regulation which . . ." (and here the text breaks off). There then follows a lacuna of six lines. Some excerpts from Deuteronomy 28, the underlying passage for what follows, must have stood at this point in the text.[66] It is most probable that the

---

62 See Schiffman, *Reclaiming,* 165–7; N. M. Sarna, *Songs of the Heart* (New York: Schocken, 1993) 11.

63 Cf. Schiffman, "*Temple Scroll,*" 46–8.

64 L. H. Schiffman, "The King, His Guard and the Royal Council in the *Temple Scroll,*" *PAAJR* 54 (1987) 247–9. M. Hengel, J. H. Charlesworth and D. Mendels, "The Polemical Character of 'On Kingship' in the Temple Scroll: An Attempt at Dating 11QTemple," *JJS* 37 (1986) 28–38 date the scroll to between 103/2 and 88 BCE.

65 Schiffman, "*Temple Scroll,*" 48–51.

66 Cf. Yadin, *Temple Scroll,* 2.265.

singular usage of the Deuteronomic chapter as a whole for the addressee led to the interpretation that it was directed at the ruler.

The body of the preserved text of this passage is 59:2–21. The text picks up by describing the scattering of the people (presumably as a result of the king's transgressions) and their being disgraced, as well their worship in exile of other gods, based primarily (and not in scriptural order) on Deut 28:36–37, 48, and 64. The text then describes the destruction of the cities based on Lev 26:31–32 and Jer 25:9. Thereafter, the text returns to Lev 26:32 to describe the astonishment of the enemies of Israel. The passage is also based on the content of Deut 31:17–18, but with language based on the Prophets.[67] The notion of God's hiding His face from Israel is then introduced (also found in Deut 31:17–18). The violation of the covenant by the people—presumably under the leadership of the king—is then described based on Deut 31:16 and Lev 26:15. Following the Deuteronomic schema, the people then repent, and God saves them and redeems them from among their enemies, so that he will be their God and they will be his people.

At this point the text returns to the motif of the king. If the king turns away from following the law, he will not have a successor and his dynasty will come to an end. But if he follows the law, then his dynasty will be passed down to his descendants. God will then be with him and save him from his enemies and from those who seek to kill him, and he will rule over all his enemies.

These themes are strikingly reminiscent of MMT. It is only by observing the laws of the Torah, as set forth in the Deuteronomic covenant, that the king will be saved from misfortune. The king can guarantee the welfare of the people by following these laws. Indeed, in MMT, at the very end, we find that the observance of the laws of the Torah is considered beneficial both for the king and the people of Israel. It is clearly implied in C 23–26 that obeying the group's interpretation of the law will lead to the ruler's being saved from trouble and misfortune.

It thus emerges that the homiletical section of MMT is also parallel to a section of the *Temple Scroll*. Both the law and the theology of the scroll have much in common with MMT, because the two texts stem from the common legal and theological tradition of the Sadducees.

---

[67] Cf. Yadin, *Temple Scroll*, 2.266–7.

Yet here also, while we find this commonality, there is no evidence of literary dependence.

Conclusions

Our study has shown that the text of MMT has much in common with various documents of the Qumran corpus. As it now stands in one of the manuscripts, it has been combined with the sectarian calendar that its authors probably favored. One of the scribes who prepared the copies of MMT which have come down to us clearly wanted to emphasize that the authors of MMT accepted the 364-day sectarian calendar of solar months and solar years.

With the *Temple Scroll* it shares a variety of sacrificial laws. These parallels are no doubt to be traced to the common Sadducean legal substratum which they share. Yet no literary dependence of either text on the other can be shown.

Regarding the *Zadokite Fragments*, this is also the case for the legal section of MMT. In this context we should call attention to our view that the Admonition of the *Zadokite Fragments* actually refers to the early pre-Teacher of Righteousness days of the sect when the group came into existence in protest over the conduct of the Jerusalem Temple regarding matters of Jewish law and interpretation. This is the very same time when the MMT document would have been composed and sent to the Jerusalem establishment according to our understanding of the early history of the Qumran sect.[68]

4Q*Florilegium*, most of which does not concern legal matters, included a similar law to that of MMT, but the extraneous details in each list of excluded persons led to the conclusion that again there was no literary dependence, only common legal rulings. We should recall that MMT exhibits no parallels with the *Rule of the Community* or other such documents which represent the teachings of the sect after it reached maturity.

These conclusions are consistent with the view that MMT reflects the formative period of the Qumran sect. It therefore shares legal rulings with the sources of the *Temple Scroll* and the early laws of the

[68] Cf. Schiffman, *Reclaiming*, 92; Strugnell, "MMT: Second Thoughts," 70–73, a section not included in his appendix to DJD X. In the oral presentation of this material at the Notre Dame Symposium on the Dead Sea Scrolls (April, 1993), Strugnell explicitly said that he now agreed with my view that MMT predates the career of the Teacher of Righteousness.

Zadokite Fragments. At the same time, it reflects the ideology of parts of the *Temple Scroll.* Yet while the earlier MMT and *Temple Scroll* (and its sources) lack the language of sectarian antagonism, this tone is found in the *Zadokite Fragments* which was completed after the split was final, and which reflects the sectarian animus which would characterize the later documents of the Qumran group.

With MMT we have clearly returned to the early days of sectarian law. The parallels with other legal texts from the Qumran corpus and with Sadducean views known from the later Rabbinic corpus open before us the Sadducean heritage of the founders of the sect. These early Hasmonean-period Sadducees, as distinct from their Hellenized brethren described by Josephus, were pious priests. This latter group are the Sadducees with whom the Pharisees and sages argue according to Talmudic sources. They strove to fulfill the words of the Torah as they understood them, seeking to find God in the meticulous performance of the sacrificial worship in His holy Temple in Jerusalem and in the constant maintenance of the highest standards of ritual purity. It is this legal system which underlies the law of the Dead Sea Scrolls.

Some Remarks on 4QMMT and the Rabbinic Tradition: or, When Is a Parallel Not a Parallel?[1]

YAAKOV ELMAN
Yeshiva University
New York, NY

The following remarks are intended to emphasize the importance of *systemic* examination in the comparative study of Qumranic and rabbinic halakhic texts. Facile parallels may mislead; consideration must be given not only to a careful examination of all texts relevant to the particular area of halakha under consideration, but also to the question of how the particular rule functions within the larger legal/ritual system of which it is part.

It is also time to re-examine a judgment which has run through discussions of Qumranic law from the days of Solomon Schechter (or even Abraham Geiger) to the very publication of MMT in 1994: that, in Yaakov Sussman's words, "As . . . Geiger already noted, and [Saul] Lieberman pointed out at greater length and depth, . . . sectarian halakha in general, and Sadducean halakha in particular, was stringent. . . . Indeed, all the halakhot in the Dead Sea scrolls which are at variance with Pharisaic halakha are stricter than the corresponding Pharisaic rulings."[2] Further, "this stringency is systematic and fully consistent, applying to all details and aspects of any given halakha."[3]

---

1 My thanks to Professors Moshe Bernstein, Baruch Levine, Lawrence Schiffman and Richard White for their helpful comments, and to Professor Schiffman for inviting me to participate in a very stimulating panel. Special thanks to Professor Bernstein for editorial services above and beyond the call of duty.

2 DJD X, p. 197.

3 DJD X, p. 190.

Stringency and Fundamentalism

Once we assert that Qumranic halakha represents a "systematic and fully consistent" stringency, which applies "to all details and aspects of any given halakha," we are asserting that the *only* consistency is one of stringency, despite the direction in which legal or ritualistic or exegetical logic may tend. This is a position which is difficult to defend when one deals with sectarian legislators who had a quasi-scholastic mind-set. Moreover, this assumption leads to another, more dubious one: that Pharisaic/rabbinic halakha tends to leniency. However, the very existence of "fences" extending beyond the biblical text in rabbinic law, which typifies it and is the apparent target of criticism in the Damascus Covenant,[4] should make us wary of such an assumption.

Beyond that, there are exceptions to the rule that "all the halakhot in the Dead Sea scrolls which are at variance with Pharisaic halakha are stricter than the corresponding Pharisaic rulings."[5] Thus, an

[4] See Chaim Rabin, ed., *The Zadokite Documents* (Oxford: Clarendon Press, 1954) 34–35 (7:12–13 [MS A] בוני החוץ; 19:25–26 [MS B] בוני החיץ).

[5] See Joseph M. Baumgarten's important "The Pharisaic-Sadducean Controversies about Purity and the Qumran Texts," *JJS* 31 (1980) 157–170, and in particular the judgment expressed on 168–169, "we have found [the Sadducean] complaints about Pharisaic laxities in the sphere of purity to be consistent with the laws found in the *Temple Scroll* and other Qumran writings." But this judgment is based on their rejection of *ṭevul yom,* their defilement of animal bones and their view on *niṣṣoq,* regarding which see below. Baumgarten does not address the broader issue of degrees or removes of impurity, presumably for the very reason that no evidence exists for the institution at Qumran. However, given the codificatory nature of the Temple Scroll, this particular argument from silence carries greater weight than might otherwise be the case, though we must not lose sight of the fact that the Temple Scroll's system of law was not identical to the sect's.

In his discussion of the Essene avoidance of oil, Baumgarten assumes the operation of the laws of removes of impurity for the Essenes; see Joseph M. Baumgarten, "The Essene Avoidance of Oil and the Laws of Purity," *RevQ* 6 (1967–69) 183–192, esp. 187–188. He bases this on 1QS 6:16–21 and 7:19–20, where a "novice . . . was admitted to the טוהורת הרבים, the pure foods of the sect, after an apprenticeship of a year," while in regard to pure liquids, two years were required. "The distinction," he asserts, "can only be rooted in the special character of liquids as carriers of impurity." However, while no one would deny the sect's concern with matters of purity, surviving texts, insofar as they are available to me, remain far from the rabbinic system of removes of impurity, which was an integral part of the institution of "fences." Moreover, as Baumgarten himself points out, oil in particular was always a sensitive matter; see 189–190.

examination of the available evidence does not bear out this judgment in the sweeping manner in which it is typically expressed.

For example, 11QT 50:4–7[6] rules that contact with the bone or blood of dead person defiles, but not, it would appear, the amputated bone of a living person.

וכול איש אשר יגע על פני השדה בעצם אדם מת ובחלל חרב או במת או בדם אדם מת או בקבר וטהר כחוק המשפט הזה....

> As for any man who shall touch upon the surface of the field a bone of a dead human or one killed by the sword, or a dead person, or the blood of a dead human or a grave, he shall be purified according to this ordinance . . . .[7]

As Yadin rightly noted, the inclusion of the word *met* modifying *ʿeṣem ʾadam* and *dam ʾadam* clearly points to a concern on the part of the drafter to exclude amputated ("living") limbs from this law. But rabbinic halakha clearly rules to the contrary, as Yadin already noted, and as Hannah K. Harrington observes in her recent comparison of the two systems of purities.[8] Thus the Temple Scroll in this instance is *less stringent* than that of the rabbis. The drafter has employed what Jacob Milgrom has called "homogenization,"[9] in this case similar to the

---

[6] Despite the consensus view of the Temple Scroll as pre-sectarian, the fairly large amount of overlap between its prescriptions and those of various sectarian ones, as well as its presence in the sect's library would seem to indicate that its concerns were congruent with theirs, even when disagreements on details existed. In this case, there is no indication, to my knowledge, of a more stringent sectarian position on the issue to be discussed than the one taken here.

[7] See Yigael Yadin, *Megillat ha-Miqdash* (Jerusalem: Israel Exploration Society, 1977) 2.156.

[8] See Yadin, *Megillat ha-Miqdash,* 1.257–259, and Hannah K. Harrington, *The Impurity Systems of Qumran and the Rabbis: Biblical Foundations* (SBLDS 143; Atlanta: Scholars Press, 1993) 60–61, and note her useful comparative tables in Appendix B, 283–291.

Among the rabbinic sources relevant to this point we need only cite *Sipre* Numbers 127 (ed. Horovits) p. 165, *m. ʿEd.* 6:3 and *m. Kelim* 1:5. Targum pseudo-Jonathan to Num 19:16 also reflects the same point of view. Note that it is R. Eliezer and R. Nehunia b. Haqaneh who uphold this opinion in *m. ʿEd.* 6:3; the role of the former in preserving older strands of halakha is well-established; see Y. D. Gilat, *R. Eliezer ben Hyrcanus: A Scholar Outcast,* (Ramat Gan: Bar Ilan University Press, 1984) 23–67, and *passim*; see also Jacob Neusner, *Eliezer b. Hyrcanus: The Tradition and the Man* (2 vols.; Leiden: E. J. Brill, 1973) 2.315–316, but also his *In Search of Talmudic Biography: The Problem of the Attributed Saying* (BJS 70; Chico, CA: Scholars Press, 1984), esp. 85–90 and 131.

[9] Jacob Milgrom, "The Qumran Cult: Its Exegetical Principles," *Temple Scroll*

rabbinic hermeneutic device referred to as *heqeš*, to define the limbs and blood of Num. 19:18 as issuing from a corpse rather than a living person, since the verse deals with "one killed by the sword or a dead person." The latter terms modify the former in the direction of a more limited application of the resultant rule, that is, *in the direction of leniency*!

It is significant that though the editors of MMT rely on the Temple Scroll for help in restoring the text of MMT in a number of places,[10] they explicitly reject the parallel in regard to MMT B 72–74. Rejecting a proposed restoration based on the Temple Scroll passage discussed above, they note that "with this reading the halakha would depart from that of the rabbis in the direction of leniency, which would be exceptional in MMT; it is not clear why the fact that the rabbis saw fit to add a prohibition should trouble the sect."[11] Does this mean that the sect would accept any stringency at all?

It would seem that MMT supplements the Temple Scroll passage. 11QT deals with the circumstances which determine the impurity of detached human limbs, namely, it excludes limbs from a living person from causing impurity. MMT deals with the *state of the limb*, i.e., whether it is whole, etc.[12] However, the editors' conclusion, that "overshadowing," the rabbinic *ṭumʾat ʾohel*, which does not apply to fleshless bones, is here intended to apply to such bones, seems forced; it depends solely on the assumption that any rabbinic stringency *ipso facto* was accepted at Qumran. What independent evidence is there for the existence of overshadowing at Qumran, in published or unpublished texts?

Perhaps even more striking is the complete absence at Qumran, at least in the published material, of the rabbinic rules of "degrees (or removes) of impurity" which make up such a large part of rabbinic law

---

Studies (ed. G. J. Brooke; JSPSup 7; Sheffield: Sheffield Academic Press, 1989) 165–180, esp. 175.

[10] See DJD X, 150, where 11QT[a] 20:12–13 is used as a "parallel" to B 9–11, or 154, where 11QT 51:1–6 is cited in connection with B 18–20, or the reference to the Temple Scroll on 157 in connection with B 27–28. Note the editors' suggestion on 156, in regard to B 18–20: "In order to understand the exact attitude of the sect to this subject and the contribution made by MMT, we should treat together all the evidence found in the DSS."

[11] DJD X, p. 171.

[12] See the discussion of this point in M. J. Bernstein's paper in this volume, "The Employment and Interpretation of Scripture in 4QMMT: Preliminary Observations," 36 n. 16.

on the subject, and which clearly and intentionally broadened the scope of the system many-fold. We might, for example, have sought such elaborations in 11QT 50:16–19. Although the Temple Scroll is not at source a sectarian document, and may predate the legislation of degrees, we might have expected something of a hint of such legislation in some other text. It is noteworthy that sectarian documents are more concerned with elaborating the purity rules of animal skins, as in B 18–24. Surely such an important part of the rabbinic purity rules as "removes" should have had a sectarian counterpart, if stringency was the guiding rule.

It may however be suggested that the rabbinic expansion of degrees of impurity began only after the destruction of the Temple. If the system of degrees and removes of impurity, which was already mentioned by the Houses of Hillel and Shammai in *m. Maʿaś. Š.* 3:9, *m. Šeqal.* 8:6, and by Hananiah, Segan ha-Kohanim, in *m. Pesaḥ.* 1:6, may be projected back in time to the era of MMT in the 150s BCE, then the Pharisaic halakha is infinitely more stringent than the Sadducean one on this pervasive feature of their system of purity. It is this possibility which seems most likely to me.

If, however, we follow Jacob Neusner, and date this feature of the rabbinic system to the Yavneh period after the Destruction, MMT could hardly mention what did not exist either for the sect or its opponents.[13] If so, *contra* Sussman, the rabbinic system did contain matters which were indeed "an artificial creation of the academy (*beit midraš*), or late rabbinic speculation which substituted for the temple."[14]

Neusner's rejection of the Houses' data proceeds from the fact that the Houses at times seem to debate matters which are also the subject of discussion in the Ushan period and thus violate his system of verifications. However, aside from the doubts which have been raised regarding Neusner's grounds for rejecting attributions to the Houses as anachronistic,[15] the evidence of R. Hananiah Segan ha-Kohanim

[13] In J. Neusner, *A History of the Mishnaic Law of Purities* (Leiden: E. J. Brill, 1977) 21.161–164.

[14] DJD X, 197–98.

[15] See my review of Neusner's *Judaism: The Evidence of the Mishnah*, "The Judaism of the Mishna: What Evidence?" *Judaica Book News* 12/2 (1982) 17–25, esp. 20, and E. P. Sanders, *Jewish Law from Jesus to the Mishnah: Five Studies* (London: SCM Press, 1990) 170–172. See also Moshe Weiss, "The Authenticity of the Explicit Discussions in *Bet Shammai—Bet Hillel* Disputes," [Hebrew] *Sidra* 4 (1988) 53–66.

noted above, which is independent of the Houses, would seem to indicate that some system of degrees of impurity was in place during late Second Temple times.

Nevertheless, given the biblical foundations on which both the rabbinic and Qumranic systems of impurity rest, there is no *a priori* reason to consider the Houses' material to be anachronistic. Given what we now know of the Temple Scroll's methods of exegesis, the Houses' universe of discourse certainly contained the methods and concerns typical of the rabbinic system.

Likewise, the drafter of 11QT 50:4–7 could have directed his interpretation in the more stringent direction, but chose not to do so, since the more compelling interpretation was one more in keeping with the literal compass of the text. Thus we have a case in which *a "fundamentalist", or, perhaps better, a more "literalist" approach to the text overcame the tendency to stringency.* And this same principle would have operated in the matter of rabbinic degrees and removes of purity.

In sum, either the sect is lenient in this important matter, or the rabbinic halakha on this matter is late, a possibility which seems unlikely for the reasons given above. Moreover, we cannot argue that the sect agreed with the Pharisees, and thus did not mention it in the polemical context of MMT, since we must then explain why this pervasive feature of the purity system does not manifest itself in any other Qumran halakhic text.

Milgrom's view of the maximalist reading of the Temple Scroll may come into play here as well. Milgrom has argued that both "maximalist" (where the application of the laws of purity is extended to all Israel) and "minimalist" views of purity (where such laws are limited to priests and those who come into contact with sancta) may be found in Scripture, in rabbinic literature and in Qumran. However, the vector of Qumranic maximalism was different from that of the rabbis; it extended to matters of *purification* rather than to *extensions of impurity at removes* and the like.[16] It is likely, therefore, that MMT did *not* agree with the rabbis on this matter, and thus, on this particular issue the rabbis were much more stringent than the sect.

It is true that these examples proceed *ex silentio*; however, we are hardly likely to find *explicit leniencies vis à vis the biblical text* in the system

---

[16] See J. Milgrom, "The Scriptural Foundations and Deviations in the Laws of Purity of the *Temple Scroll*," *Archaeology and History in the Dead Sea Scrolls: The New York University Conference in Memory of Yigael Yadin* (ed. L. H. Schiffman; JSPSup 8; JSOT/ASOR Monographs 2; Sheffield: Sheffield Academic Press, 1990) 83–99.

of a sectarian fundamentalist mentality. The rabbis might legislate certain rules out of existence; the sectarian interpreters sought to find a place for all Scripture within their halakhic system, as witness, for example, their use of the *millu'im* in their Temple service.[17]

A Systemic Approach to *Niṣṣoq* and *Muṣaqot*

Rabbinic literature on the laws of purities, even when restricted to the Mishnah and Tosefta, is both extensive and complex in its ramifications and interconnections. It is for that reason one of the areas of rabbinic law which perhaps demonstrably existed *as a system* in tannaitic times, that is, as a consistent set of principles and applications. Bearing that in mind, I would like to examine one of the most interesting, compelling—and apparently inevitable—parallels adduced from it to a section of 4QMMT, the matter of *niṣṣoq*[18]-*muṣaqot*. However, as we shall see, once we go beyond the examination of single terms which appear linguistically cognate, and proceed on a systemic basis, the apparent simplicity of the parallel dissolves. This is because that single equation of *niṣṣoq* = *muṣaqot*, when viewed systemically, yields contradictory consequences in both the rabbinic/Pharisaic and Qumranic systems of purities. As we shall see, when we consider in addition the semantic range of these terms, the *Sitz im Leben* in which these rules would have operated, and the archaeological remains as well, the equation becomes anything but simple.

When we look beyond the mesmerizing lexical equation of *muṣaqot* and *niṣṣoq*, there appears in its place a wealth of possibilities, of varying degrees of likelihood; some, I think, are more probable than the one currently accepted. Even more important, this examination grants us an insight into the sectarian mentality *from the inside.*

Let us begin by examining the two clauses of this most spectacular revelation of MMT.

---

17 See the conversion of the dedication ceremony of Lev 8–9 to an annual event in 11QT 17:1–5.

18 I have chosen to follow the vocalization of Hanokh Yalon in *Šiššah Sidrei Mishnah* (ed. Hanokh Albeck; Jerusalem: Mosad Bialik, 1959) 6.486, but see Elisha Qimron, in his "Halakhic Terms in the Dead Sea Scrolls and Their Contribution to the History of Early *Halakhah*," [Hebrew] *The Scrolls of the Judaean Desert: Forty Years of Research* (eds. Magen Broshi et. al.; Jerusalem: Mosad Bialik, 1992) 128–138, esp. 133–134. There is a brief glossary of the significant rabbinic terms employed in this paper in Appendix Four below.

ואף על המוצקות אנחנו אומרים שהם שאין בהם טהרה ואף המוצקות אינם מבדילות בין הטמא לטהור כי לחת המוצקות והמקבל מהמה כהם לחה אחת.

> And concerning (unbroken) streams of a liquid (poured from a clean vessel into an unclean vessel): we are of the opinion that they are not pure, and that these streams do not act as a separative between impure and pure liquids, for the liquid of the streams and that of the vessel which receives them are alike, being a single liquid.[19]

The editors suggest that the repetition of the word *weʾap* indicates that two rules are being presented: first, that streams poured into an unclean vessel are unclean, and second, that these streams are considered as connectives, so that even the liquid in the upper vessel, if originally clean, becomes unclean.

Several assumptions now come into play. First, since this is a polemical document, with the polemic directed at the Pharisees, we must seek a parallel in early rabbinic literature. Furthermore, since we assume that the sect took a stringent position, we must seek our parallels among the corpus of rabbinic leniencies.

Elisha Qimron and John Strugnell take *m. Yad* 4:7 as the parallel to the first ruling, and *m. Ṭohar.* 8:9 for the second.[20] The first of these identifications seems to echo MMT both linguistically and form-critically: אומרים צדוקים קובלין אנו עליכם פרושים שאתם מטהרין את הנצוק ("The Sadducees say: We protest against you, Pharisees, for you declare clean the unbroken stream!") Our rabbinic parallel thus fulfills the role of providing a Pharisaic leniency, but requires that we equate Qumran *muṣaqot* with Middle Hebrew *niṣṣoq,* in the sense of "a stream (of liquid) poured out," in this case, a stream of liquid poured from a ritually pure container to a ritually impure one. According to MMT, the impurity travels up the stream into the upper container, and, since the liquid constitutes a single unit—"for the liquid of the streams and that of the vessel which receives them are alike, being a single liquid" as the text explains, all is impure.

---

19 DJD X, 161.

20 The major rabbinic texts cited in the ensuing discussions are found below, with translation, in Appendix Three: Sources.

Rabbinic Inconsistency?

The contrast with the Pharisaic view is not without its difficulties, however. On the one hand, it is clear that the Pharisees, and the rabbis after them, held that a *niṣṣoq*, a free-falling stream of liquid, did not constitute a *ḥibbur*, a connective in the absolute sense seemingly required by MMT. On the other hand, judging from *m. Makš.* 5:9, some tannaim before the Destruction, including Beth Shammai and their opponents, here not named, held that the rim of the upper container served as a boundary or separation between pure and impure, as the Tosafist R. Samson of Sens (12th-13th cent.) notes in his commentary to the mishnah *ad loc.* The issue in this mishnah concerns a particular type of *niṣṣoq*, one made up of a viscous liquid, such as honey or thick batter. When the upper container is righted, some of the honey, which had passed beyond the boundary and thus had become impure, returns to the volume encompassed by the upper vessel and transfers impurity to its contents. Note first of all that there *are* indeed rabbinic cases where *niṣṣoq does* cause impurity, and these cases represent an area of *agreement* between the House of Shammai and its opponents, here apparently not the House of Hillel, which would presumably otherwise be named.

Naturally, one could argue, such minor exceptions regarding a *niṣṣoq* which causes impurity would be lost in polemical contexts, either that of *m. Yad* or MMT; even if this is so, however, *we* should not lose sight of that fact. In short, the Pharisaic/sectarian disjunction is not as absolute as *m. Yad* 4:7 alone would have it.[21]

Qimron and Strugnell take *m. Ṭohar.* 8:9 as the parallel of the second ruling of MMT on *muṣaqot*, though what it adds to *m. Yad* is irrelevant to the MMT ruling. *M. Ṭohar.* 8:9 merely states that a *niṣṣoq* does not constitute a *ḥibbur*, a "connective," either for transmitting impurity or producing purity. That is, it cannot join two separate ritual baths, neither of which contains the minimum required quantity of water (forty *seʾah*) into a single, halakhically valid ritual pool. However, since according to Qimron and Strugnell's own interpretation, MMT

21 R. Leszynsky, *Die Sadduzäer* (Berlin: Mayer & Mueller, 1912) 38–43 utilized the partial parallel of *m. Makš.* 5:9 to interpret *m. Yad* 4:7, but restricted the dispute to bees' honey; see however B. Revel's critique in *JQR* 7 (1916–1917) 438. It should perhaps be noted in this connection that S. Zeitlin's view, expressed in "Takkanot Ezra," *JQR* 8 (1917–1918) 68–69, is totally excluded by MMT's assertion that אינם מבדילות בין הטמא לטהור.

here speaks specifically of the first option—transmitting impurity—and not of producing purity, the parallel of *m. Ṭohar.* does not go beyond the information presented by *m. Yad.* There is thus only one parallel, evidenced by two mishnayot, and not two separate parallels, and *m. Ṭohar.* 8:9 adds nothing to the interpretation of MMT beyond what we have already gained from *m. Yad.*

Yaakov Sussman, apparently recognizing this problem, takes *m. Yad* 4:7 (and *m. Makš.* 5:9) as parallel to the second MMT ruling, and *m. Miqw.* 6:8 as parallel to the first.[22] Sussman infers that "MMT rules strictly about both of these laws," in particular that "Unbroken columns of liquid 'have no purity'—viz., the water in the upper *miqweh* is not rendered fit for ritual immersion by virtue of the unbroken column connecting this water with the lower *miqweh*."[23] He comments in passing, however, that "the matter still requires further investigation."

Though he does not detail his reasons for this hesitation, several difficulties come to mind. First of all, *m. Miqw.* 6:8 refers to two ritual pools, a lower one which contains the requisite amount of forty *se'ah*s of water undrawn by human effort, and an upper one which contains drawn water, normally invalid for purification. If these are joined by a clay or lead pipe, which is lowered into the lower pool and then lifted so as to cause at least a hair-breadth's flow of water into the upper pool, thus connecting the two, the upper pool becomes valid.

Sussman's hesitation would seem to be due to the fact that (1) the term *niṣṣoq* is not used here; (2) this connection via pipe is definitely *not* a *niṣṣoq*, which refers to a stream of water which falls through the air and not to one which runs through a pipe, as the Tosafists note in several places, e.g., *b. Git.* 16a s.v. *ha-niṣṣoq*.

Finally, there is a third serious problem with this interpretation; it assumes an inconsistent use of the principle of *ḥibbur* by the Rabbis, since if *niṣṣoq* is not a connective for impurity, it should not serve as a connective otherwise as well. Indeed, *m. Ṭohar.* 8:9 states explicitly that a *niṣṣoq* cannot serve as a connective either for impurity *or purity*. Thus, the Mishnah itself unequivocally rejects the inconsistency which Sussman hesitantly proposes. It also indicates in passing that in all likelihood, as the Tosafists noted, a stream of water passing through a pipe was not categorized as a *niṣṣoq*.

---

22 DJD X., 188. For the text of *m. Miqw.* 6:8, see Appendix Three.

23 Ibid., 188.

"Streams of Water" in Middle Hebrew

Here is where the assumption of stringency comes into play, both directly and indirectly. The assumption seems to be that both the sect and the rabbis will rule stringently or leniently even at the expense of inconsistency with regard to fundamental principles. Sussmann assumes that the rabbis will reject *niṣṣoq* as a connective to impurity, but not for purposes of purification (despite *m. Ṭohar.* 8:9), while the sect will alway opt for stringency. But as far as the rabbis are concerned, it is clear that they defined *niṣṣoq* as excluding piped water, and so, at least according to their own lights, there was no inconsistency.

An examination of the semantic range of *niṣṣoq* and related terms bears this out. When we examine the complex of terms for "streams of water" in Middle Hebrew, and the semantic range of each one, an interesting fact emerges. The rabbis apparently distinguished among several different types of streams, each of which had its own term. As noted above, *niṣṣoq* apparently refers specifically to a free-falling stream unencumbered by a container, and not to water passing through a pipe. Another term, *qaṭapres* (Greek *kataphoros*) refers to a stream of water running along sloping ground (a *midron*, see *b. Pesaḥ* 42a) but not running in a riverbed or aqueduct. *ʾEšboren*, which is counterposed to the others in *m. Ṭohar.* 8:9, refers to a declivity in which water gathers; it differs from the others in that it *may* act as a connective.

Both *qaṭapres* and *ʾēšboren*, however, refer not to the stream or body of liquid, but to the ground over which it flows, just as *sillon* ("pipe") or *ʾammah* in the phrase "*ʾammat hammayim*," ("ditch, aqueduct") refers to that which constrains the water, and not to the water itself. The water must be specified, as in the phrase *ʾammat hammayim*, or inferred, as in "[*mei*] *sillon*."

Niṣṣoq seems to be the exception in not being employed in connection with a channel or pipe which constrains and directs it or with the ground over which it flows; it must therefore refer to a stream of water which is thus unconstrained. It cannot refer to water in a *sillon*, which would presumably be called *mei sillon*, along the lines of the *mei gebaʾim*, *mei borot*, *mei šiḥin* and *mei meʿarot*—the water of various types of ditches—of *m. Miqw.* 1:4.

Finally, the word *qilluaḥ*, which can also refer to a free-falling stream of water passing from one vessel to another, is not employed in matters involving purities. Its usage is limited to issues of invalidation, usually of *terumah* by touch, but *not* of transmitting impurity (*meṭamme*ʾ). Thus, for example, in *m. T. Yom* 2:7, המערה מכלי אל כלי ונגע טבול יום בקילוח: אם יש בו, יעלה באחד ומאה. ("as to one who pours [liquid *terumah*] from [one] vessel to [another] vessel, and a *ṭevul yom* touched the stream, [if the vessel] had something in it, it is neutralized in a [proportion of] a hundred and one").

Likewise, the verbal form of קלח is employed in *m. Miqw.* 4:4 in regard to invalidation of a ritual pool, היו מקלחין בתוך המים, אם ידוע שנפל לתוכו ארבעים סאה מים כשרים עד שלא ירדו לתוכו שלשה לגין מים שאובים—כשר. ואם לאו, פסול.

> If [invalidating drawn water and rainwater] fell into the water [of a ritual pool], if it was known that forty *se*ʾ*ah*s of valid water fell [into the ritual pool] before three *log*s of drawn water [did], [the ritual pool] is valid [even though ordinarily three *log*s of drawn water invalidates a ritual bath]; if [it is] not [known], it is invalid.

When the question is one of purities strictly defined, the term employed is *niṣṣoq*; otherwise, it is *qilluaḥ*.[24]

To summarize: The result of all this is to call into question Sussman's tentative equation of the first clause of our MMT passage with *m. Miqw.* 6:8, which involves validating a ritual pool by means of a pipe and in which the term *niṣṣoq* does not appear. Further, his interpretation contradicts *m. Yad* 4:7 and *m. Ṭohar.* 8:9, in which *niṣṣoq* clearly refers to a free-standing stream of water. Moreover, when we examine the semantic range of the panoply of terms for streams of water in Middle Hebrew, his assumption that *niṣṣoq* may refer to water running through a pipe becomes linguistically improbable, as well as disregards the medieval interpretive tradition, which serves as the basis

---

[24] It is only in amoraic times that the word passes into more general use, as in the unique occurence of *y. ʿAbod. Zar.* 4:8 (44a) in regard to *yein nesekh*, where R. Ze'era points up an inconsistency: רב הונא בשם רב: הקילוח כבור. ר׳ זעירה בעי: בכל אתר לית את עבד הנצוק חיבור. והכא את עבד הנצוק חיבור? Indeed, the use of *qillu*ᵃ*ḥ* in *b. ʿAbod. Zar.* 75a = *b. Nid.* 65b illustrates the distinction between water flowing in a pipe and that which consitutes a free-falling stream: מניחין תחת [ה]צינור שמימיו מקלחין—that water becomes a *qillu*ᵃ*ḥ* only *after* leaving the pipe. It must be admitted, however, that this third-generation amoraic use of *niṣṣoq* blurs the Middle Hebrew I distinction between *niṣṣoq* and *qillu*ᵃ*ḥ*, and in so doing creates a contradiction between its non-use as a connective in matters of purity and its validity as such in the context of *yein nesekh*. There is no evidence for this in our period, however.

of his interpretation of *niṣṣoq* in the first place. Thus Sussman's hesitation in proposing this equation is clearly in place, and our response should likewise be cautious.

Qumranic Inconsistency?

On the other hand, if we assume that the sect rules stringently in both cases, that is, that *muṣaqot* are connectives for impurity but not for producing purity, this consistent stringency is also attained at the expense of the logical and legal contradiction. We have already seen, in the case of 11QT 50:4–7, that the drafter eschewed a consistent stringency in favor of exegetical consistency. Even though the Temple Scroll and MMT may represent different sectarian approaches, the biblical background of *muṣaqot,* as we shall see, clearly supports a sectarian literal approach to those biblical sources, no matter what interpretation of the several offered below is accepted.

In short, there are systemic objections, certainly on the rabbinic side and possibly on the sectarian, to the equation of *muṣaqot* with *niṣṣoq*. However, upon further reflection, these very problems on the rabbinic side may lead to a more nuanced interpretation of *muṣaqot*— if we abandon the tempting *niṣṣoq–muṣaq* equation. It is time to examine the bases for the equation once again.

The parallel to *niṣṣoq* is suggested not only by the use of a passive from *yaṣaq,* but the polemical context and, in particular, the form of the two statements. Now, the first problem regarding Sussman's interpretation of *m. Miqw.* 6:8—the fact that the *sillon* of *m. Miqw.* 6:8 cannot refer to the *niṣṣoq* of *m. Yad* 4:7—might be solved by assuming that Qumranic *muṣaqot* had a wider meaning than rabbinic *niṣṣoq,* and encompassed both transference of liquid by means of both a *niṣṣoq* and a *sillon,* a pipe. Thus, according to the Mishnah, a *sillon* cannot be a *niṣṣoq,* but MMT would view all streams as coming under that rubric.[25] However, while this solves the problem of *m. Miqw.* 6:8, it only strengthens the contradiction between the Qumranic view of *niṣṣoq* as a connective in the one instance and not in the other.

[25] This consideration would support Daniel R. Schwartz' thesis that Qumranic halakha represents a "realist" point of view, in contrast to the rabbinic nominalist approach; see his "Law and Truth: On Qumran-Sadducean and Rabbinic Views of Law," *The Dead Sea Scrolls: Forty Years of Research* (eds. D. Dimant and U. Rappaport; Leiden: E. J. Brill, 1992) 229–240, esp. 232 #5. For a brief comment on his thesis in the context of our passages, see below, Appendix One.

Moreover, such an assumption combines two divergent biblical uses of the same word, which while not impossible, is hardly desirable. The word *muṣaq* may derive from either or both of two biblical texts; as a consequence, there are two ways of understanding the rule. *Muṣaqot* calls to mind the description of Solomon's bronze sea in I Kings 7:23//II Chron 4:2, which was made *muṣaq* ("of cast metal"), i.e., of metal poured out, as noted already by Joseph Baumgarten.[26] The biblical use of the term may have indicated to the author(s) of MMT that *muṣaqot* indeed constitute, to use the rabbinic term, a *ḥibbur,* a connective.

On the other hand, *muṣaq* in Zech 4:2 clearly has the meaning, "pipe," corresponding to Middle Hebrew *ṣinnor, sillon.* If this is the meaning intended, it opens up a whole new world of interpretive possibilities, and we shall investigate them below. First let us continue our investigation of the equation *niṣṣoq* = *muṣaq.*

If Sussman is correct, the Pharisees are as inconsistently lenient as their adversaries are inconsistently stringent, since though the *niṣṣoq* cannot transmit impurity, it may produce purity. This contradiction may be resolved by taking *m. Miqw.* 6:8 at face value as not referring to *niṣṣoq,* but to the transfer of water by means of a pipe (*sillon*) and not a free-standing stream. However, if we do so, *we have lost our rabbinic parallel for the first of this pair of MMT rulings.* This dilemma brings us to the methodological point I raised at the outset of this paper; at what price do we attain our rabbinic parallels, and at what cost do we maintain the sect's overall stringency *vis à vis* Pharisaic halakha? In this case, the cost of maintaining the parallel is the production of incoherence in the rabbinic system, namely, that *niṣṣoq* functions as *ḥibbur* in regard to purification but not in regard to transference of uncleanness, despite the testimony of *m. Ṭohar.* 8:9. It brings with it as well as a departure from the medieval Tosafist tradition of understanding this term, a tradition not lightly to be disregarded, as Sussman would certainly agree.

The picture is not brighter on the Qumran side, either, since the biblical antecedents of *muṣaqot* seem to argue for its function as a connective, both for purity and impurity. However, here the problem is less severe, since we do not, in fact, have at our disposal in the Qumran material on purities anything comparable to the wealth of material available on the rabbinic side. It may be, for example, as

---

[26] See his "The Pharisaic-Sadducean Controversies" (above, n. 5) 64 n. 26.

Patrich argued in another context,[27] that Sadducean (and by extension, we may argue, Qumranic) halakha did not accept the Pharisaic/ rabbinic rule that water flowing in the requisite quantities from a ritual pool or similar water source cannot become impure. In Sadducean/ Qumran law, water streams of whatever sort might serve as a connective to impurity but not to purity.

A consideration of the *Sitz im Leben* of these rules will, however, rule out that possibility, since if water canals may transmit impurity, the aqueduct which served Qumran itself would be susceptible to contamination.[28] The very existence of an aqueduct at Qumran argues against Patrich's supposition, if Qumran represents a species of Sadducean halakha. But if so, the original inner Qumranic contradiction re-emerges, and we must search further.

What then is the meaning of the phrase "they have no purity in them," which led to Sussman's troublesome parallel to *m. Miqw.* 6:8 in the first place? According to Qimron, it is equivalent to "they are impure." According to Sussman, however, as already noted, it means that *muṣaqot* do not serve to join pools to make them effective or valid purificatory agents, as if to say: "they have no purification in them." However, since Sussmann's interpretation encounters the difficulty of the absence of *niṣṣoq* in *m. Miqw.* 6:8, it might perhaps be better to accept Qimron's equation of "no purity" = "impurity."

Unfortunately, this understanding of the phrase cannot be supported either from Qumran Hebrew or Middle Hebrew. Stegemann's unpublished concordance does not list another attestation of it, and its meaning is quite different in Middle Hebrew. In rabbinic literature it means "they have no purity [in a ritual pool]," i.e., they cannot be purified by immersion but must be broken in order to purify them, as is the rule with regard to earthenware vessels, which can only be purified by being broken beyond the point of being employed in their usual way.

If MMT is employing the rabbinic idiom, the point of the phrase is that *muṣaqot* have no possibility of purification of impure liquids. This would imply that the author(s) of MMT reject the rabbinic mode of

---

[27] Y. Patrich, "The Aqueduct from Etam to the Temple and a Sadducean Halakhah," [Hebrew] *Cathedra* 17 (1981) 11–23.

[28] See Z. Ilan and D. Amit, "The Aqueduct of Kumran [sic]," [Hebrew] in *The Aqueducts of Ancient Palestine: Collected Essays* (eds. D. Amit, Y. Hirschfeld, and Y. Patrich; Jerusalem: Yad Izhak Ben-Zvi, 1989) 283–288. See also the remarks of E. P. Sanders, *Jewish Law from Jesus to the Mishnah*, 356 n. 48.

purifying liquids by "touching," *haššaqah,* where the impure liquid is merely brought into contact with the pool and thus becomes pure. The reason for the impossibility is clear; the requirement of total immersion would in the case of liquids lead to the loss of the impure liquids for drinking purposes. However, if this is the point of the line, we may well wonder why the word *muṣaqot* is employed rather than the more general *leḥot* ("liquids").

Another possibility is that the authors of MMT rejected the rabbinic mode of partial purification of a sick person who had suffered a seminal emission by means of "*tišᶜah qabbin,*" a shower of nine-*qabs* worth of water, a mode of purification which is alluded to in *m. Miqw.* 3:4, mentioned in *t. Ber.* 2:11, and which appears in both talmuds (*b. Ber.* 22a-b, *b. Git.* 16a and *y. Ber.* 3 [6c]). This possibility has two distinct advantages: it maintains the semantic range of the rabbinic *niṣṣoq,* i.e., a free-falling stream of water, and it provides an interpretation for *muṣaqot* and *niṣṣoq which does not require us to posit a contradiction within the two respective purity systems,* since the purification of *tišᶜah qabbin* does not involve any use of the principle of *ḥibbur,* connection.

It is time now to examine the question of whether we do, in fact, have two rulings here in MMT. The editors note that each is prefaced by the word *ʾap,* but, although *ʾap* does indeed appear twice in these lines, as Qimron, Strugnell and Sussman note, it appears only once in combination with the word *ᶜal,* which in the rest of MMT serves to introduce a new topic. Moreover, there is no absolute formulaic consistency in MMT. At times, only a zero-element introduces a new topic; see B 58, the very next law. Conversely, at times there is an excess of such particles, as in the preceding lines, where the rules regarding the blind and the deaf, though they share a common conclusion, are separately introduced by *weʾap ᶜal,* as the editors note.[29] If that is so, it may very well be that these lines constitute a unit, and that there is a sense of "not only do they not have any purity in them, but they do not interpose against impurity." If so, however, we have an excess of motive clauses; *muṣaqot* are impure because they have no purity in them, and because the liquid of the *muṣaqot* constitutes one unit. Nevertheless, such an excess is hardly fatal to our proposal, given the polemical context in which it appears. Indeed, such rhetorical devices are to be expected.

---

[29] DJD X, 160, and see the chart on 137. It should however be noted that almost all the attestations of these phrases are actually restorations.

Muṣaqot: Other Possibilities

However, as we shall see, we have hardly exhausted our wealth of interpretive possibilities. Perhaps we ought not allow tempting rabbinic parallels to determine the meaning of the Qumranic term, but rather look to the biblical background for it, and only then seek a rabbinic parallel.

Since, in biblical usage, the term *muṣaq* describes objects made of molten metal, a substance which may be viewed as analogous to a viscous liquid, Qumran Hebrew *muṣaqot* may refer to a joining mechanism consisting of such a liquid. If so, the more likely rabbinic parallel is not to a non-viscous *niṣṣoq* which does not, according to *m. Yad*, transmit impurity, but to a viscous one, such as honey, which does transmit impurity.

Proof for this possibility may be found in the aforementioned *m. Makš.* 5:9, where it would seem that Beth Shammai and their opponents hold that viscous liquids such as honey or batter, and also (*ʾap*), according to Beth Shammai, thick pottage of grits or beans, do transmit impurity. The reason for this is, as expressed by Beth Shammai but probably applying to both positions, that the *niṣṣoq* springs back into the upper vessel when the flow is stopped. When it is not viscous, however, once it leaves the upper vessel it inevitably flows directly into the lower vessel into which it is being poured, and thus the liquid in the upper vessel retains its purity.[30]

What then, one may ask, is the dispute between the Pharisees and the Sadducees? After all, if *muṣaqot* refers to a viscous liquid, MMT must hold with one of the positions of *m. Makš.* 5:9. If, however, their position is that of the Shammaites, would they single out the other side when the two are so close to each other on this matter? In answer I might point out this is indeed the nature of religious controversy. What are to an outsider merely minor differences assume a major proportion to insiders; moreover, as Schiffman has demonstrated, Qumranic halakha may well parallel one side of a rabbinic dispute.[31]

It may be argued that there is no compelling reason to equate *muṣaqot* with any particular type of *niṣṣoq*. But on any interpretation

---

30 It should be noted that R. Leszynsky, *Die Sadduzäer*, 38–43, interpreted *niṣṣoq* as "honey."

31 See for example his discussion of the dispute over the slaughter of pregnant animals in L. H. Schiffman, "*Miqṣat Maʿaśeh Ha-Torah* and the Temple Scroll," *RevQ* 14 (1990) 435–457, esp. 450–451.

there is something missing in all these statements: "something poured out," the assumed literal meaning of both *niṣṣoq* and *muṣaq*, hardly does justice to the technical ramifications of the term. And *m. Yad* hardly prepares us for the revelation of viscosity in *m. Makš.* 5:9. Added to this is the peculiar status of oil among the Essenes, which, as Baumgarten has noted, is due precisely to its viscous character.[32]

Qimron and Strugnell themselves have, perhaps inadvertently, suggested two other possibilities, both worthy of attention. First, they note that "the fact that the controversy [over *niṣṣoq*] is mentioned both in MMT and in the Mishna shows how important it was. It probably involved the purity of the pools . . . and the purity of the water channels of the Temple," noting in this connection *t. Miqw.* 4:6. This potentially fruitful suggestion was not followed up, however; indeed, the impression one gets from the discussion is that the editors may not have been aware of the fact that they were proposing an entirely separate set of interpretations for *muṣaqot.* As we shall see, this suggestion is not new; Louis Finkelstein already suggested this interpretation for Middle Hebrew *niṣṣoq* in 1929.[33]

As a second possibility, they momentarily consider another meaning for *muṣaqot*, namely, "pipes," but this is dismissed as being "less plausible" than the interpretation of *muṣaqot* as "streams." Yet here, again, it crops up in regard to the Temple's water distribution system, at least implicitly. The editors of MMT seem to have wanted it both ways; while ostensibly interpreting *muṣaqot* as *niṣṣoq*, they refer to texts which refer to pipes on the one hand, and to water courses on the other. Both of these possibilities seem to take us out of the realm of the rabbinic *niṣṣoq*, which refers, as I noted above, to free-falling streams of water and not water in pipes or aqueducts. However, as we shall see, these suggestions, muted though they may be, offer intriguing possibilities for a more nuanced understanding of Qumranic halakha.

Let us examine the editors' second, "less plausible" possibility—*muṣaqot* as pipes, first. It has a clear biblical referent in Zech 4:2, where *muṣaq* is clearly a "pipe," as noted above. Its lack of plausibility is presumably due to the explicit mention of *leḥah*—"liquid"—in MMT's justification for the impurity of the entire *muṣaq*. The term *muṣaqot* must therefore refer to liquids and not to pipes. But could it not refer

---

[32] See his "The Essene Avoidance of Oil and the Laws of Purity" (n. 5 above).

[33] See nn. 47–48 below.

to the liquid contained in the pipe? After all, we do have the phrase *leḥat hammuṣaqot*—"the liquid of the pipes," according to this interpretive possibility—the equivalent of Middle Hebrew *mei sillon.* Indeed, it is somewhat more likely that one would refer to the "liquid of the pipes" than the tautologous "liquid of the streams," since the streams *are themselves* the liquid!

Such an interpretation would serve to explain the first ruling, that *muṣaqot* do not contain purity. The meaning would seem to be either that a *sillon* cannot serve to join ritual pools, parallel to *m. Miqw.* 6:8 above, without the difficulty that Sussmann's interpretation engenders, or that a *sillon,* if made of clay, "does not have *ṭohorah* [in a *miqveh*]," a rejection of *m. Kelim* 2:3, which makes clay *sillonot* serving as gutters insusceptible to impurity. The problem with the latter is that "clay" is not specified, but since the two common materials for the construction of pipes in the Roman world were clay and lead,[34] both mentioned in *m. Miqw.*, this objection is not insuperable.[35]

If this is so, the proper translation of this section of MMT is as follows: "And concerning [liquids flowing in] pipes: we are of the opinion that they contain no purity (i.e., cannot produce purity), and that pipes do not act as a separative between impure and pure liquids, for the liquid of the pipes and that of that which receives them are alike, being a single liquid."

This second ruling would then refer to *sillonot* (Latin *tubuli fictiles*)[36] which, according to *t. Miqw.* 4:6, carried water from the *castellum,* a water tower, which in turn carried it from the aqueduct or the local water storage facility.[37] Indeed, Moshe Fisher and Tzvi Shacham may have found the remains of a *castellum* adapted for desert and field use at the Ein Boqeq oasis.[38] The point of the ruling would seem to be related to the matter of *niṣṣoq,* after all, since when water

---

34 See J. G. Landel, *Engineering in the Ancient World* (Berkeley and Los Angeles: University of California Press, 1978) 43.

35 For stone water mains, see Amihai Mazar, "A Survey of the Aqueducts Leading to Jerusalem," in *The Aqueducts of Ancient Palestine* (above n. 28), 169–195, esp. 180–183, and the illustration on 182.

36 See Landel, 43–44.

37 Y. Brand, *Ceramics in Talmudic Literature* [Hebrew] (Jerusalem: Mosad Harav Kook, 1953) 380.

38 See their "The Water System of the En Boqeq Oasis," *The Aqueducts of Ancient Palestine* (above, n. 28) 289–298, esp. 295–296.

runs from a faucet (Latin *calix*, or nozzle)[39] into an unclean receptacle, MMT may very well hold that the water in the storage facility is itself affected, thus seriously compromising the purity of an entire neighborhood! Indeed, this consideration, which would have affected the purity of the sect's "pure food," may have constituted one of the essential motives for removing themselves to the desert and becoming an "*Austrittsgemeinde.*"

This interpretation, however, cannot be accepted without qualification, since the Qumranic water system did not seem to rely on pipes as far as I can determine at the present time, nor is the tower located near any of the water channels which run through the installation. Water seems not to have been distributed by means of pipes or nozzles, even for drinking purposes. Either no need for such elaborate measures was felt, or dangers of ritual contamination of the entire system would have been too great to allow installation of such a system. Of course, this does not mean that the sect did not encounter the problem of dealing with a system already in place, say in Jerusalem, and the rejection of *muṣaqot* in MMT may predate the construction of the Qumran complex. On the whole it seems safer not to assume that MMT refers to pipes for whose existence we have no evidence.

But it may be that the absence of pipes at Qumran stems precisely from their role in spreading impurity throughout a water system, as I shall explain. If so, *muṣaqot* may still refer to pipes *à la* Zech 4:2.

If pipes are connectives to impurity, then in Qumran, whose 15 cisterns and ritual pools seem to have been served by only one aqueduct fed by rainwater,[40] a single misstep could lead to unmitigated disaster, since the sect's only water source would then have been contaminated. The only remedy would have been to stop up the aqueduct, use up the impure water, and wait for rain to provide new, pure water.[41] In the meantime, the purity of the ritual meal would have been compromised. Indeed, any plausible interpretation

---

39 See Landel, 42–53, for a description of Roman water supplies and, in particular, 49–50 for a discussion of the way in which the water was delivered to private consumers. "The supply pipe was attached to the outlet of the nozzle. Frontinus notes that the position of the nozzle affected the amount drawn off. If set at an angle 'facing the flow' it would obviously collect more, and if slanted the other way, less" (p. 50).

40 See Ilan and Amit, "The Aqueduct of Kumran" (above, n. 28) n. 9.

41 See E. P. Sanders, "Did the Pharisees Eat Ordinary Food in Purity?" in *Jewish Law,* 224, for an analogous situation.

of MMT must consider the *Sitz im Leben* of the provision of water to the Qumran community.[42] I shall return to this point below.

All of this brings us to a problem raised long ago in connection with *m. Yad* 4:7, and recently discussed by Patrich, as noted in passing above.[43] The Pharisees' response to the Sadducean challenge rings strange within the context of rabbinic halakha. According to the Mishnah, the Pharisees raise the matter of an aqueduct which passes between graves, according to the Palestinian Mishnah tradition, or from a cemetery, according to the Babylonian tradition. What does an aqueduct have to do with a stream of water issuing from a vessel? They are not analogous, since streams of water which are *meḥubbar leqarqaᶜ* ("connected to the ground") cannot be made unclean, while a *niṣṣoq* is by definition unclean by Sadducean rules. Thus some commentators assumed that this leniency of *meḥubbar leqarqaᶜ* was not operative in Sadducean halakha, despite Lev 11:31.[44] However, now that we have MMT, the problem becomes more acute, since, if the Sadducees rejected the implication of Lev 11:31 where a cemetery was concerned, we might well expect this issue to be taken up in MMT as one of the important differences between the sects. Patrich's suggestion, that the early Pharisees themselves held the view that even streams originating in and flowing along the ground might become unclean, thus becomes attractive, though only by an argument from silence. Nevertheless, as he points out, this was not a theoretical matter, for there was indeed an aqueduct which passed over burial caves in the vicinity of the Sultan pool; this aqueduct supplied water to the Temple already in Hasmonean times, according to Patrich. It is likely, however, that this aqueduct had not yet been constructed at the time of MMT, nor were the tombs, which Patrich dates to the 30s BCE, yet cut out.[45]

---

42 There is a remote possibility that the Qumran installation was not built in accordance with the dictates of MMT, but it would seem more likely that it was, and the remote possibility that it was not should not preclude interpretations which conform to the information to be gleaned from the archaelogical record.

43 Above, n. 27.

44 See the commentary of Rabbi Shlomo ha-Edeni, *Melekhet Shelomo,* ad loc., and Patrich, "The Aqueduct from Etam" (above n. 27), 13.

45 Patrich, "The Aqueduct from Etam," (above, n. 27) 15–17, esp. nn. 24 and 25; the tombs seem to date from the 30s of the first century BCE, long after the date of MMT, though some date the beginning of the aqueduct to Solomon's time. At any rate, the tombs would seem to provide a firm dating for this Pharisaic response to the Sadducee challenge.

If so, then, the Pharisaic answer in *m. Yad* 4:7 post-dates MMT by more than a century, thus calling the parallel into question even more![46]

The problematical analogy of the two statements, that of the Sadducees and the Pharisaic answer—brings us to another, sixth, possibility, one originally raised by Louis Finkelstein in 1929, in attempting to deal with the problematic debate of *m. Yad* 4:7. He suggested that *niṣṣoq* refers to an aqueduct, in line with the analogy drawn to *ʾammat hammayim.*[47] Unfortunately, he refers to this solution only in passing, and notes that he does not have the space to deal with the matter there.[48] However, while this solution has its attractions, it requires disregarding entirely an undisputed rabbinic tradition (the Geonic commentary on Toharot,[49] Maimonides, Rashi, the Tosafists, etc.), not an easy matter, as experience has shown.[50] Moreover, Finkelstein's interpretation collapses the argument from analogy to one of identity, since according to his reading, *niṣṣoq* = *ʾammat hammayim.*[51] Finally, why should two synonyms be used in close proximity within a polemic context? The more potent expression of the Pharisaic argument would require the use of the same word—*niṣṣoq*—in order to

---

46 Needless to say, though the existence of the Qumran aqueduct indicates that the sect did not reject the rabbinic concept of *meḥubbar leqarqaʿ*, as Patrich suggested for the Sadducees, his dating of the tombs remains unaffected.

47 See "The Pharisees," *HTR* 22 (1929) 185–261, esp. 217 n. 81, and *The Pharisees: The Sociological Background of Their Faith* (3d ed.; Philadelphia: JPS, 1962) 2.813.

48 In *HTR* n. 81 he writes: "With some hesitation I offer the suggestion that by 'nizoq' the Mishnah means 'aqueduct,' but the discussion of the matter would take us too far afield."

49 See Y. N. Epstein, *Perush ha-Geonim le-Seder Toharot im Mavo ve-He'arot* (Jerusalem: Magnes, 1981/2) 129.

50 To give an interesting illustration of the reliability of the medieval commentatorial tradition: Rashi on *b. B. Meṣ.* 39a s.v. *maḥamat mardin* correctly defines the Babylonian Aramaic loanword from Middle Persian *murdu(n)*; see D. Sperber, "On the Unfortunate Adventures of Rav Kahana: A Passage of Saboraic Polemic from Sassanian Persia," in *Irano-Judaica: Studies Relating to Jewish Contacts with Persian Culture Throughout the Ages* (ed. G. Shaked et al.; Jerusalem: Ben-Zvi Institute, 1982) 83–100, esp. 86–87. See also Rashi's rendering of the Aramaic *bistarki* from Pehlevi *v(i)starg, wistar(ag)* (New Persian *bistar*) as Old French *tapid* in *b. B. Qam.* 117a s.v. *bistarki*. These minutiae of realia, even in non-halakhic contexts, demonstrate the tenacity of the tradition which lies behind the medieval commentators.

51 It would seem also that the Pharisees' argument by analogy loses much of its force thereby, although it could be argued that the argument is intended as a *reductio ad absurdum* or perhaps an argument *ad majorem*, since the cemetery might be considered as a greater source of impurity than any other source with which a *niṣṣoq* might come into contact.

drive the analogy home. Of course, if Patrich's dating of the Pharisaic response to the 30s of the first century BCE—some 120 years or so after the formulation of the Sadducean challenge—is accepted, this may explain the linguistic discrepancy, though one might have expected a redactional hand to have smoothed it out.[52]

At any rate, two possible solutions present themselves. We can achieve the same effect without the impediments just noted if we understand *muṣaqot* as referring to pipes, as suggested above. Pipes were an integral part of the Roman system of water distribution.[53] The question becomes one of whether impurity might be transmitted up the stream and through the pipe to the *castellum*,[54] and from there to the aqueduct. This would seem to be a much more important matter than the rare, presumably accidental pouring of liquid into an unclean container by means of a *niṣṣoq*, which would have only a limited effect.

On the other hand, if *muṣaqot* are pipes, we must abandon our wonderful parallel at *m. Yad*, unless we wish to reinterpret the mishnah there, since Middle Hebrew for "pipe" is *sillon* and not *niṣṣoq*; we must also abandon our assumption that MMT's interlocutors are more lenient, for here both the authors of MMT and the Pharisees may well agree that clay pipes may be transmitters of impurity and cannot themselves be purified—as MMT has it, אין בהם טהרה and אינם מבדילות בין הטמא לטהור. Indeed, if our letter seeks to convince its recipient, why should we assume that it is purely polemical? Clearly, the author wishes to open some common ground!

What pipes would be referred to in this context? Presumably, the pipes which were connected to the *castellum*, which served as a neighborhood water tower. *T. Miqw.* 4:6 refers to "drawn water" which can invalidate a ritual pool if connected to it by the standard *šepoperet hannod*, the pipette attached to a waterskin which serves as the

---

52 Is this then a proof for Ḥ. Albeck's view that Rabbi Judah the Prince merely arranged his sources but did not edit them? See his *Mavo la-Mishnah* (Jerusalem: Mosad Bialik, 1967) 99–115.

53 See Landel, 42–53; R. J. Forbes, *Studies in Ancient Technology* (Leiden: E. J. Brill, 1964) 1.172–177, and D. Sperber, *Material Culture in Eretz-Israel During the Talmudic Period* [Hebrew] (Jerusalem and Ramat Gan: Yad Ben-Zvi and Bar-Ilan University Press) 33–41.

54 See the illustration in Forbes, 167, and Oded Irsai, "The Discussion of Water Installations and Aqueducts in Rabbinic Literature—Characteristics and Terminology," in *The Aqueducts of Palestine*, (above n. 28) 47–56, esp. 49 s.v. *qastlin*.

standard measure to connect two ritual pools in a valid manner.[55] If the *sillon* is of this measure, then the pool is valid, since the pipette does not constitute a vessel which would then make the water which it directs into the pool "drawn water"—*mayim še'ubim*—which invalidates a pool. If the opening is smaller, the water does not invalidate the pool. Likewise, water flowing directly from a *sillon* without the interposition of a vessel from which to pour is invalid for *neṭilat yadayim,* hand-ablution, according to R. Yose in *t. Yad* 1:14, though there is also a contrary, anonymous position.

However, since the *castellum* produces drawn water, this would indicate that the water is no longer considered in its natural state, and so it is perhaps susceptible to impurity, in which case, once again, *this ruling would reflect common ground between the two groups.* The difference inheres in the possibility of the *castellum* becoming ritually impure; this possibility did not exist for the Pharisees, while it did for the Sadducees.

This places the whole question in a different light. As I noted above, the Qumranic water system did not apparently make use of pipes, at least not in connection with what certainly appear to be ritual baths. Whether water for other purposes was carried by means of pipes requires investigation. If pipes were used, the probability of interpreting *muṣaqot* in the light of Zech 4:2 would become, I should think, overwhelming.

However, it may be that the Qumranites prefered *not* to connect their household water system directly to an aqueduct precisely for this reason. That is, if the Sadducees accepted the possibility of ritual contamination of water sources that were *meḥubbar leqarqa*ʿ ("connected to the ground"), they would be careful not to connect *muṣaqot* to their aqueduct, in order to prevent the disaster of ritual contamination of all their water by a careless use of water drawn into an unclean vessel. In this wider sense, then, *muṣaqot* may refer to water which is drawn from any source, that is, drawn water in contrast to water which collects naturally in pools, which alone may not be subject to impurity.

This possibility returns us to one of our earlier suggestions, the first, as it happens. Rather than referring to pipes *à la* Zech 4:2, *muṣaqot,* which is after all derived from the root *yaṣaq* ("to pour out"), may refer to that which is "poured," as opposed to *leḥot,* which would

---

55 The standard rabbinic understanding of this measure is that of two fingers rotated around the inside of the opening; see *m. Miqw.* 6:7.

then refer to liquid at rest. *Muṣaqot* would thus correspond not only to the rabbinic *niṣṣoq*, but to *ʾammat hammayim* and *mei sillon* as well, and perhaps the *qaṭapres*, but not *ʾešboren*, which, like *leḥot*, refers to liquid at rest. Note that this interpretation has the advantage of paying due attention to the semantic range of each of these referents and of being systemic in nature. Moreover, an interpretation along these lines not only obviates the problems which the narrower parallels bring in their wake, but also corresponds to the archaeological facts of the Qumranic case, as far as we know them. The wider consequences of such an interpretation must be considered, as well. Systemic consistency in the interpretation of sectarian texts should be preferred over both the sect's undoubted tendency to strictness and the temptation of rabbinic parallels.

The diachronic aspect must also be considered. Pre-Mishnaic *niṣṣoq* may perhaps have had this wider sense of a stream of water from wherever it might flow. It only became more specialized when employed in conjunction with *qaṭapres*. If this is so, Sussman's interpretation might be sustained on linguistic grounds for both MMT and *m. Yad* 4:7, in its original sense. The cost of doing so is considerable, however, for now we would be dealing with three systems of purities: that of MMT, that of the pre-Mishnaic Pharasaic halakha and that of the Mishnah. In this case, the Pharisaic halakha may be less stringent than the later rabbinic one, since *qaṭapres* would not serve as a connective if subsumed under this projected original meaning of *niṣṣoq*. Only when *qaṭapres* was distinguished from *niṣṣoq* did it take on the character of a connective. For the time being, however, this must remain a matter of speculation.

Finally, to return to the "pipes alternative," despite all this, the legal inconsistency engendered by Sussman's parallels would remain, since by understanding *niṣṣoq* as "pipe," we equate *niṣṣoq* and *sillon*. Why should *niṣṣoq/sillon* serve as a *ḥibbur* for *ṭohorah* but not *ṭumʾah* for the rabbinic system, and vice versa for MMT? For this I would reiterate one of the possibilities raised above. MMT rejects *haššaqah* as a means of purifying liquids, or *tišʿah qabbin* as an alternative to immersion for those who cannot immerse. In essence, there is no contradiction because the two clauses beginning with *weʾap* in our MMT passage refer to two different matters. Finally, there is the possibility that the Qumranites did not make use of pipes in its water distribution system precisely because of the possibility of ritual contamination of its entire water supply, and thus its food, etc. Futhermore, there may have been the question of "drawn water," a matter on which both sects may have agreed.

As to the meaning of *muṣaqot* itself, two of the possibilities just examined seem most worthy of consideration. Either we can accept the equation *muṣaqot* = *niṣṣoq* within the context of water distribution, and interpret "they have no purity" in one of the ways suggested above, namely, as rejecting *haššaqah* and/or *tišᶜah qabbin*, or as a rhetorical flourish, or alternately, we can adopt the more expansive semantic range for *muṣaqot*, which would include within it both *niṣṣoq* and *mei sillon*, among possible others. These others might even include Finkelstein's "aqueduct" suggestion as well. If we adopt the first possibility, the Qumran halakha on this matter is stricter than the corresponding rabbinic one; if we adopt the second, it has points both of stringency and leniency.

Appendix One: Nominalism and Realism at Qumran?

Daniel Schwartz recently applied the realist/nominalist dichotomy in a phenomenological examination of the rabbinic and sectarian outlooks on the nature of law.[56] He suggests that the sectarians were realists, the rabbis nominalists, and that the latter tendency was accentuated after the Destruction and the rise of Christianity.

His analysis of the dispute over the impurity of animal bones is relevant to our concerns. Since Pentateuchal legislation mentions only human bones,

> shall one say that the law on human bones shows that bones are sources of impurity, and that God need not list all types of bones? Or should one say, rather, that if God mentioned human bones only, the law is limited to them alone? That is, are human bones impure because bones are impure, as realists might say, or are they impure because the Torah calls them impure, as nominalists would say? And it is not surprising to find the rabbinic nominalists limiting the law to human bones, while priestly realists, as shown by the *Temple Scroll* (LI) and, apparently, by the Mishnah's report of the position of the צדוקים (m. *Yadaim* 4:7) as well, viewed animal bones too as sources of impurity.[57]

---

[56] See Daniel R. Schwartz, "Law and Truth: On Qumran-Sadducean and Rabbinic Views of Law," (above, n. 25). Add to the literature cited in his n. 3 the discussion of the medieval controversy in Norman F. Cantor, *The Civilization of the Middle Ages* (New York: Harper, 1993) 333–337.

[57] *Ibid.*, 232.

However, as noted at the outset of this paper, the positions taken by both the respective parties on the matter of amputated limbs—the rabbinic view that limbs from a living animal are as defiling as those from a dead carcass, as well as the Temple Scroll's opinion that only the latter is defiling—contradict his premise.

Schwartz' disjunction between the rabbis as nominalists and the Qumran sect as realists becomes blurred when applied to the matters of connectives for purity or impurity if we accept the editors' interpretation. Both systems seem to distinguish between connectives when used for purification and when used for transmission of impurity. For the rabbis, whereas it is most likely that a *niṣṣoq* is not a *sillon,* despite the fact that both may refer to streams of water, a stance we recognize as nominalist, we nevertheless find a realist position in regard to viscous streams according to Beth Shammai. Likewise, in MMT *muṣaqot* are connectives for impurity but not for purity, a nominalist position on the part of the sect. In the language of legal philosophy, both systems of purities would then have nominalist and realist elements. However, if any of the interpretations or modifications suggested above be accepted, the Qumran system may be construed as realist.

Appendix Two

A. Summary of Interpretive Options

muṣaqot:

1. free-falling stream of liquid
2. free-falling stream of viscous liquid
3. streams of liquid of various natures, encompassing *niṣṣoq, qaṭapres, mei sillon, qilluaḥ*
4. pipe (*sillon*)
5. water channels in the ground
6. aqueduct

ʾein bahem ṭohorah:

1. clay pipes cannot be purified
2. rejection of *haššaqah* as mode of purification for unclean liquids
3. rejection of *tišʿah qabbin* as mode of purification for those unable to immerse
4. rhetorical flourish without legal significance

B. Summary of Interpretive Analysis of Muṣaqot

1. free-falling stream of liquid.

Pro: apparent etymological relationship (*muṣaqot* = *niṣṣoq*).

Con: If MMT has two clauses, how can the clause of B 55–56 be interpreted so as not to contradict B 56–58, i.e., how can *ḥibbur* work only in one direction, both in rabbinic and Qumranic sources? If, on the other hand, the entire section constitutes one unit, why so many motive clauses?

In any case, what does "they have no *ṭohorah*" mean? (This problem must be faced for all suggestions; see below). Why does the Pharisaic response to the Sadducean challenge (*m. Yad* 4:7) refer to an aqueduct if the issue is a free-falling stream of water? Finally, why is this isssue so important, since it seems to be a matter which occurs rarely? (Despite its rarity, however, Beth Shammai and its interlocutor seem to debate a related issue.)

2. free-falling stream of *viscous* liquid.

Pro: obviates inconsistency on rabbinic side since viscous liquid may serve as a connective; MMT then would agree with *m. Makš.* 5:9, and the basis of the sectarian-rabbinic dispute is even narrower and rarer than #1.

Con: the very narrowness of the dispute makes it less likely to have been a significant area of contention.

3. streams of liquid of various natures, encompassing *niṣṣoq, qaṭapres, mei sillon.*

Pro: since the implication is that flowing water from whatever source and in whatever channel, serves as a connective, there is no inconsistency on the Qumran side.

4. pipe.

Pro: apparently no pipes at Qumran; thus conforms to archaeological evidence *ex silentio.*

Con: no parallel with *niṣṣoq* at *m. Yad* 4:7 despite similar dispute-form, unless we disregard strong medieval rabbinic tradition on the meaning of *niṣṣoq.*

5/6. aqueduct or water channel.

Pro: inconsistencies removed.

Con: aqueduct and water channels used at Qumran despite danger of contamination. If we equate *muṣaqot* = aqueduct with *niṣṣoq,* the argument in *m. Yad* 4:7 is considerably weakened by collapse of analogy to identity; why is Pharisaic response cast in different terms from Sadducean challenge? Do both sects allow impurity to affect water courses which are *meḥubbar leqarqa*ʿ? Finally, we must disregard strong medieval rabbinic tradition on *niṣṣoq* unless we detach *m. Yad* 4:7 from MMT despite similar dispute-form.

Appendix Three: Sources

MMT B 55–58

ואף על המוצקות אנחנו אומרים שהם שאין בהם טהרה
ואף המוצקות אינם מבדילות בין הטמא לטהור כי לחת המוצקות
והמקבל מהמה כהם לחה אחת.

And concerning (unbroken) streams of a liquid (poured from a clean vessel into an unclean vessel): we are of the opinion that they are not pure, and that these streams do not act as a separative between impure and pure liquids, for the liquid of the streams and that of the vessel which receives them are alike, being a single liquid.[58]

m. Yad 4:7 (from MS Kaufman)

אומרין צדוקין: קובלין אנו עליכם פרושין שאתם מטהרין את הנצוק.
אומרין פרושין: קובלין אנו עליכם צדוקין שאתם מטהרין את אמת המים
הבאה מבית הקברות.

Say the Zadokites: We complain of you, Pharisees, since you declare the *niṣṣoq* clean. Say the Pharisees: We complain of you, Zadokites, since you declare clean the water course (=aqueduct?) which comes from the tombs.

m. Makš. 5:9 (from MS Kaufman)

כל הנצוק טהור חוץ מדבש זיפים והצפחת.
בית שמי אומ': אף מיקפה שלגריסים שלפול מפני שהיא סולדת לאחריה.

All the *niṣṣoq* is ritually clean aside from the honey of the Ziphites and the batter (or: honey of Zapahat). Beth Shammai say: Also the thick pottage of grits, or of beans, because it springs backwards.

58 DJD X, 161.

m. Tohar. 8:9 (from MS Kaufman)

הנצוק והקטפרס ומשקה טופח אינן חיבור לא לטומאה ולא לטהרה והאשבורן חיבור לטומאה ולטהרה.

The *niṣṣoq,* the (water running) down an incline, or dripping moisture (too minute to moisten something else) do not serve as a connective either for uncleanness or cleanness. But a [stagnant] pool [of water] serves as a connnective both for uncleanness and cleanness.

m. Miqw. 6:8 (from MS Kaufman)

מטהרין את המקוות העליון מן התחתון הרחוק מן הקרוב. כיצד? מביאין סילון שלחרס או שלאבור ומניח את ידיו תחתיו עד שהוא מתמלא מים ומושכו ומשיקו אפילו כשערה דיו.

Ritual pools may be made clean [by joining drawn water from] a higher [pool to valid water] from a lower [pool or drawn water from] a distant [pool to valid water] in a [pool] near at hand. How? One brings an earthenware pipe or of lead and puts his hand beneath it until it is filled with water; then he draws it along until [the two pools] touch—even by a hairs' breadth it is sufficient.

Appendix Four: Glossary

ʾammah (*ʾammat hammayim*) ditch or aqueduct (conveying water).

haššaqah in the rabbinic (ritual) purity system, the purification of an impure liquid by bringing it into contact with a pool of pure liquid.

ḥibbur connective of pure and impure.

ʾešboren a declivity in which water gathers; stagnant pool.

midron the sloping ground along which a *qaṭapres* runs.

muṣaqot see Appendix Two for six possibilities.

niṣṣoq free-falling stream of water unencumbered by a container.

qaṭapres a stream of water running along sloping ground (*midron*).

qilluaḥ a term, usually not employed in context of purities, for a free-falling stream of water.

sillon pipe (generally fashioned of clay or lead).

ṭevul yom literally, "one who has immersed during the day"; the status until nightfall of an impure individual who has immersed before nightfall on the final day of his purificatory process. In rabbinic halakha, he is pure to a limited degree, while in the Qumranic system he remains impure.

tišʿah qabbin a shower of nine-*qab*s of water which effects partial purification under certain circumstances in the rabbinic system.

ṭumʾat ʾohel impurity transmitted by overshadowing.

4QMMT and New Testament Studies

JOHN KAMPEN
Payne Theological Seminary
Wilberforce, Ohio

Virtually all discussion about 4QMMT is important for New Testament studies. All of the historical and literary issues concerning a major document which impinges on our understanding of Jewish history during the Second Temple period, particularly concerning the growth and development of Jewish sectarianism, are, or at least should be, considered significant by the New Testament scholar. It is not the purpose of this paper to address the myriad historical and literary issues discussed elsewhere in this volume and in other forums. My purpose is to identify more specifically New Testament texts and issues which could be affected directly by material found in 4QMMT.[1] I will focus on three specific issues.

Polemical Formulae

Responding to the initial description of this text by Elisha Qimron and John Strugnell at the 1984 Jerusalem Congress on Biblical Archaeology, Moshe Weinfeld made mention of the similarity of the formula in 4QMMT ועל . . . אנו אומרים ("and concerning . . . we say") or אנו חושבים ("we consider") and אתם יודעים ("you know") to the form of the antitheses in the Matthean Sermon on the Mount:

[1] I shall refer to the content in its central portion as legal rather than halakhic literature, not to remove it from consideration as a product of Jewish literary creativity during the Second Temple era, but to limit the former term to the material it orginally designated, the legal rulings of the rabbis and the literature which discussed them. On this point in 4QMMT note the comments of John Strugnell, "MMT: Second Thoughts on a Forthcoming Edition," *The Community of the Renewed Covenant: The Notre Dame Symposium on the Dead Sea Scrolls* (eds. Eugene Ulrich and James VanderKam; Notre Dame: University of Notre Dame Press, 1994) 65–66.

ἠκούσατε . . . ἐγὼ δὲ λέγω ("you have heard . . . but I say").[2] I have noted elsewhere that these arguments in 4QMMT are closer to the antitheses in the Sermon on the Mount than the שומע אני syllogism, a parallel previously advanced by those scholars who looked to rabbinic literature to explain features in that gospel which were considered to be rooted in Palestinian Judaism.[3]

Preliminary discussions of 4QMMT already noted the manner in which the arguments in this remarkable document are framed using pronouns for all three persons.[4] While the first and third person references are always in the plural, the second person includes both the singular and plural. Schiffman has noted that it is in the extant fragments of the concluding hortatory section that the second person singular is used.[5] That the second person refers to a specified group and its leader is clear from line C 27: לטוב לך ולעמך ("for the welfare of you and your people").[6] The reasons for assuming this leader to be one of the cast of Hasmonean characters which appear when we discuss the identity of the Wicked Priest in some other

---

[2] Elisha Qimron and John Strugnell, "An Unpublished Halakhic Letter from Qumran," *Biblical Archaeology Today* (ed. J. Amitai; Jerusalem: Israel Exploration Society, 1985) 400–407; for the response of Moshe Weinfeld see p. 430. This is also mentioned by G. M. Stanton, *A Gospel for A New People: Studies in Matthew* (Edinburgh: T & T Clark, 1992) 93.

[3] John Kampen, "A Reexamination of the Relationship between Matthew 5:21–48 and the Dead Sea Scrolls," *SBLSP* 29 (1990) 36–37; id., "The Sectarian Form of the Antitheses Within the Social World of the Matthean Community," *DSD* 1 (1994) 343–45.

[4] See E. Qimron and J. Strugnell, "An Unpublished Halakhic Letter from Qumran," *The Israel Museum Journal* 4 (1985) 9–12; id., "An Unpublished Halakhic Letter," *Biblical Archaeology Today*, 402. Note that the use of הייתם יודעים ("you knew") in *ʾAbot R. Nat.* B is similar to the last of these formulas (see S. Schechter, ed., *Aboth de Rabbi Nathan* [Vienna, 1887] 26 or Ben Zion Wacholder, *The Dawn of Qumran: The Sectarian Torah and the Teacher of Righteousness* [Cincinnati: HUC Press, 1983] 265, n. 12 for text).

[5] Lawrence H. Schiffman, "The New Halakhic Letter (4QMMT) and the Origins of the Dead Sea Sect," *BA* 53 (1990) 67. His reference to the use of the second person singular in the introductory sentence of the letter now appears to be inaccurate as is the implication that only the second person singular is used in the concluding section.

[6] B. Z. Wacholder and M. G. Abegg, *A Preliminary Edition of the Dead Sea Scrolls* (Washington: Biblical Archaeology Society, 1995) 3.xxiii. I thank the authors for supplying me with a copy of the preface to their volume in advance of the November 1994 SBL Annual Meeting. Note also 4QMMT C 31–32.

sectarian compositions from Qumran are less than convincing.[7] The fact that David is held up as a model for the addressee has been used as evidence of his royal status.[8] In MMT C 25–26, however, David is held up as איש חסדים ("a man of piety" or of "righteous deeds"), a figure which tended to be of religious rather than political significance during the Second Temple era.[9] David, however, functions as a model for a variety of figures in Second Temple Judaism.[10] The supposition that the addressee is part of the same movement as the writer, but geographically and/or theologically somewhat removed from the author's group is much more likely, given that the addressee is recognized for his prudence and knowledge of Torah.[11] Important for

---

7 Schiffman, *BA* 53 (1990) 67. Note also the papers by Daniel R. Schwartz, "MMT, Josephus and the Pharisees," and Hanan Eshel, "4QMMT and the History of the Hasmonean Period," elsewhere in this volume. See now Strugnell, "MMT: Second Thoughts," 71.

8 DJD X, 117–19.

9 See J. Kampen, *The Hasideans and the Origin of Pharisaism: A Study in 1 and 2 Maccabees* (SBLSCS 24; Atlanta: Scholars Press, 1989) 2–17 concerning the term חסיד. In that study I also argue that the use of the term חסדים in Qumran literature reflects its biblical usage and is not an allusion to the group of *Asidaioi* mentioned in 1 Macc 2:42, 7:13 and 2 Macc 14:6.

A similar interpretation of this passage in MMT has been argued by G. J. Brooke, "The Significance of the Kings in 4QMMT," in *Qumran Cave IV and MMT: Special Report* (ed. Z. J. Kapera; Kraków: Enigma, 1991) 109–13.

10 E.g., "David," *EncJud* 5.1327–28; Louis H. Feldman, "Josephus' Portrait of David," *HUCA* 60 (1989) 129–74. In his article on "David" in the *Encyclopedia of Religion* (4.243–44), J. Van Seters notes:

> The most important development in the Davidic tradition in postbiblical Judaism was the regarding of David as the author of the Psalter, or at least as author of most of the psalms within it. This meant that David, as the composer of Israel's sacred hymns and prayers, was a model of Jewish piety.

He also notes the use of David as representative of the spiritual life of all Israel, as an authority on the law and as a prophet, in addition to the messianic aspects of the use of that figure.

A similar case regarding the use of the figure of Solomon underlies the presentation of the purpose of the Wisdom of Solomon by D. Winston, *The Wisdom of Solomon* (AB 43; Garden City: Doubleday, 1979) 63–64.

11 4QMMT C 28. See Martin Abegg, "Paul, 'Works of the Law' and MMT," *BARev* 20, no. 6 (November/December 1994) 54. I thank Dr. Abegg for providing me with a copy of the typescript of his article in advance of my presentation of this paper at the Annual Meeting of the SBL in November, 1994. I have amended my comments concerning his paper to correspond with its published version. See also Wacholder and Abegg, *Preliminary Edition,* 3.xxiii-xxv. In these studies it is suggested that 4QMMT C 7 should be reconstructed to read, פרשנו מרוב הע[דה]

the analysis of the antitheses below is the fact that the central portion of the document itemizing the legal issues is in the second person plural.[12]

The first person plural also refers to a specified group, in this case to be identified with the anonymous author of this document. That this anonymous author is the Teacher of Righteousness is sheer conjecture. Such a hypothesis probably obscures our ability to understand the historical and sociological matrix of the document, unless that identification can be more adequately established. Since I assume both the importance and the pervasiveness of halakhic differences within Second Temple Judaism, I see no necessary reason to connect this document with the reference to the Teacher of Righteousness in 4QpPs[a], where the Wicked Priest sought to kill the Teacher, apparently because of ". . . the law which he sent to him,"[13] as proposed by Qimron and Strugnell. Of great significance is the similarity of the legal stance frequently taken in this document to positions ascribed to the צדוקים ("Zadokites" or "Sadducees") in later rabbinic materials.[14] The third person plural is used to document the practices of the opponents; included are descriptions of those things which "they" do that upset the author of 4QMMT and which are considered to be contrary to the proper way for a Jew to live. Frequently those practices are known to us from later sources as Pharisaic. This viewpoint is characteristic of the opponents of those persons included in both the first and second person references in this document. The writer is saying, "*I* am talking to *you* about *them.*"

("we have separated from the majority of the con[gregation]") rather than הע[ם] ("the pe[ople]"), as proposed by Qimron and Strugnell (DJD X, 58). Since the adherents of the addressee are referred to as "the people" in C 27 I am not convinced that "the congregation" is a better reconstruction. The textual evidence suggests the same meaning for either proposal: that the author and the addressee are, or at least were, part of the same movement. The first person references are also discussed in the next paragraph.

12 While the second person plural appears only at MMT B 68 and partially at B 80, there are no appearances of the second person singular. The fact that all references to the first person are also in the plural suggests that the text is composed in such a manner as to contrast the viewpoints of two different groups.

13 Contra Qimron and Strugnell, DJD X, 119–21, and H. Eshel, "4QMMT and the History of the Hasmonean Period," elsewhere in this volume; also rejected by Schiffman, *BA* 53 (1990) 68. See now Strugnell, "MMT: Second Thoughts," 71. A lacuna before התורה prevents us from reading more of that line.

14 Schiffman, *BA* 53 (1990) 69.

The discourse concerning legal issues in the central section of 4QMMT is, on formal grounds, the closest parallel to the antitheses in Jewish literature of the Second Temple era. I am here referring to the form of the individual logia and not of the document as a whole.[15] The primary exemplars of Jewish legal literature for the Second Temple period are found in the literature of the Rabbis. David Daube, that astute observer of forms in legal literature, already pointed out the difference between the antitheses and the scholastic tone of rabbinic debates: "The tone [of the antitheses] is not academic but final, prophetic, maybe somewhat defiant. Nor is there any reasoning."[16] Texts attributed to Qumran are the other primary Jewish documents which discuss items of a legal nature (in addition to 4QMMT, the Damascus Document, the Community Rule, the Book of Jubilees and the Temple Scroll). While similarities in the content of the antitheses to these other Qumran materials have been noted, nowhere do we find likenesses in the mode of argumentation.

4QMMT gives us a picture of a mode of argumentation closer to the antitheses than anything previously attested in Second Temple Judaism. Such similarities permit us to probe the subtle arguments of the antitheses from a different perspective. The addressee of ἠκούσατε ("you have heard") in the antitheses is remarkably similar to ואתם יודעים ("and you know") in 4QMMT; the author of the gospel is addressing some other group with which he/she has a close connection.

When we evaluate the third person references, however, we note a telling difference between the two compositions. While 4QMMT uses the active voice with third person plural forms to describe the activities of the opposition, the opinions of the opponents of Matthew's group are described in the quotation-like statements following the passive form, שנאמר ("it was said"). The use of the passive form suggests that the source of these viewpoints was thought, or at least argued by some, to be divine revelation.[17] In those two instances where the Matthean formulation is expressed in full and third person references appear, the dative is employed to indicate the identity of the opponents: τοῖς

---

15 See Qimron and Strugnell, DJD X, 205, concerning the form of the document as a whole.

16 David Daube, *The New Testament and Rabbinic Judaism* (London: Athlone Press, 1956) 57–58.

17 Kampen, "The Sectarian Form of the Antitheses," 351–52.

ἀρχαίοις ("to the first ones").[18] I have elsewhere identified these recipients of earlier revelation as the Qumran sectarians.[19] In the Matthean antitheses the persons addressed in the second person plural are the successors of those recipients of that earlier revelation referred to in the third person. The arguments being refuted by Matthew can be attributed to the adherents of an ideology expressed in the sectarian literature known to us from the fragments found at Qumran. One important difference in the use of the first person in these two texts is also evident.

The response ἐγὼ δὲ λέγω ὑμῖν ("but I say to you") placed on the lips of Jesus is found in the first person singular, rather than in the plural as in 4QMMT. Scholars of the first gospel have noted the manner in which these statements represent a Matthean viewpoint, i.e., the antitheses as found in the Gospel of Matthew are the creation of its author.[20] The author of Matthew uses the hero of the story to counter an opposing viewpoint presumably important within the Jewish community in which these early followers of Jesus were located.

One of the joys and agonies of working with these new texts is that we are constantly finding new data and reading it in different ways. In this case, this argument for the form of 4QMMT and its consequent conclusions for our analysis of the Matthean antitheses contradicts some of my earlier analysis.[21] In that argument I understood the form of 4QMMT to be similar to the form of the disputes between the Sadducees and the Pharisees recorded in texts such as *m. Yad* 4:8–9, a debate between two parties, rather than this attempt to take seriously all three persons mentioned in the text.

As a footnote to this section I must note the article by David Flusser in which he argues that the ברכת המינים ("the blessing concerning the heretics") was originally directed against the Essenes.[22]

---

[18] Matt 5:21, 33.

[19] Kampen, "The Sectarian Form of the Antitheses," 353–56.

[20] That the formulation of the antitheses is the responsibility of the Gospel writer is documented very well by Robert H. Gundry, *Matthew: A Commentary on His Literary and Theological Art* (Grand Rapids: Eerdmans, 1982) 82–84, as well as in his subsequent commentary on each section.

[21] Kampen, "The Sectarian Form of the Antitheses."

[22] D. Flusser, "Some of the Precepts of the Torah from Qumran (4QMMT) and the Benediction Against the Heretics" [Hebrew] *Tarbiz* 61 (1992) 333–74, II. He had already argued for the identification with the Essenes in his article, "The Jewish-Christian Schism: Part II," *Judaism and the Origins of Christianity* (Jerusalem: Magnes Press, 1988) 635–44.

Professor Flusser has clearly noted that 4QMMT provides evidence of the kind of sectarian polemics in which Jews of the first century of the common era were engaged. That the first century Jewish followers of Jesus also engaged in these polemics should not come as any surprise.

"Fornication" (זנות) in Second Temple Judaism

This term is of considerable importance for understanding the rationale behind certain legal stipulations in the Damascus Document and has distinct implications for the analysis of several passages in the New Testament.[23] Collectively זנות the noun and זנה the verb also appear four times in the composite text of 4QMMT.[24] Of the greatest consequence in the preserved fragments is 4QMMT B 75–82. This section begins . . . ועל הזנות הנעסה בתוך העם והמה ("and concerning fornication which is done in the midst of the people, they . . ."),[25] thereby designating the beginning of a new ruling. After the lacuna at the end of the line the first word in the next line is קדש ("holy"). The text then goes on to render opinions on cattle, clothing and fields, only to return to the term זנות or הזונות[26] when providing the rationale for all of the stipulations. The prohibitions with regard to cattle שלוא לרבעה כלאים ("to not mate two kinds"), clothing [שלוא] יהיה שעטנז ("[not shall] it be of mixed stuff") and fields ושלוא לזרוע שדו וכ[רמו כלאים] ("to not sow his field or his vin[eyard with two kinds]") all concern the mixing of species and are found in Lev 19:19. In v. 29 of that same chapter we return to the issue of זנות: "Do not defile your daughter by making her a prostitute (להזנותה) so that the land will not be prostituted (ולא תזנה) and filled with depravity."

4QMMT B 79 provides the rationale for this legislation concerning the mixing of two kinds: [ב]גלל שהמה קדושים ובני אהרון ק[דושי] [קדושים] ("[be]cause they are holy and the sons of Aaron are m[ost

[23] Note my preliminary discussion of the appearance of this term in 4QMMT: "The Matthean Divorce Texts Reexamined," *New Qumran Texts and Studies: Proceedings of the First Meeting of the International Organization for Qumran Studies, Paris 1992* (ed. G. Brooke with F. García Martínez; STDJ 15; Leiden: E. J. Brill, 1994) 149–67.

[24] 4QMMT B 9,75,82; C 5.

[25] The orthography of the composite text follows 4Q396 1–2 iv 4. The alternative reading הזונות is found in 4Q397 6–13 12.

[26] I will leave this term untranslated for the moment.

holy]").[27] This line supports the conjecture of Qimron contra Baumgarten that the initial reference in B 75 as well as the conclusion in B 82 both concern intermarriage between the priests and the laity.[28] The appearance of both קדש and קודש in B 76 supports the hypothesis that the בני אהרון ("sons of Aaron") as the "holy ones" are also the referents at the end of line 75. Similar concerns about mixing the sacrifices of priests and Israelites is found in 11QT 35:12 and 37:11. In other words the central issue for this entire section about the mixing of "two kinds" is the intermarriage of priests and common Israelites. Crossing these boundaries is considered to be a violation of the laws of זנות.

The reading of the verbal form in B 9 is less certain. If it is the correct reading, it is found within the context of the act of sacrifice by the gentiles, presumably to the Jewish god, and thus is considered prostitution, a concept familiar to us from the Hebrew Scriptures. The other reference to the term is found in line C 5 of the final hortatory section. Here the term הזנות can be read clearly in the preserved text but the surrounding context is fragmentary. Qimron has reconstructed the beginning of the previous line as ועל הנשי[ם] ("Concerning the wome[n]"), based primarily on the appearance of זנות in the following line.[29] But in CD 5:1 we read ועל הנשיא ("and concerning the prince"), another possible reconstruction. This is found in the context of CD 4–5, those folios particularly interested in defining the term זנות for the sectarians. The term זנות in CD has a rather broad definition including at least bigamy, divorce, and incest.[30] In that document it is clearly a term used to define the ideological boundaries of the group.

In 4QD^f the biblical precedent with regard to כלאים is applied to unlawful intercourse.[31] The term also appears in 4QD^e//4QD^b where it refers to a man who approaches לזנות אל אשתו אשר לא כמשפט ("for fornication his wife in a manner which is not according to the

27 Or קודש הקדושים, as in 11QT 35:9, which is more common but does not match the morphology of the term earlier in the line.

28 Qimron and Strugnell, DJD X, 55, 171–75. Joseph Baumgarten's opinion that this refers to intermarriage between Israelites and aliens is attributed to private communication in the DJD volume.

29 DJD X, 58.

30 Kampen, "Matthean Divorce Texts," 152–57.

31 Kampen, "Matthean Divorce Texts," 155.

rule").[32] Punishment for this offense is expulsion from the sect. It is clear that in the Damascus Document זנות is one of the major terms used to describe activity not acceptable to the new covenant in the land of Damascus. In other words, the term is used as a boundary marker to determine who is and who is not a member of the sect. The use of this term in this manner, then, is similar to that found in 4QMMT, where it describes behavior which violates the boundary between the priests and the Israelites.

This sectarian context for the term, now spelled out more clearly because of its appearance in 4QMMT, impinges on its use in the New Testament. The exception clause in the Matthean divorce texts has continued to leave New Testament scholars in a quandary: παρεκτὸς λόγου ("except on the grounds of") πορνείας in 5:32 and μὴ ἐπὶ ("except for") πορνείας in 19:9. The exception is usually considered to be either fornication, incest, or adultery.[33] Davies and Allison note that it might "be a term with general import. It might refer, that is, to sexual irregularity of any kind."[34] They then reject such a possibility, suggesting that the interpretation of those verses would not be much different from adultery. If, however, the term is used to refer to disputed laws of sexual and marital behavior which varied among sectarian groups within first century Judaism, the term simultaneously has a more focused and broader meaning. It refers to זנות as defined by Matthew in contrast to other sectarian definitions of the term. In other words, the exception allowed by Matthew is the violation of זנות as understood within the Matthean community as opposed to how it was understood by other sectarians. Divorce was permitted if the wife did not hold to those teachings which characterized the beliefs of the Matthean community in contrast to the other varieties of Judaism available to Jews in the first century CE.

Note that in the later rabbinic tradition the term "applies not merely to all extra-marital intercourse but also to intercourse in marriages which run contrary to Rabbinic decisions."[35] זנות is a boundary marker term whose definition was a source of disagreement

---

[32] Kampen, "Matthean Divorce Texts," 157.

[33] W. D. Davies and Dale C. Allison, Jr., *A Critical and Exegetical Commentary on the Gospel According to Saint Matthew* (ICC; 3 vols.; Edinburgh: T. & T. Clark, 1988–) 1.529–32.

[34] *Critical and Exegetical Commentary*, 1.531.

[35] *TDNT* 6.589–90; cf. *m. Yebam.* 6:5, *Sanh.* 7:4.

among first century Jewish sects. The breadth of the meaning of πορνεία is represented elsewhere in the New Testament when we see that in 1 Cor 5:1 it clearly refers to incest. Its frequent pairing with ἀκαθαρσία ("uncleanness" – טומאה in Hebrew), a major issue in a number of Qumran compositions including 4QMMT, bears subsequent investigation.[36]

"Works of the Law"

The recognition of the similarity between the phrase מעשי התורה in 4QMMT[37] and ἔργων νόμου in the Pauline letters[38] has been noted by a number of researchers.[39] Evidence of its appearance in other Qumran literature has also been argued, especially the disputed reference in 4Q174 (Florilegium) 1:7.[40] One of the reasons for such

---

[36] This pairing is found in 2 Cor 12:21, Gal 5:19, Eph 5:3, Rev 17:4.

[37] The phrase actually only appears once in the text in line C 27.

[38] Rom 3:20; Gal 2:16; 3:2,5,10. In Rom 3:28 the prepositional phrase is χωρὶς ἔργων νόμου. In Rom 2:15 it appears in the singular with the article: τὸ ἔργον τοῦ νόμου.

[39] David Flusser, "Paul's Jewish-Christian Opponents in the Didache," *Gilgul: Essays on Transformation, Revolution and Permanence in the History of Religions. Dedicated to R. J. Zwi Werblowski* (eds. S. Shaked, D. Shulman, G. G. Stroumsa; Studies in the History of Religions 50; Leiden: E. J. Brill, 1987) 82 n. 20; Peter J. Tomson, *Paul and the Jewish Law: Halakha in the Letters of the Apostle to the Gentiles* (CRINT III:1; Assen: Van Gorcum/Minneapolis: Fortress, 1990) 66 (for his acquaintance with the text he cites David Flusser, *Judaism and the Origins of Christianity* [Jerusalem: Magnes, 1988] 722, ill. 8); Robert Eisenman and Michael Wise, *The Dead Sea Scrolls Uncovered: The First Complete Translation and Interpretation of 50 Key Documents Withheld Over 35 Years* (Rockport: Element, 1992) 182–84; James D. G. Dunn, *The Theology of Paul's Letter to the Galatians* (Cambridge: Cambridge University Press, 1993) 78–79; Abegg, "Paul," 54–55.

[40] On whether it should read מעשי תורה or מעשי תודה see Steven D. Fraade, "Interpretive Authority in the Studying Community at Qumran," *JJS* 44 (1993) 63 n. 56, where he claims that Strugnell, on the basis of the appearance of the phrase in 4QMMT, is now inclined to read תורה rather than תודה, which he proposed in his article concerning the text as it is found in DJD V: "Notes en marge du Volume V des 'Discoveries in the Judaean Desert of Jordan'," *RevQ* 7 (1970) 221. The original publication of this fragment by John Allegro read תורה (DJD V, 53). Note the discussion of Heinz-Wolfgang Kuhn, "Die Bedeutung der Qumrantexte für das Verständnis des Galaterbriefes aus dem Münchener Projekt: Qumran und das Neue Testament," *New Qumran Texts and Studies: Proceedings of the First Meeting of the International Organization for Qumran Studies, Paris 1992* (ed. G. Brooke with F. García Martínez; STDJ 15; Leiden: E. J. Brill, 1994) 173–75, 202–209, where he supports the reading תודה based on a reexamination of the original fragment. In her recent study Annette Steudel continues to read the phrase מעשי תודה

interest in the potential identification of this phrase is the apparent absence of the phrase in other extant Jewish literature.[41] A careful analysis of this identification is required.

The consistent anarthrous nature of the Greek phrase as it is found in the writings of Paul could pose a problem for the identification of the term with מעשי התורה in 4QMMT.[42] The article does not appear in the Pauline phrase ἐξ ἔργων νόμου. The fact, however, that the Pauline usage is found in a prepositional phrase could explain its anarthrous nature.[43] C. F. D. Moule suggests that the context of a particular use of νόμος in Paul is more important than the presence or absence of the article.[44] The absence of the article in the Greek phrase is not necessarily an argument against a hypothesis suggesting that Paul knew this particular composition or its adherents.

It does seem unlikely that the Pauline phrase would be a reference to this specific document by name since we do not know its title. As

---

arguing that תורה is paleographically impossible (*Der Midrasch zur Eschatologie aus der Qumrangemeinde [4QMidrEschat$^{a.b}$]: Materielle Rekonstruktion, Textbestand, Gattung und traditionsgeschichtliche Einordnung des durch 4Q174 ["Florilegium"] und 4Q177 ["Catena A"] repräsentierten Werkes aus den Qumranfunden* [Leiden: E. J. Brill, 1994] 44). In support of this view she cites the extensive study of this text by George Brooke, *Exegesis at Qumran: 4QFlorilegium in its Jewish Context* (JSOTSup 29; Sheffield: JSOT Press, 1985) 87, 108. In his recent translation, on the other hand, Florentino García Martínez reads "the works of the law" (*The Dead Sea Scrolls Translated: The Qumran Texts in English* [Leiden: E. J. Brill, 1994] 136). But see his discussion of this text in Section III of his article in this volume, "4QMMT in a Qumran Context."

41 E.g., Markus Barth, *Ephesians: Introduction, Translation and Commentary on Chapters 1–3* (AB 34; Garden City: Doubleday, 1974) 245. Flusser's references are grouped around "doing the law" rather than "the works of the law," even though he does cite T.Dan 6:9 as containing the latter phrase ("Paul's Jewish-Christian Opponents," 82 n. 20). This text appears rather to refer to the "law of God" (*OTP* 1.810). Other less apparent references are cited by Dunn, *Paul's Letter to the Galatians,* 79 n. 29. 1QS 5:21 and 6:18 both read מעשיו בתורה and 5:23 contains only the term מעשיו.

42 The omission of the article in 4Q 174 1–2 i 7 is also apparent. See Steudel, *Der Midrasch zur Eschatologie,* 44.

43 BDF, 133–34; Herbert Weir Smyth, *Greek Grammar* (rev. Gordon M. Messing; Cambridge: Harvard University Press, 1956) 288–89. The possibility of greater specificity hinted at by H. E. Dana and Julius R. Mantey is not convincing (*A Manual Grammar of the Greek New Testament* [Toronto: MacMillan, 1927] 150).

44 C. F. D. Moule, *An Idiom Book of New Testament Greek* (2d ed.; Cambridge: University Press, 1968) 113. For an attempt to do a careful analysis of the article with νόμος in Galatians he points to Ernest de Witt Burton, *A Critical and Exegetical Commentary on the Epistle to the Galatians* (ICC; New York: Scribners, 1920) 447–60.

already noted, מעשי התורה is only to be found once in the extant fragments.[45] If the work bore a heading, or came to have a title as it was reissued, it would appear more probable that it was derived from the continuation of the words found at the beginning of section B: אלה מקצת דברינו ("These are a portion of our words") as an adaptation of Deut 1:1—אלה הדברים ("These are the words"). The use of Deuteronomy in the concluding hortatory section would constitute some evidence for such a claim.[46] There is no evidence to suggest that מעשי התורה was part of the actual heading for the work or that such a title was ascribed to it. In that case it appears doubtful that Paul's use of the phrase was a direct reference to the text of 4QMMT.

In his presidential address to the Society of Biblical Literature, my teacher, Samuel Sandmel of blessed memory, issued his since often-repeated warning against "parallelomania."[47] Less frequently noted is the fact that a major concern of that address was the relationship between the Dead Sea Scrolls and the New Testament. Sandmel concluded that address by calling on scholars of both the scrolls and the New Testament, as well as the entire community involved in biblical scholarship, to "draw away from the extravagance [of parallelomania] which has always been a latent danger and which the scrolls have made an imminent and omnipresent one."[48] Sandmel's cautions included the point that apparent literary parallels require additional corroboration. It is on the face of it difficult to see the connection between Paul's concern with regard to circumcision and kosher food and the material known to us from the scrolls.[49] Instructive in this regard is Michael Newton's study of purity at Qumran and in the letters of Paul, in which he notes the major differences in their use of purity/righteousness terminology.[50] Clearly

---

45 C 27. The plural form of מעשה is also to be found at B 2 and C 23, but it is not in the construct form nor is it used in conjunction with the term תורה.

46 This is also proposed by Strugnell, "MMT: Second Thoughts," 62–63.

47 Samuel Sandmel, "Parallelomania," *JBL* 31 (1962) 1–13; reprinted in, id., *Two Living Traditions: Essays on Religion and the Bible* (Detroit: Wayne State University Press, 1972) 291–304.

48 Sandmel, *Two Living Traditions*, 304. Perhaps I am fortunate that Dr. Sandmel is not commenting on the earlier sections of this paper.

49 Kuhn, "Die Bedeutung der Qumrantexte," 174–75, 209–13.

50 Michael Newton, *The Concept of Purity at Qumran and in the Letters of Paul* (SNTSMS 53; Cambridge: Cambridge University Press, 1985) 116. The entire

a more careful analysis of the stipulations with regard to the Gentiles in both 4QMMT and the Damascus Document is required, but it is by no means apparent how the results of such a study would lead to an argument which would make the Pauline connection more convincing. My suspicion, however, of the specific legal and literary connections of this phrase in 4QMMT with the Pauline literature does not dispense with all of the issues requiring consideration.

In his recent article Martin Abegg claims, "MMT, however, provides the 'smoking gun' for which students have been searching for generations . . . ."[51] Earlier in the same article he provides a less dramatic disclaimer: "I do not mean to suggest that Paul knew of MMT or of the zealous members of the Qumran community, but simply that Paul was reacting to the kind of theology espoused by MMT, perhaps even by some Christian converts who were committed to the kind of thinking reflected in MMT."[52] The claim that Paul was aware of the kind of ideology reflected in 4QMMT requires more careful evaluation.

Arguments for a connection between certain themes in the letters of Paul and in Qumran compositions have been advanced since the discovery of the scrolls.[53] Prominent have been hypotheses concerning the ethical dualism of Paul, the idea of the community as temple, and the emphasis on God's righteousness.[54] The recognition that the texts from Qumran can provide a more adequate context for the interpretation of certain Pauline concepts needs to be accounted for in the case presently under consideration. For example, Mark Seifrid, who observes certain similarities between 1QS and the writings of Paul in his study of justification by faith, notes that "despite the proximity of Paul's understanding of grace to that of Qumran Essenism, it is unlikely that his preconversion thought was shaped in a fundamental

---

volume provides evidence for this conclusion. This work reflects no awareness of 4QMMT, which had only received preliminary notices around that time.

51 Abegg, "Paul," 55.

52 Abegg, "Paul," 54.

53 Note the bibliography collected by Joseph A. Fitzmyer, S.J., *The Dead Sea Scrolls: Major Publications and Tools for Study* (rev. ed.; SBLRBS 20; Atlanta: Scholars Press, 1990) 176–77.

54 Note the recent summary by Heinz-Wolfgang Kuhn, "The Impact of the Scrolls on the Understanding of Paul," *The Dead Sea Scrolls: Forty Years of Research* (eds. Devorah Dimant and Uriel Rappaport; STDJ 10; Leiden: E. J. Brill, 1992) 327–39. An evaluation of each of these hypotheses is outside the scope of this paper.

manner by Essenes."[55] Abegg's observations concerning the use of various forms of the phrase from Gen 15:6 and Ps 106:31 translated "reckoned to him as righteousness" in 4QMMT C 31 and Gal 3:5 suggest a literary complex of similar terms in the two compositions presently being evaluated.[56] This analysis suggests that 4QMMT provides additional evidence for the existence of an ideology which left its distinctive mark on Second Temple Judaism, most notably on traditions associated with Qumran, and that the writings of Paul reflect some awareness of the existence of this same view.

Studies concerning the Jewish provenance of Paul frequently divide over their interpretation of Acts 22:3, where the questionable claim is made that Paul was raised in Jerusalem and studied at the feet of Gamaliel.[57] Where that claim is accepted as historically valid it is argued that Paul was thoroughly familiar with Palestinian Judaism, and that his claims for being a Pharisee are rooted in that experience, since Gamaliel is said to be a Pharisee and teacher of the law in Acts 5:34. Advocates of this view could expect that Paul learned about the phrase מעשי התורה from the sectarian adherents in that Palestinian context. Since, however, Paul's education as a Palestinian Jew is a doubtful hypothesis, the assumed Palestinian provenance of the Qumran writings pose a problem for the proposed identification. Those who reject Acts 22:3 as evidence of his early Palestinian background are left with a different problem: trying to explain his claim for being "as to the law, a Pharisee" in Phil 3:5 when almost all of our sources concerning Pharisaism are Palestinian.[58] New perspectives on the history of Second Temple Judaism are required to account for these considerations.

---

[55] Mark A. Seifrid, *Justification by Faith: The Origin and Development of a Central Pauline Theme* (NovTSup 68; Leiden, E. J. Brill, 1992) 181. In n. 168 of that same page he does state: "It is not impossible, of course, that Paul did encounter Essenes and was familiar with their thought."

[56] Abegg, "Paul," 55. He also cites Gal 2:16, but this reference employs the verb δικαιόω. The related terms are presented in a less convincing form in Eisenman and Wise, *Dead Sea Scrolls Uncovered*, 183–84. The expression ותחשב לו צדקה "it was reckoned for him as righteousness" also appears in 4Q225 2 i 8 (psJub^{a}; ed. J. C. VanderKam, DJD XIII, 145).

[57] Hans Dieter Betz, "Paul," *ABD* 5.187. My discussion at this point is meant to be programmatic and introductory. The issues merely hinted at in these paragraphs have been the subject of extensive discussion and require additional analysis.

[58] See A. J. Saldarini, "Pharisees," *ABD* 5.294–95.

If further research would suggest other linguistic and legal similarities between Paul and the literature from Qumran, it would force us to raise further questions about the spread of ideas known to us from that literature. Diaspora Judaism has for the most part made a very limited entree into the vocabulary of Qumran studies. Yet just as Paul's claim of being a Pharisee, probably in Tarsus, disrupts the historical paradigms for understanding Pharisaism in the Second Temple era, so does evidence of Qumran literature or ideology in upper Syria or Asia Minor in the middle of the first century CE.[59] Although there are limited sources concerning the nature of Jewish life in these areas at that time, one is forced nonetheless to ask further questions concerning the possibility for and nature of Jewish sectarianism in the life of the Jewish Diaspora in Asia Minor in the first century.

Conclusion

4QMMT gives us new evidence concerning Jewish legal teaching during the late Second Temple period. This is important for our understanding of the New Testament, not primarily because of a few more isolated parallels which might be identified, but because Jewish groups in the first centuries BCE and CE distinguished themselves from one another by the practices which they observed. Calendrical observance and other legal issues related to the practice of Jewish life were fundamental indicators of one's identity within the various groups in existence within late Second Temple Judaism. The significance of 4QMMT for New Testament studies can only be evaluated within this context.

When we recall that those earlier followers of Jesus at an important formative stage in their history comprised a Jewish sect, the scope of the discussion becomes evident. 4QMMT is a major document that both describes the practices of one Jewish sect and disputes those of another a century or two before the majority of the works comprising the New Testament were written. It is then instructive concerning both the form in which Jewish sectarianism could express itself and the content of the legal rulings about which Jews could disagree. The impact of this document thus is the same for Jewish and New Testament studies, because it advances the understanding of Jewish

---

59 Kuhn suggests that he could have learned these ideas while residing in the Nabatean kingdom or at Damascus in Syria ("Impact of the Qumran Scrolls," 336).

sectarianism, a fundamental issue in both fields of study. 4QMMT adds a few more pieces to that puzzle entitled "Jewish Life in the Graeco-Roman Era." The pieces added to that puzzle are the most important part of this document's contribution to New Testament studies. Everything else is commentary.

A Bibliography of MMT[1]

1) Volumes Devoted Completely to 4QMMT and Referred to by Short Title

DJD X — E. Qimron and J. Strugnell (in consultation with Y. Sussmann and with contributions by Y. Sussmann and A. Yardeni). *Qumran Cave 4, V: Miqṣat Maʿaśe Ha-Torah.* Discoveries in the Judaean Desert X; Oxford: Clarendon, 1994.

Special Report — Z. J. Kapera (ed.). *Qumran Cave IV and MMT: Special Report.* Kraków: The Enigma Press, 1991.

2) Inventories of photographs

Reed, S. A. (comp.). *Dead Sea Scroll Inventory Project: List of Documents, Photographs and Museum Plates,* Fascicle 9, 15–16. Claremont: Ancient Biblical Manuscript Center, 1992.

Reed, S. A. (comp.), M. J. Lundberg (ed.) with M. B. Phelps. *The Dead Sea Scrolls Catalogue. Documents, Photographs and Museum Inventory Numbers,* 107–8. SBLRBS 32. Atlanta: Scholars Press, 1994.

3) Reproductions of photographs

Eisenman, R. H. and J. M. Robinson. *A Facsimile Edition of the Dead Sea Scrolls. Prepared with an Introduction and Index.* Washington, D.C.: Biblical Archaeology Society, 1991 [Volume I: Plates 78, 79, 114, 213, 287, 359, 422, 424, 442, 496, 557, 793, 871, 906. Volume II: Plates 925, 931, 1024, 1045, 1426, 1427, 1439, 1440, 1441, 1442, 1471.]

Qimron, E., and J. Strugnell. DJD X, Plates I-VIII.

[1] This bibliography is substantially dependent on a bibliography of 4QMMT provided to the editors by Florentino García Martínez.

Sussmann, A., and R. Peled (eds.). *Scrolls from the Dead Sea: An Exhibition of Scrolls and Archaeological Artifacts from the Collections of the Israel Antiquities Authority,* 67 [4Q396]. New York: George Braziller, 1993.

Tov, E. (ed.) with S. J. Pfann. *The Dead Sea Scrolls on Microfiche. A Comprehensive Facsimile Edition of the Texts from the Judean Desert.* Leiden: IDC–E. J. Brill, 1993. [4Q394 PAM 40.618, 41.208, 41.760, 41.780, 42.472, 43.477, 43.492, 43.521 IAA: 190450, 190451; 4Q395 PAM 40.964, 41.762, 42.472, 43.477 IAA 190451; 4Q396 PAM 40.619, 41.638, 42.602, 42.631, 42.815, 43.490 IAA 190449; 4Q397 PAM 41.412, 41.582, 41.762, 41.891, 42.472, 43.476, 43.489 IAA 190453, 190454, 206039; 4Q398 PAM 41.992, 42.183, 42.368, 42.557, 42.838, 43.489, 43.491 IAA 190448, 190452; 4Q399 PAM 41.823, 43.491].

4) Transcriptions of the Hebrew Text (with or without translation)

Anonymous. "An Anonymously Received Pre-Publication of 4QMMT." *The Qumran Chronicle* 1 (1990–91) Appendix "A" No. 2, 1–9.

Dombrowski, B. W. W. *An Annotated Translation of Miqṣāt Maᶜaśēh ha-Tôra (4QMMT)*. Weenzen: Privately printed, 1992.

Eisenman, R. and M. Wise. *The Dead Sea Scrolls Uncovered,* 180–196. Rockport: Element, 1992.

———. *De Dode-Zeerollen onthuld,* 175–191. Houten: De Haan, 1993.

———. *Jesus und die Urchristen. Die Qumran-Rollen entschlüsselt,* 187–205. P. Davies and Birgit Mänz-Davies (Trans.). München: C. Bertelsmann, 1993.

Qimron, E. and J. Strugnell. "The Texts." DJD X, 3–42; "The Composite Text." DJD X, 43–63.

[Qimron, E. and J. Strugnell.] "For this you waited 35 Years. MMT as reconstructed by Elisha Qimron and John Strugnell." *BARev* 20 (November/December 1994) 56–61. [reprinted from DJD X]

Strugnell, J. and E. Qimron. "Some Torah Precepts. Miqṣat Maᶜase ha-Torah. 4Q396 (MMTᶜ)." In *Scrolls from the Dead Sea: An Exhibition of Scrolls and Archaeological Artifacts from the Collections of the Israel Antiquities Authority,* 64–66. Edited by A. Sussmann and R. Peled. New York: George Braziller, 1993.

Wacholder, B. Z. and M. G. Abegg (eds.). *A Preliminary Edition of the Unpublished Dead Sea Scrolls. The Hebrew and Aramaic Texts from Cave Four.* Fascicle Three, 271–296. Based on a Reconstruction of the Original Transcriptions of Jozef T. Milik and John Strugnell. Washington D.C.: Biblical Archaeology Society, 1995.

5) Other Translations

Dombrowski, B. W. W. (trans.). "Miqṣāt Maʿaśēh hattôrâ (4QMMT) in English." *The Qumran Chronicle* 4 (1994) 28–36.

García Martínez, F. (ed.). *The Dead Sea Scrolls Translated. The Qumran Texts in English,* 77–85. W. G. E. Watson (trans.). Leiden/New York/Cologne: E. J. Brill, 1994.

———. *Textos de Qumrán,* 127–136. Madrid: Trotta, 1993.

García Martínez, F. and A. S. van der Woude (eds.). *De Rollen van de Dode Zee. Ingeleid en in het Nederlands vertaald,* Deel 1, 121–132. Kampen/Tielt: Kok/Lannoo, 1994.

Krupp M. (ed.). *Qumran-Texte zum Streit um Jesus und das Urchristentum,* 119–127. GTB Siebenster Taschenbuch 1304. Gütersloh: Gütersloher Verlaghaus, 1993.

Maier, J. (trans.). *Die Qumran-Essener: Die Texte vom Toten Meer,* Band II, 362–376. UTB 18673. München-Basel: Reinhard, 1995.

Vermes, G. (trans.). *The Dead Sea Scrolls in English,* 181–182 [a portion of 4Q399]. New York: Penguin, 1995.

6) Bibliographies

Kapera, Z. J. "A Preliminary Bibliography of 4QMMT: 1956–1990." *The Qumran Chronicle* 1 (1990–91) Appendix A, No. 2, 10–12.

———. "A Preliminary Subject Bibliography of 4QMMT: 1956–1991." *Special Report,* 75–80.

———. "A Preliminary Subject Bibliography of 4QMMT. Part II: Summer 1991–Spring 1994." *The Qumran Chronicle* 4 (1994) 53–66.

Qimron, E., "Bibliography of the Halakha at Qumran." DJD 10, 124–130.

7) General Studies

Dexinger, F. "Qumran. Ein Überblick." In *Qumran. Ein Symposion*, 29–62. Edited by J. B. Bauer, J. Fink, H. D. Galter. Grazer Theologische Studien 15. Graz: Eigenverlag des Instituts für Ökumenische Theologie und Patrologie an der Universität Graz, 1993.

García Martínez, F. "Estudios Qumránicos 1975–1985: Panorama crítico (IV)." *EstBíb* 46 (1988) 545–548.

———. "Une secte dans le judaïsme de l'époque." *Le Monde de la Bible* 86 (1994) 24–27.

Harrington, D. and J. Strugnell. "Qumran Cave 4 Texts: A New Publication." *JBL* 112 (1993) 491–499.

Kapera, Z. J. "How not to publish 4QMMT in 1955–1991." *Special Report*, 55–67.

———. "How not to publish 4QMMT. Part II: Spring 1991–Spring 1994." *The Qumran Chronicle* 4 (1994) 41–52.

Lange, A. and K. F. D. Römheld, "Dokumentation neuer Texte." *Zeitschrift für Althebraistik* 8 (1995) 111–113.

Mędala, S. "Some Remarks on the Official Publication of MMT." *The Qumran Chronicle* 4 (1994) 193–202.

Milevski, I. "Algunos de los preceptos de la Torá. Manifiesto fundacional e historia de la secta de Qumrán." *Revista de Arqueología* 15/153 (1994) 30–32.

Qimron, E. "Miqṣat Maʿase Hatorah." *ABD* 4.843–45. New York: Doubleday, 1992.

Qimron, E. and J. Strugnell. "An Unpublished Halakhic Letter from Qumran." In *Biblical Archaeology Today. Proceedings of the International Congress on Biblical Archaeology Jerusalem, April 1984*, 400–407. Edited by J. Amitai. Jerusalem: Israel Exploration Society, 1985.

———. "An Unpublished Halakhic Letter from Qumran." *Israel Museum Journal* 4 (1985) 8–12.

Schiffman, L. H. [Yehudah]. "The Battle of the Scrolls" [Hebrew]. *Cathedra* 61 (1991) 3–23.

———. "From the Caves of Qumran. New Light On The History Of Rabbinic Judaism From The Dead Sea Scrolls." *Jewish Action* (Spring 1992) 24–27.

Shanks, H. "MMT as the Maltese Falcon." *BARev* 20 (November/December 1994) 48–51, 80–81.

Strugnell, J. "The Qumran Scrolls: A Report on Work in Progress." In *Jewish Civilization in the Hellenistic-Roman Period,* 94–106. Edited by S. Talmon. JSPSup 10. Sheffield: JSOT Press, 1991.

Tomson, P. "Halachise brieven uit de oudheid: Qumran, Paulus en de Talmud." *Nederlands Theologisch Tijdschrift* 46 (1992) 248–301.

Zangenberg, J. "Some Remarks on the Special Report on Qumran Cave Four and MMT: Review Article." *The Qumran Chronicle* 4 (1994) 67–72.

8) Language

Dombrowski, B. W. W. "A Short Reply [to P. Muchowski]." *The Qumran Chronicle* 4 (1994) 39–40.

Grelot, P. "Les oeuvres de la Loi (A propos de 4Q394–398)." *RevQ* 16/63 (1994) 441–448.

Morag, S. "Qumran Hebrew: Some Typological Observations." *VT* 38 (1988) 148–164.

Muchowski, P. "Dombrowski's Translation of MMT. A Few Remarks." *The Qumran Chronicle* 4 (1994) 37–39.

Nebe, W. "Zwei vermeintliche Ableitungen von *twk* 'Mitte' im Qumran-Hebräischen." *Zeitschrift für Althebraistik* 5 (1992) 218–223.

Qimron, E. *The Hebrew of the Dead Sea Scrolls.* Harvard Semitic Studies 29. Atlanta: Scholars Press, 1986.

———. "The Language." DJD X, 65–108.

———. "Observations on the History of Early Hebrew (1000 B.C.E. – 200 C.E.) in the Light of the Dead Sea Documents." In *The Dead Sea Scrolls. Forty Years of Research,* 349–361. Edited by D. Dimant and U. Rappaport. STDJ 10. Leiden/Jerusalem: E. J. Brill/Magnes, 1992.

Smith, M. S. "The *Waw*-Consecutive at Qumran." *Zeitschrift für Althebraistik* 4 (1991) 161–164.

9) Literary Character and Historical Setting

Abegg, M. G. "Paul, 'Works of the Law' and MMT." *BARev* 20 (November/December 1994) 52–55, 81.

Baumgarten, A. I. "Rabbinic Literature as a Source for the History of Jewish Sectarianism in the Second Temple Period." *DSD* 2 (1995) 14–57.

———. "The Rule of the Martian as Applied to Qumran." *Israel Oriental Studies* 12 (1992) 121–142.

Baumgarten, J. M. "Some Remarks on the Qumran Law and the Identification of the Community." *Special Report,* 115–117

Betz, O. "The Qumran Halakhah Text *Miqṣat Maʿaśe Ha-Tôrah* (4QMMT) and Sadducean, Essene, and Early Pharisaic Tradition." In *The Aramaic Bible. Targums in their Historical Context,* 176–202. Edited by D. R. G. Beattie and M. J. McNamara. JSOTSup 166. Sheffield: JSOT Press, 1994.

Brooke, G. J. "The Significance of the Kings in 4QMMT." *Special Report,* 109–113.

Burgmann, H. "4QMMT: Versuch einer historisch begründbaren Datierung." *Folia Orientalia* 27 (1990) 43–62.

———. "4QMMT: Versuch einer historisch begründbaren Datierung." In *Weitere lösbare Qumranprobleme,* 83–105. Qumranica Mogilanensia 9. Kraków: Enigma Press, 1992.

———. "A Historically Justifiable Date of 4QMMT." *Special Report,* 114.

Davies, P. R. "Sadducees in the Dead Sea Scrolls?" *Special Report,* 85–94.

Dombrowski, B. W. W. *Ideological and Socio-structural Developments of the Qumran Association as Suggested by Internal Evidence of Dead Sea Scrolls. Part I: Major texts mainly from Qumran Cave 1, CD and 4QMMT.* Qumranica Mogilanensia 11. Kraków: Enigma Press, 1994.

Eisenman, R. "A Response to Schiffman on MMT." *Special Report,* 95–104.

Eshel, E. "4QLev^{d}: A Possible Source for the Temple Scroll and *Miqṣat Maᶜaśe ha-Torah.*" *DSD* 2 (1995) 1–13.

Flusser, D. "Some of the Precepts of the Torah from Qumran (4QMMT) and the Benediction Against the Heretics" [Hebrew]. *Tarbiz* 61 (1992) 333–373.

García Martínez, F. "Orígenes del movimiento esenio y orígenes de la secta qumránica." In: *II Simposio Bíblico Español,* 527–556. Edited by V. Collado Bertomeu and V. Villar Hueso. Valencia-Córdoba, 1987.

———. "Orígenes del movimiento esenio y orígenes de la secta qumránica." In *Los Hombres de Qumrán,* 91–117. Edited by F. García Martínez and J. Trebolle Barrera. Madrid: Trotta, 1993.

———. "Dos notas sobre 4QMMT." *RevQ* 16/62 (1993) 293–297.

Kampen, J. "The Sectarian Form of the Antitheses within the Social Word of the Matthean Community." *DSD* 1 (1994) 338–363.

Mędala, S. "The Character and Historical Setting of 4QMMT." *The Qumran Chronicle* 4 (1994) 1–27.

———. "List do arcykaplana z czwartej groty w Qumran (4QMMT)." *Szczecinskie Studia Kościelne* 4 (1993) 29–45.

———. "Próby ustalenia charakteru i okoliczności powstania dokumentu qumra'nskiego o wypeldianiu Tory (4QMMT)." In *Studia Orientalia Thaddaeo Lewicki Oblata,* 143–164. Kraków: Enigma Press, 1994. [English summary: Attempts to establish the nature and the circumstances of origin of the Qumran document on practicing the Torah (4QMMT), p. 165.]

Qimron, E. "Halakhic Terms in the Dead Sea Scrolls and their Contribution to the History of Early *Halakha.*" [Hebrew] In *The Scrolls of the Judaean Desert: Forty Years of Research* [Hebrew], 128–138. Edited by M. Broshi, S. Talmon, S. Japhet and D. Schwartz. Jerusalem: Bialik Institute, 1992.

Qimron E., and J. Strugnell, "The Literary Character and the Historical Setting." DJD X, 109–121.

Schiffman, L. H., "4QMMT - Basic Sectarian Text." *Special Report*, 81–83.

———. "The New Halakhic Letter (4QMMT) and the Origins of the Dead Sea Sect." *BA* 55 (1990) 64–73.

———. "The New Halakhic Letter (4QMMT) and the Origins of the Dead Sea Sect." In *Mogilany 1989. Papers on the Dead Sea Scrolls*, 1.59–70. Edited by Z. J. Kapera. Qumranica Mogilanensia 2. Kraków: Enigma Press, 1993.

———. "New Light on the Pharisees. Insights from the Dead Sea Scrolls." *Bible Review* 8 (June 1992) 30–33, 54. [Reprinted, virtually unchanged, in "New Light on the Pharisees." In *Understanding the Dead Sea Scrolls*, 217–224. Edited by H. Shanks. New York: Random House, 1992.]

———. "Origin and Early History of the Qumran Sect," *BA* 58 (1995) 37–48.

———. "Origins and Early History: Evidence of the Halakhic Letter." In *Reclaiming the Dead Sea Scrolls*, 83–95. Philadelphia/Jerusalem: The Jewish Publication Society, 1994.

———. "Qumran and Rabbinic Halakhah." In *Jewish Civilization in the Hellenistic-Roman Period*, 138–146. Edited by Shemaryahu Talmon. JSPSup 10. Sheffield: JSOT Press, 1991.

———. "The Significance of the Scrolls: The Second Generation of Scholars - or is it the Third?- Offers a New Perspective on the Texts from Qumran Caves." *Bible Review* (October 1990) 18–27, 52. [Reprinted, virtually unchanged, in "The Sadducean Origins of the Dead Sea Scroll Sect." In *Understanding the Dead Sea Scrolls*, 35–49. Edited by H. Shanks. New York: Random House, 1992.]

Schwartz, D. R. "Law and Truth: On Qumran-Sadducean and Rabbinic Views of Law." In: *The Dead Sea Scrolls. Forty Years of Research*, 229–240. Edited by D. Dimant and U. Rappaport. STDJ 10. Leiden/Jerusalem: E. J. Brill/Magnes, 1992.

Stegemann, S. "The Qumran Essenes - Local Members of the Main Jewish Union in Late Second Temple Times." In *The Madrid Qumran Congress* 1.83–166. Edited by J. Trebolle Barrera and L.

Vegas Montaner. STDJ 11. Leiden/Madrid: E. J. Brill/Editorial Complutense, 1992.

Strugnell, J. "Appendix 3: Additional Observations on 4QMMT." DJD 10, 203–206.

———. "MMT: Second Thoughts on a Forthcoming Edition." In *The Community of the Renewed Covenant: The Notre Dame Symposium on the Dead Sea Scrolls*, 57–73. Edited by E. Ulrich and J. VanderKam. Christianity and Judaism in Antiquity Series 10. Notre Dame, IN: University of Notre Dame Press, 1994.

VanderKam, J. C. "The People of the Dead Sea Scrolls. Essenes or Sadducees?" *Bible Review* 7 (April 1991) 42–47 [Reprinted, virtually unchanged in *Understanding the Dead Sea Scrolls*, 50–62. Edited by H. Shanks. New York: Random House, 1992.]

———. "The Qumran Residents: Essenes not Sadducees!" *Special Report*, 105–108.

Wise, M. O. "4QMMT and the Sadducees: A Look at a Recent Theory." *The Qumran Chronicle* (forthcoming).

10) Halakha

Baumgarten, J. M. "The Laws of *ʿOrlah* and First Fruits in the Light of Jubilees, the Qumran Writings, and Targum Ps. Jonathan," *JJS* 38 (1987) 195–202.

———. "Liquids and Susceptibility to Defilement in 4Q Fragments." *Proceedings of the Eleventh World Congress of Jewish Studies. Jerusalem, June 22–29, 1993. Division A: The Bible and its World*, 193–197. Jerusalem: The World Union of Jewish Studies, 1994.

———. "The Pharisaic-Sadducean Controversies about Purity and the Qumran Texts," *JJS* 31 (1980) 157–170.

———. "Recent Qumran Discoveries and Halakhah in the Hellenistic-Roman Period." In *Jewish Civilization in the Hellenistic-Roman Period*, 147–58. Edited by S. Talmon. JSPSup 10. Sheffield: JSOT Press, 1991.

———. "Sadducean Elements in Qumran Law." In *The Community of the Renewed Covenant. The Notre Dame Symposium on the Dead Sea Scrolls*, 27–36. Edited by Eugene Ulrich and James VanderKam.

Christianity and Judaism in Antiquity Series 10. Notre Dame, IN: University of Notre Dame Press, 1994.

Broshi, M. "Anti-Qumranic Polemic in the Talmud." In *The Madrid Qumran Congress,* 2.589–600. Edited by J. Trebolle Barrera and L. Vegas Montaner. STDJ 11. Leiden/Madrid: E. J. Brill/ Editorial Complutense, 1992.

Davies, P. R. "Halakhah at Qumran." In *A Tribute to Geza Vermes. Essays on Jewish and Christian Literature and History,* 37–50. Edited by P. R. Davies and R. T. White. JSOTSup 100. Sheffield: JSOT Press, 1990.

Deines, R. "Die Abwehr der Fremden in den Texten aus Qumran." In *Die Heiden. Juden, Christen und das Problem des Fremden,* 59–91. Edited by Reinhard Feldmeier und Ulrich Heckel. WUNT 70. Tübingen: J. C. B. Mohr, 1994.

García Martínez, F. "Les limites de la Communauté: pureté et impureté à Qumrân et dans le Nouveau Testament." In *Text and Testimony. Essays on New Testament and Apocryphal Literature in honour of A. F. J. Klijn,* 111–122. Edited by T. Baarda, A. Hilhorst, G. P. Luttikhuizen, A. S. van der Woude. Kampen: Kok, 1988.

———. "El problema de la pureza: la solución qumránica." In *Los Hombres del Mar Muerto,* 165–186. Edited by F. García Martínez and J. Trebolle Barrera. Madrid: Trotta, 1993.

———. "Il problema della purità: la soluzione qumranica." In *Israele alla ricerca di identità tra il III sec. a.C. e il I sec. d.C. Atti del V Convegno di studi Veterotestamentari,* 169–191. Edited by G. L. Prato. Ricerche Storico Bibliche 1. Bologna: Edizioni Dehoniane, 1989.

Harrington, H. K. *The Impurity Systems of Qumran and the Rabbis. Biblical Foundations.* SBL Dissertation Series 143. Atlanta: Scholars Press, 1993.

Kister, M. "Some Aspects of Qumranic Halakha." In *The Madrid Qumran Congress,* 2.571–588. Edited by J. Trebolle Barrera and L. Vegas Montaner. STDJ 11. Leiden/Madrid; E. J. Brill/ Editorial Complutense, 1992.

Muchowski, P. "Introductory Remarks on 4QMMT by Professor Sussman." *Special Report*, 69–73.

Qimron, E. "The Halakha." DJD X, 123–177.

———. "The Holiness of the Holy Land in the Light of a New Document from Qumran." In *The Holy Land in History and Thought. Papers Submitted to the International Conference on the Relations between the Holy Land and the World outside it*, 9–13. Edited by M. Sharon. Leiden: Brill, 1988.

Schiffman, L. H. "Miqsat Maʿaśe ha-Torah and the Temple Scroll." *RevQ* 14 (1989–1990) 435–458.

———. "New Halakhic Texts from Qumran." *Hebrew Studies* 34 (1993) 21–33.

———. "Pharisaic and Sadducean Halakhah in Light of the Dead Sea Scrolls. The Case of the Tevul Yom." *DSD* 1 (1994) 285–299.

———. "The Prohibition of the Skins of Animals in the *Temple Scroll* and *Miqṣat Maʿaseh ha-torah*." In *Proceedings of the Tenth World Congress of Jewish Studies. Jerusalem, August 16–24, 1989. Division A: The Bible and Its World*, 191–198. Jerusalem: World Union of Jewish Studies, 1990.

———. "Sacral and Non-Sacral Slaughter According to the *Temple Scroll*." In *Time To Prepare the Way in the Wilderness*, 69–84. Edited by Devorah Dimant and Lawrence H. Schiffman. STDJ 16. Leiden/New York/Cologne: E. J. Brill, 1995.

———. "The Temple Scroll and the Systems of Jewish Law of the Second Temple Period." In *Temple Scroll Studies*, 239–255. Edited by George J. Brooke. JSPSup 7. Sheffield: JSOT Press, 1989.

Sussmann, Y. "The History of Halakha and the Dead Sea Scrolls. Preliminary Observations on *Miqṣat Maʿaśe Ha-Torah* (4QMMT)" [Hebrew]. *Tarbiz* 59 (1989–90) 11–76.

———. "The History of *Halakha* and the Dead Sea Scrolls" [Hebrew]. In *The Scrolls of the Judaean Desert: Forty Years of Research*, 99–127. Edited by M. Broshi, S. Japhet, D. Schwartz, and S. Talmon. Jerusalem: Bialik Institute/Israel Exploration Society, 1992.

———. "The History of the Halakha and the Dead Sea Scrolls. Preliminary Talmudic Observations on Miqṣat Maʿaśe Ha-Torah (4QMMT)." DJD X, 179–200.

Modern Author Index

Citation Index

HEBREW BIBLE

Genesis
2:23–24 35
15:6 35, 36, 142

Leviticus
4:13–14 44
5:1–4 44
5:2 44, 45
5:3 45
5:15 60
7:15 10
8–9 105
11:31 119
11:39–40 32
13:46 42
14:8 42, 43
15:25–30 90
17:3 39
19:19 45, 135
19:23–24 37
19:25 37
19:29 135
19:30 34
22:16 36
22:28 40, 88
23 84
26:15 96
26:31–32 96
27:32 37

Numbers
15:27 44
15:27–31 44
15:30–31 44
19:8 34
19:10 34
19:16 36
19:18 36, 102
19:21 34
28–29 85

Deuteronomy
1:1 5, 140
4:30 48
6:18 35
6:24–25 35
7:26 47
12:2 47
12:28 35
12:31 47
22:6–7 88
22:9 46
22:10–11 92
23:2–4 37
23:2–9 94
28 95
28:36–37 96
28:48 96
28:64 96
30:1 20, 21, 48
30:1–2 48, 49
30:1–3 95
30:16 49
31:16 96
31:17–18 96
31:29 21, 48, 49, 95
32:7 49

1 Samuel
2:12–17 76
2:22 76
2:35 76
2:36 76

2 Samuel
7:15 35

1 Kings
2:27 76
7:23 112

NEW TESTAMENT

APOCRYPHA

PSEUDEPIGRAPHA

DEAD SEA SCROLLS

RABBINIC LITERATURE

OTHER GREEK AUTHORS